INGLÉS
PARA
ESPAÑOLES

BASIL POTTER

EX DIRECTOR DE ESTUDIOS DEL INSTITUTO BRITÁNICO EN MADRID Y BARCELONA
LICENCIADO DE LAS UNIVERSIDADES DE OXFORD Y DE PARÍS

INGLÉS
PARA
ESPAÑOLES

CURSO MEDIO

EDITORIAL JUVENTUD, S. A.

PROVENZA, 101 - BARCELONA

© BASIL POTTER
© de la edición española:
EDITORIAL JUVENTUD, S.A.
Provença, 101 - 08029 Barcelona
info@editorialjuventud.es
www.editorialjuventud.es
Trigésimo segunda edición, 2004
ISBN 84-261-0081-3
Depósito legal: B: 36.184-2004
Núm. de edición de E. J.: 10.480
Impreso en España - Printed in Spain
Ediprint, c/ Llobregat, 36 - Ripollet (Barcelona)

INTRODUCCIÓN

Es éste el segundo volumen del tratado *Inglés para Españoles,* que ha de comprender en total cuatro volúmenes: Elemental, Medio y Superior, que enseñarán al alumno desde los rudimentos del idioma hasta los conocimientos necesarios para aspirar al examen para el *Lower Certificate* de la Universidad de Cambridge, el más fácil de los exámenes universitarios para los cuales prepara el Instituto Británico en España. El cuarto volumen consiste en un *Curso complementario de perfeccionamiento y repaso,* que contribuirá a un más profundo conocimiento del idioma.

He procurado seguir, en líneas generales, el mismo método que en mi primer libro y pretendo que para estudiar el volumen segundo hay que tener un completo conocimiento del primero. El vocabulario del alumno se aumenta gradualmente y se le dan oportunidades no sólo de aprender, sino de utilizar las nuevas palabras. A medida que los pasajes de lectura se hacen más complicados, aparecen a veces palabras de uso poco frecuente. Se deja a juicio del profesor no insistir demasiado en estas palabras. Por ejemplo, un alumno no necesita recordar *icicle* o *phenomenon* a esta altura.

Al explicar la gramática se ha tenido especial cuidado de no introducir muchos temas nuevos en una misma lección. Comúnmente, la lección gramatical sobre un asunto determinado, por ejemplo pronombres relativos, completa el conocimiento del alumno sobre el tema. Las partes más sencillas de la lección deben haber sido aprendidas antes y practicadas en las construcciones más fáciles que ya ha estudiado. Por el mismo motivo, se han evitado las largas listas de palabras a aprender de memoria. Los verbos irregulares, por ejemplo, se aprenden en grupos de tres o cuatro, diseminados en el conjunto del libro, y no se hacen aprender al alumno listas de treinta o cuarenta verbos a un tiempo. En cada cinco lecciones se inserta una lección de revisión con ejercicios de pronunciación.

Las aclaraciones gramaticales han sido colocadas inmediatamente después de los vocabularios y antes del trozo de lectura. Sin embargo, algunos profesores prefieren pasar directamente de las nuevas palabras a la lectura, dejando la explicación de la gramática para después, permitiendo al alumno deducir la gramática, en cuanto sea posible, por el texto.

Los ejercicios han sido concebidos para dar la mayor facilidad posible en la formación de ejemplos. Se han evitado casi por completo los textos puramente gramaticales, puesto que el objeto del libro es enseñar inglés, no gramática, la cual sólo puede utilizarse como un medio para conseguir aquel fin.

Este volumen, lo mismo que el anterior, ha sido publicado con la autorización del profesor Walter Starkie, representante que fue en España del Consejo Británico, y que los recomendó a los alumnos de los Institutos Británicos en España.

BASIL POTTER

LESSON ONE

Vocabulary and Pronunciation

i: wéek-énd (fin de semana), the cléaners' (tintorería), réading-lamp (portátil, lámpara para lectura).

i márried (casado), to remémber (acordarse), cárpet (alfombra), mánager (administrador, director).

e dréssing-táble (peinadora, tocador), bédside táble (mesita de noche), desk (escritorio), pléasant (agradable), eléctric (eléctrico), séttled (arreglado), to remémber.

a márried, bank (banco), mánager, réading-lamp.

a: cárpet.

o moróccan (marroquí).

o: wárdrobe (ropero).

ʌ cómfortable (cómodo), rug (estera, tapete).

u room (sitio), spare róom (cuarto de huéspedes), bóokcase (estante), cúshion (cojín).

ə mánager, sófa (sofá), fúrniture (muebles), cómfortable, to be afráid (tener miedo), cúshion, pléasant, séttled, cúrtains (cortinas).

ə: fúrniture, cúrtains, to work (funcionar).

ei maid (criada, muchacha), to be afráid, dréssing-táble, bóokcáse.

ai bédside táble.

ou sófa, wárdrobe, stove (estufa).

eə spáre róom.

ʃ cúshion.

tʃ fúrniture.

Frases

as long as:	tanto tiempo como
on the ground floor:	en la planta baja
on the left:	a la izquierda
on the right:	a la derecha

Grammar

Present Indicative

Auxiliary verbs

	Affirmative	Negative	Interrogative
To be	I am he is we are, etc.	I am not he is not we are not, etc.	am I? is he? are we?, etc.
To have	I have he has we have, etc.	I have not he has not we have not, etc.	have I? has he? have we?, etc.
To have (forma continua)	I am having he is having we are having, etc.	I am not having he is not having we are not having, etc.	am I having? is he having? are we having?, etc.

La forma continua del verbo *to be* se usa poco.

Ordinary verbs

	Affirmative	Negative	Interrogative
	Forma «habitual»		
To help	I help he helps we help, etc.	I do not help he does not help we do not help, etc.	do I help? does he help? do we help?, etc.
To go	I go he goes we go, etc.	I do not go he does not go we do not go, etc.	do I go? does he go? do we go?, etc.
	Forma «continua»		
To help	I am helping he is helping we are helping, etc.	I am not helping he is not helping we are not helping, etc.	am I helping? is he helping? are we helping?, etc.
To go	I am going he is going we are going, etc.	I am not going he is not going we are not going, etc.	am I going? Is he going? are we going?, etc.

Uso del presente de indicativo

1. La forma «habitual» sólo se emplea cuando se habla, en general, de costumbres o de acciones repetidas.

Por ej.: He does not work on Sundays: he stays at home.
No trabaja los domingos: se queda en casa.

2. La forma «continua» se emplea para el verdadero presente, es decir, para las acciones que ocurren en el momento en que hablamos.

Por ej.: He is writing a letter.   Está escribiendo una carta.
What are you doing here?   ¿Qué hace usted aquí?

3. La forma continua se emplea a menudo como futuro, sobre todo en el estilo familiar. (Como el presente en castellano.)

Por ej.: When is he coming?   ¿Cuándo viene? (vendrá).

4. La forma continua del verbo *to go* se emplea para formar un futuro compuesto, como ocurre con el verbo *ir a* en español.

Por ej.: I am going to eat fish for lunch.
Voy a comer pescado para el almuerzo.

5. Los verbos de percepción y algunos otros como *to belong, to seem,* etc., no se emplean en la forma continua.

Por ej.: Do you know Mr. Brown? He is very intelligent.
¿Conoce usted al señor Brown? Es muy inteligente
Do you see me?   ¿Me ve usted?
I think he is very tired. Creo que está muy cansado.

6. El presente de indicativo se emplea normalmente en vez del presente de subjuntivo, que casi no existe en inglés.

Por ej.:   I do not think he is intelligent.
No creo que sea inteligente.
Perhaps he is there now. Quizás esté allí ahora.
Tell me when he comes. Cuando venga dígamelo.

Nótese que:

El presente de indicativo se emplea después de las conjunciones de tiempo: when (cuando), while (mientras), as soon as (tan pronto como), as long as (tanto tiempo como), etc., donde en castellano se pone subjuntivo.

Por ej.: When I arrive I shall see your brother.
Cuando llegue veré a su hermano.
Wait until he comes. Espere hasta que venga.

PRACTICE TABLE

When		goes to work	let me know
		arrives	
	he	leaves the house	tell Charles
As soon as		wakes up	
	she	comes down to breakfast	we shall be glad
		gets better	
If		goes to sleep	I shall phone you.

7. El verbo *to have* se emplea sólo en forma continua, cuando es verbo principal y no auxiliar y no traduce la idea de posesión.

Por ej.: We are having lunch. Estamos almorzando.
Are you having a good time?
¿Están ustedes divirtiéndose?

Pero   Have you my book? ¿Tiene usted mi libro?
o   Have you got my book? (Véase párrafo 8).

8. Como se ve en 7, el presente del verbo *to have,* en sentido de posesión se emplea más a menudo seguido de la palabra *got* (participio pasado del verbo *to get,* obtener).

Por ej.: Have you got any money? ¿Tiene usted algún dinero?
No, I have not got any. No, no tengo.

9. El modismo *to have to* o *to have got to* se emplea para traducir el modismo castellano *tener que.*

Por ej.: I have to go to work every day.
Tengo que ir al trabajo cada día.
I have got to write a letter to my aunt.
Tengo que escribir una carta a mi tía.

Contracciones verbales

do not	— don't	I am	— I'm
does not	— doesn't	you are	— you're
is not	— isn't	he is	— he's

are not	— aren't	she is	— she's
has not	— hasn't	it is	— it's
have not	— haven't	we are	— we're
		they are	— they're
I have	— I've		
you have	— you've		
he has	— he's		
she has	— she's		
it has	— it's		
we have	— we've		
they have	— they've		

Reading

HOME

Mr. Armstrong has a nice house in Oxford where he lives with his wife and family. He has four children, Peter, Joan, Andrew and David, but Peter does not live in Oxford now. He is married and lives with his wife in Cambridge. However, he sometimes comes to see his parents when he has a week-end free. Joan goes to school in Oxford but has to take a bus to get there as the school is at the other end of the town. Andrew goes to a boys' school quite near the house. He walks there in about ten minutes. David does not go to school as he is too young: he is only four.

Mr. Armstrong leaves the house every morning at about half-past nine to go to his work at the bank. He is the manager of one of the banks in Oxford. However, Joan and Andrew have to be at school at nine o'clock, so that the family all have breakfast together at eight o'clock. Mrs. Armstrong gets up first and comes down to the kitchen to prepare the breakfast. Mrs. Armstrong has a maid who comes every morning to help her, but she does not sleep in the house. She comes in at about ten o'clock. Joan and Andrew don't generally get up until they have to.

The Armstrongs' house is not a big house. On the ground floor there is a hall with the dining-room on the right and the drawing-room on the left. Behind the dining-room there is the kitchen. Upstairs there are four bedrooms and a bathroom. Mr. and Mrs. Armstrong sleep in the large bedroom with the baby, David. Joan and Andrew each have a bedroom and there is one spare room for visitors.

This morning the Armstrong family are having breakfast. The postman has come to the house and has left several letters for Mr. Armstrong which he is now reading.

11

«Do you know who is writing to me now?» he asks his wife. «Young Charles Lee. He wants to know if he can stay with us. He is coming to Oxford to study at the Bodleian Library for a book which he is writing and is going to stay here about a month. Do you think there is room for him in the house? Remember Peter and his wife are coming every week-end next month.»

«That doesn't matter. We can put Andrew on the sofa in the sitting-room for the one night when Peter and Mary come. Then Peter and Mary can have Andrew's room and Charles the spare room.»

«What furniture is there in the spare room? When Charles comes, he will want to be comfortable if he is going to read and study a lot.»

«I'm afraid there isn't much furniture in the spare room. We shall have to add some. There is only a bed, a wardrobe, a dressing-table and a small bedside table.»

«Have we got any more to give him?»

«Oh, yes. Joan has a nice desk in her room which we can put in the spare room and there are too many armchairs in the sitting-room. We can put a comfortable one in Charles's room.»

«Have we got a good carpet to give him?»

«Yes. When the carpet from Andrew's room comes back from the cleaners' we'll put it in the spare room. It will be just the right size and will make the room warm and comfortable.»

«Then he must have a reading-lamp and a bookcase to keep his books in.»

«Yes. I am going to buy a small bookcase, as we haven't got enough bookcases in the house and I know where I can buy one cheaply. Then we have got two reading-lamps in our bedroom and one is enough. We'll give Charles the other. So with the pretty curtains and the moroccan rugs and cushions he will have a pleasant room.»

«Yes, and if it's too cold we can light a fire in the fireplace or give him an electric stove. The electric stoves we've got work very well.»

Well, that is settled then. I shall write to Charles and say that he can stay here as long as he likes. He will no doubt tell us when he is coming Now I must go to work. Good-bye, mother.»

«Good-bye.»

Ejercicios

A) «You leave the house every morning at half-past nine.»

1. **Escríbase esta oración substituyendo como sujeto:**
   a) The children   *b)* We all   *c)* Mr. Armstrong.

2. **Escríbanse estas cuatro oraciones:**
   a) en forma negativa   *b)* en forma interrogativa.

B) **Answer the following questions (with complete sentences):**
   1. Where does Mr. Armstrong live?
   2. Does Joan live in Cambridge?
   3. Who lives in Cambridge?
   4. Where does Joan go to school?
   5. How does Andrew go to school?
   6. Does David go to school?
   7. At what time does Mr. Armstrong leave the house?
   8. Where does Mr. Armstrong work?
   9. At what time do Andrew and Joan have to be at school?
   10. Who gets up first?
   11. Does Andrew get up first?
   12. Does the maid sleep in the house?
   13. How many bedrooms are there in Mr. Armstrong's house?
   14. What is the Armstrong family doing?
   15. What is Mr. Armstrong doing?
   16. Who is coming to stay in Oxford?
   17. Why is he coming to Oxford?
   18. How long is he going to stay in Oxford?
   19. What furniture is there in the spare room?
   20. What has Joan got in her room?
   21. What must Charles have to keep his books in?
   22. Where will Mrs. Armstrong find a bookcase?
   23. How will Charles keep warm?
   24. Do Mr. Armstrong's electric stoves work well?
   25. What will Mr. Armstrong tell Charles in his letter?

C) **Rewrite the following sentences using the contracted forms of the verbs:**
   1. My child does not go to school.
   2. He is not old enough.
   3. Our friends are not coming today.
   4. That does not matter.

13

5. I am afraid there is not much furniture in the spare room.
6. We have not got any more.
7. If it is too cold, we can light a fire.
8. These stoves do not work well.
9. He will tell us when he is coming.
10. He has not got a bookcase.

D) **Describe:**

1. The furniture in your sitting-room.
2. The furniture in your bedroom.
3. The furniture in the room you are in now.

E) **Put the verb in the correct form of the present (the infinitive is given):**

1. He (to go) to give me his reading-lamp.
2. (To know) you when he is coming?
3. Today the Armstrongs (to wait) for Charles who (to come) from Cambridge by car.
4. (To have) you a good time at the Armstrongs' house today?
5. When you play with the Armstrong children (to have) you a good time?
6. How long (to go) Charles to stay with the Armstrongs?
7. I (to think) not he (to be) very strong.
8. We (to have) not got enough money to go to the cinema.
9. I shall stay at home until Peter (to arrive).
10. Mr. Armstrong (to have) to go to work every day.

Translate into English:

Hoy estamos muy contentos porque nuestro amigo Pedro va a venir a pasar el fin de semana en nuestra casa. No viene muy a menudo porque tiene que descansar los domingos y el viaje es muy largo. Viene en el tren que llega a las cinco y media, y ahora estamos preparando su cuarto. Hemos puesto un escritorio y un sillón cómodo cerca de la ventana. La alfombra parece nueva, porque ha vuelto de la tintorería, y mamá va a comprar una estantería nueva. Hay un buen fuego ardiendo en la chimenea y no hace frío en el cuarto. Abajo en la cocina, mamá y la criada preparan la cena. Cuando llegue Pedro todo estará listo.

Pedro es estudiante en la Universidad de Cambridge y trabaja muchísimo. Cuando venga a nuestra casa, por cierto traerá un libro para estudiar por la noche en su cuarto. Creo que trabaja demasiado y que no descansa bastante. A mí no me gusta estudiar mucho. Cuando llegue el invierno iré a muchos bailes. Me gusta bailar.

LESSON TWO

Vocabulary and Pronunciation

i: to teach (enseñar).

i   to becóme (llegar a ser), vícar (párroco), evént (acontecimiento), impórtant (importante), léarned (sabio), ícicle (cerrión, carámbano), for exámple (por ejemplo), ábsentmínded (distraído).

e   lécture (conferencia), to lécture (dar una conferencia) professor (profesor, catedrático), evént.

a: for exámple.

o   wrong (falso, equivocado).

o: impórtant, taught (de 'to teach').

ʌ   púzzled (desconcertado, perplejo), públic-hóuse (taberna), dull (aburrido), to becóme.

u   púlpit (púlpito).

ə   fámous (famoso), ábsent-mínded, lécture, to amúse (divertir), vícar, impórtant, púzzled, to méntion (mencionar), professor, sérmon (sermón).

ə: sérmon, léarned, to turn (volver).

ei   fámous, mistáke (equivocación), Mediterránean (Mediterráneo).

ai   ábsent-mínded, ícicle, to réalíze (darse cuenta).

au   públic-hóuse.

oi   to boil (hervir), to oil (engrasar).

iu: to amúse.

eə   to réalize.

ʃ   to méntion.

tʃ   lecture.

Consonante muda

gh   muda en taught.

Frases

> In this way.: de este modo, de esta manera.
> For example: por ejemplo.

Verbos irregulares

> to teach: taught: taught: enseñar.
> to become: became: become: llegar a ser.

Grammar

Preterite and Present Perfect

AUXILIARY VERBS

	Affirmative	Negative	Interrogative
To be (Preterite)	I was you were he was, etc.	I was not you were not he was not, etc.	was I? were you? was he?, etc.
To be (Present Perfect)	I have been he has been we have been, etc.	I have not been he has not been we have not been, etc.	have I been? has he been? have we been?, etc.
To have (Preterite)	I had you had, etc.	I had not you had not, etc.	had I? had you?, etc.
To have (Present Perfect)	I have had he has had we have had, etc.	I have not had he has not had we have not had, etc.	have I had? has he had? have we had?, etc.

ORDINARY VERBS

	Affirmative	Negative	Interrogative
To help *To go* (Preterite)	I helped, etc. I went, etc.	I did not help, etc I did not go, etc.	did I help?, etc. did I go?, etc.
To help *To go* (Present Perfect)	I have helped, etc. I have gone, etc.	I have not helped, etc. I have not gone, etc.	have I helped?, etc. have I gone?, etc.

Uso del pretérito y del presente perfecto

a) El pretérito se emplea para una acción acabada en fecha determinada.

Por ej.: I saw her three days ago. La vi hace tres días.

b) El presente perfecto se emplea para una acción acabada pero en fecha indeterminada.

Por ej.: I have seen her before, but I don't remember where, La he visto antes, pero no me acuerdo dónde.

c) El presente perfecto se emplea para una acción que sigue en el momento de hablar o que acaba de terminar.

Por ej.: I have lived for ten years in Madrid. Vivo en Madrid desde hace diez años (y sigo viviendo allí). Llevo diez años viviendo en Madrid. Hace diez años que vivo en Madrid.

I have just written a letter.
Acabo de escribir una carta.

d) Si la acción se hizo dentro de un período de tiempo no acabado, se emplea el presente perfecto.

Por ej.: I have seen her today. La he visto hoy.

Pero   I saw her yesterday. La vi ayer.

I have studied very much this morning and I want to rest before lunch.

He estudiado mucho esta mañana y quiero descansar antes de comer.

Pero   I studied very much this morning and did not have time to rest before lunch.

Estudié mucho esta mañana y no tuve tiempo para descansar antes de comer.

PRACTICE TABLE

Has	the teacher the post the train the bus the plane your friend	arrived come	yet?	*Form answers* No, he (it) hasn't... Yes, he (it) has just arrived...

PRACTICE TABLE

Have you		been to England?	Form answers
		passed an examination in English?	
Has **he**	ever	taught Latin?	Yes, I (he, she)
		learnt Greek?	...
		ridden a motorcycle?	
Has she		ridden a horse?	No, I (he, she)
		visited Rome?	...

Nótese bien:

1. El modismo con *just* para traducir el español *acabo de...* (Véase *c.*)

He has just arrived.   Acaba de llegar.

We have just seen Peter.   Acabamos de ver a Pedro.

They have just come back from the cinema.
Acaban de regresar del cine.

También se emplea *I had just* para traducir *Acababa de...*

I had just come home when he arrived.
Acababa de regresar a casa cuando llegó.

2. La traducción con presente perfecto inglés de las frases como:

Vivo en Madrid desde hace diez años (y sigo viviendo allí).
Llevo diez años viviendo en Madrid. Hace diez años que vivo en Madrid.

I have lived in Madrid for ten years, o I have been living in Madrid for ten years (forma continua).

PRACTICE TABLE

	have you been waiting for me?	Form answers
	have you been learning to drive a car?	I have ....
	have you been helping him?	
How long	have you been studying English?	....
	have you studied English?	
	have you lived inthis street?	and I am still
	have you been living in this street?	....

Reading

DR. SPOONER

In the last years of the 19th century Dr. Spooner lived and worked in Oxford where he was a professor at the University. He became famous because he was very absent-minded and often used wrong words when he spoke. He also very often changed the first letters of two following words, saying, for example, «I must have a well-boiled icicle» instead of «I must have a well-oiled bicycle.»

To change the first letters of two words in this way is called a «spoonerism». and Dr. Spooner is one of the few who have given their name to a new word. While he was a professor at Oxford, he often made spoonerisms during a lecture or a class, and when the students came out they said to their friends, «Have you heard what (lo que) old Spooner said in his lecture this morning? He has been lecturing for ten years and every year he amuses his students by his spoonerisms.»

Dr. Spooner was not only a professor at the University but also the vicar of a small church outside Oxford where he gave a sermon once every year. When Dr. Spooner came to give his sermon it was an important event and everybody went to listen to him. Once he started at the beginning of his sermon to talk about Aristotle. The people in the church thought that Dr. Spooner was a very intelligent and learned man, but they did not understand him as they did not know who Aristotle was. However, there were one or two people in the church who had studied Greek a long time ago and knew something about Aristotle. When Dr. Spooner said that in a certain year Aristotle arrived in Malta, one man turned to another and said, «Have you ever heard that Aristotle went to Malta? I have been teaching Greek for twenty years, but I have never read that Aristotle went to Malta.» Dr. Spooner continued his sermon and told the people how Aristotle made several journeys across the Mediterranean. The teacher of Greek became very puzzled. At last Dr. Spooner came to the end of his sermon and started to get down from the pulpit, but as he was getting down he seemed to realize something, went up again, and said, «If I have mentioned Aristotle in my sermon, it was a mistake. I was talking about St. Paul.»

There is another story about Dr. Spooner which says that he made an appointment one day to meet a friend at a public-house called «The Green Man» at Dulwich (dʌlidʒ), a suburb of London. At the end of the day he came back to his home very tired and said, «I have been waiting all afternoon at, «The Dull Man», Greenwich (grénidӡ), and my friend has not come.»

Exercises

A) 1. You made an appointment to meet me yesterday outside the cinema in Dulwich High Street.
   2. One or two people in the church knew something about Aristotle.
   3. The new electric stove in the study worked very well.
   Escríbanse estas tres oraciones: a) en forma negativa, b) en forma interrogativa.

B) 1. You have been teaching Greek for ten years at the University.
   2. You have just come home from church.
   a) Escríbanse estas oraciones poniendo como sujeto: 1) Mr. Brown, 2) The two professors, 3) We.
   b) Escríbanse las oraciones en forma afirmativa, negativa e interrogativa.

C) Answer the following questions:
   1. Who was Dr. Spooner?
   2. Where did he live?
   3. Why did he become famous?
   4. What is a spoonerism?
   5. Where did Dr. Spooner give a sermon once a year?
   6. When Dr. Spooner talked about Aristotle, why didn't the people understand him?
   7. What did the teacher of Greek say?
   8. Why did the teacher become very puzzled?
   9. What did Dr. Spooner do at the end of his sermon?
   10. Have you ever studied Greek?
   11. Where did Dr. Spooner one day make an appointment to meet a friend?
   12. Why didn't he meet his friend?

D) Use the following words and phrases in sentences:
   to turn, mistake, wrong, famous, to become, event, to realize, for example, important, in this way.

E) Form questions for the following answers:
   1. Yes, Mr. Smith lives here.
   2. Yes, I studied in Oxford last year.
   3. He became famous because he was absent-minded.
   4. No, I have never studied Greek.

5. No, the stove doesn't work very well.
6. Yes, I saw him go to the Bodleian Library at five o'clock.
7. Yes, he gets up early as he has an appointment every day at nine o'clock.
8. Because he waited at the wrong public-house.
9. He has been lecturing for ten years.
10. Yes, I have just seen him go down the street.

F) **Dictation:**

Del trozo de lectura «Dr. Spooner», desde «Dr. Spooner was not only a professor...» hasta «...and knew something about Aristotle.»

G) **Describe:**

1. Dr. Spooner's sermon in the village church.
2. How Dr. Spooner went to the wrong public-house.
   Este ejercicio se hará: 1) ayudándose con el texto, y después 2) con el libro cerrado.

H) **Complete the following sentences:**

1. He is a professor — the University.
2. He went to The Dull Man, Greenwich, instead — to The Green Man, Dulwich.
3. I live — the ground floor.
4. He started — the beginning of his sermon to talk — Aristotle.
5. Dr. Spooner said that Aristotle arrived — Malta.
6. He made several journeys — the Mediterranean.
7. — last he came to the end of his sermon.
8. You must do it — this way.
9. — the left, there is the sitting-room.
10. Turn — the right — the Town Hall.

Translate into English:

A) Hola, Jaime, ¿cómo estás? No sabía que estuvieses en Londres.
B) Pero hace más de dos meses que estoy aquí. ¿Por qué no te he visto antes?
A) Acabo de regresar de Manchester, adonde tuve que ir para ver a un hombre muy importante y muy sabio. ¿Le conoces? Se llama doctor Toms.

B) Sí, le conozco bien. Es un hombre muy distraído, pero dicen que es muy buen profesor. Me acuerdo que una vez tenía que encontrarle en una taberna en los suburbios de Londres. Esperé algún tiempo, pero no vino. Al día siguiente me dijo que había estado esperándome en la taberna, pero que después de una hora se dio cuenta que estaba en una taberna equivocada. De esta manera se hizo bastante famoso en Manchester, donde vive desde hace veinte años.

A) Me divirtió mucho por sus equivocaciones. Por ejemplo, una vez pidió ratones en el restaurante en vez de hielo (ice). El camarero se quedó (fue) bastante desconcertado al principio, pero después se dio cuenta de que quería hielo. Cuando regresó con el hielo preguntó si el profesor quería el hielo con o sin azúcar.

LESSON THREE

Vocabulary and Pronunciation

i: to r*ea*ch (alcanzar, llegar hasta).

i mús*i*cal (musical), *i*nclúd*i*ng (incluso, incluyendo), sérv*i*ce (servicio), rec*í*tal (recital).

e to t*e*ll (decir, contar).

a: f*a*r (lejos), to l*a*st (durar).

o: a*ú*dience (auditorio).

u: incl*ú*ding.

ə músic*a*l.

ə: s*é*rvice.

ei st*a*ge (escenario).

ai w*i*de (ancho), rec*í*tal.

aiə to h*i*re (alquilar), soc*í*ety (sociedad).

ju: m*ú*sical.

iə á*u*d*i*ence.

Frase

On the corner: en la esquina.

Verbo irregular

To tell, told, told: decir, contar.

Grammar

Medidas

Para preguntar la edad se emplea el pronombre interrogativo *how* seguido del adjetivo *old* — «How old are you?»

De la misma manera para preguntar la altura, longitud, etcétera, se emplea *how* seguido del adjetivo apropiado (*high, long*, etc.) y el verbo *to be*.

How old are you?	¿Qué edad tiene usted?
How high is this house?	¿Qué altura tiene esta casa?

Como se dice *I am twenty years old*, también se dice *It is twenty metres high*, empleando el verbo *to be* y colocando el adjetivo apropiado después de la expresión de medida.

I am twenty years old.	Tengo veinte años.
It is twenty metres long.	Tiene veinte metros de largo.

Nótese bien que para las personas se emplea el adjetivo *tall* (alto) en vez de *high* (alto), que se usa para cosas.

Comparación de los adjetivos

Los grados de comparación se forman en inglés de dos maneras:

A) Añadiendo las terminaciones *-er* y *-est* al adjetivo. Esta forma se emplea con los adjetivos de una sílaba, y con algunos de dos sílabas, de origen anglosajón.

El *comparativo* se forma con la terminación *-er* y se emplea sólo cuando se comparen *dos* personas o cosas. El adverbio de comparación *que* se traduce siempre por *than*, después del adjetivo en grado comparativo.

tall, alto — taller, más alto (de dos).

Peter is *taller than* Jimmie.

Pedro es más alto que Jimmie.

El *superlativo* se forma con la terminación *-est*, y se emplea cuando se comparan *más de dos* personas o cosas. El pronombre relativo *que*, después de un adjetivo en grado superlativo se traduce sólo por *that*.

tall, alto — taller, más alto — tallest, el más alto (de todos).

Peter is the tallest boy in the class: he is taller than Jimmie and taller than David.

Pedro es el chico más alto de la clase: es más alto que Jimmie y más alto que David.

Peter is the tallest boy that I have ever seen.
Pedro es el chico más alto que jamás he visto.

Nótese:

1. Que *de* después de superlativo se traduce por *in* delante de un substantivo de lugar y por *of* delante de los demás substantivos.

Oxford is the nicest town *in* England.
Oxford es la ciudad más agradable de Inglaterra.
Peter is the most intelligent of the family.
Pedro es el más inteligente de la familia.

2. Que un adjetivo que termina en *-e* pierde la *-e* al añadir *-er* o *-est*.

nice, nicer, nicest.
large, larger, largest.
wide, wider, widest.

3. Un adjetivo que termina en *-y* precedida de consonante cambia la *y* en *i* al añadir *-er* o *-est*.

happy, happier, happiest: alegre.

Pero un adjetivo que termina en *-y* precedida de vocal sigue la regla general.

grey, greyer, greyest: gris.

4. Los adjetivos monosílabos terminados en consonante después de vocal breve doblan la consonante al añadir *-er* o *-est*.

big,   bigger,   biggest: grande.
hot,   hotter,   hottest: caliente.

B) Añadiendo los adverbios *more* y *most* (más) delante del adjetivo. Esta forma se emplea generalmente con los adjetivos de más de dos sílabas.

El *comparativo* se forma poniendo *more* delante del adjetivo.

intelligent, inteligente — more intelligent, más inteligente (de dos).
Peter is more intelligent than Jimmie.
Pedro es más inteligente que Jimmie.
The cinema is more comfortable than the theatre.
El cine es más cómodo que el teatro.

El *superlativo* se forma poniendo *most* delante del **adjetivo.**

intelligent, more intelligent, the most intelligent — el más inteligente (de todos).

Peter is the *most* intelligent boy *in* his class.
Pedro es el chico más inteligente *de* su clase.

Paris is the most beautiful city that I have ever visited.
París es la ciudad más hermosa que jamás he visitado.

Nótese que el adjetivo se coloca siempre delante del substantivo en inglés, tan largo como sea.

One of the most extraordinary houses that I know.
Una de las casas más extraordinarias que conozco.

Comparación de igualdad

La comparación de igualdad se expresa en inglés por medio de las palabras *as ... as* para oraciones afirmativas y negativas, y *so ... as* para oraciones negativas solamente.

Peter is *as* intelligent *as* Jimmie.
Pedro es tan inteligente como Jimmie.

David is *not as* intelligent *as* Peter.
David is *not so* intelligent *as* Peter.
David no es tan inteligente como Pedro.

También se construye *such* (tal, tan), y *the same* (el mismo) con *as* cuando haya comparación.

I have never seen *such* a house *as* this.
Nunca he visto una casa tal como ésta.

I have never seen *such* a beautiful house *as* this.
Nunca he visto una casa tan bonita como ésta.

We live in *the same* road *as* the Smiths.
Vivimos en la misma calle que los Smith.

Adjetivos con comparativo y superlativo irregulares

good	— bueno	— better	best
bad	— malo	— worse	worst
old	— viejo	— { older / elder mayor)	oldest / eldest
far	— lejos	— { farther / further	farthest / furthest

PRACTICE TABLE

John		the nicest		in the room.
		the tallest		in the town.
		the stupidest	person	that I know.
Betty	is	the most amusing		that has ever
		the most intelligent	student	lived here.
My friend		the most friendly		of all.
		the most musical		

PRACTICE TABLE

David			intelligent amusing friendly musical		than	Peter
		more (a)			(a)	
	is	=====			=====	
My father	isn't	as (b)	absent-minded famous important		as (b)	

Combine (a) with (a) and (b) with (b).

Bastante en sentido de suficiencia se traduce por *enough* (inʌf), que se pone *después* del *adjetivo,* pero *delante* del *substantivo.*

> That is not good enough for me.
> No es bastante bueno para mí.
>
> I have not enough money.
> No tengo bastante dinero.

Which se emplea como pronombre interrogativo en sentido selectivo y se traduce generalmente en castellano por *¿cuál?*

> Which of these books do you want?
> ¿Cuál de estos libros quiere usted?
>
> Which book do you want? (selectivo).

pero
> What book do you want? (general).
> ¿Qué libro quiere usted?

Reading

Jimmy and Andrew wanted to hire a hall for a concert which their local Musical Society was going to give. They could not use the school hall as it was not big enough, so they asked about other halls in the town. They visited a theatre and a cinema but they were too expensive, so they decided to see the Church Hall which they thought would not be as expensive as the theatre or the cinema. They did not know the way to the Church Hall, so they stopped and asked a policeman.

«Can you please tell us the way to St. Peter's Church Hall?» asked Andrew. «Yes, go along the High Street until you reach the market square, then turn to the left and you will see the Church Hall on the corner of St. Michael's Road and London Avenue.»

«How far is it?» asked Jimmy.

«Not very far; about ten minutes on foot,» answered the policeman.

When they arrived at the hall, they talked to the porter.

«How much does it cost to hire the hall?» said Andrew.

«Three pounds a night, including service and light,» said the porter.

«How many seats has it?»

«It has seats for 310 people.»

«How long is it from the stage to the back?»

«It is 196 feet long and 66 feet wide.»

«Then it is longer than the cinema, but not so wide as the theatre or the cinema,» said Jimmy. «Yes, but it has seats for more people than the school hall, although it doesn't seem bigger. And it is much more comfortable and pleasant, although, of course, the cinema is the most comfortable of all.»

«How long will the concert last?» asked the porter.

«It will last about two hours, beginning at seven o'clock in the evening.»

«How often do you give a concert?»

«Only once a year, but we also give piano and song recitals to smaller audiences.»

«Shall we hire this hall then, Andrew?» said Jimmy. «Yes, I think it is the best of all we have seen.»

* * *

How tall are you? I am one metre 75 centimetres tall.

How tall is your sister Betty? Betty is one metre 40 centimetres tall.

Who is taller, you or Betty? I am taller than Betty.

How tall is your brother John? John is one metre 77 centimetres tall.

Who is the tallest of the three? John is the tallest of the three.
Which is more comfortable, the cinema or the theatre?
The cimena is more comfortable than the theatre.
Which is the most comfortable hall in the town?
The cinema is the most comfortable hall in the town.
Which is the biggest town that you have ever visited?
London is the biggest town that I have ever visited.
Which is the most beautiful town you have ever visited?
Paris is the most beautiful town that I have ever visited.

Answer the following questions:

1. Why did Jimmie and Andrew want to hire a hall?
2. Why couldn't they use the school hall?
3. Why did they decide to visit the Church Hall?
4. Where was the Church Hall?
5. How much did it cost to hire the Church Hall?
6. How long was the Church Hall?
7. Which was the most comfortable hall, the cinema, the theatre, the school hall or the Church Hall?
8. Which is the highest building in your town?
9. Which is the longest river in Spain?
10. Is Madrid bigger than Barcelona?

Complete the following sentences with the correct form of the adjective given in brackets:

1. Spain is (large) than Portugal.
2. Portugal is (small) than Spain.
3. London is the (big) city in the world.
4. Madrid is (far) from Barcelona than from Santander.
5. The south of Spain is (sunny) than the north of France.
6. I always buy the (good) cigarettes that I can find.
7. This ink is too expensive; I don't want the (expensive), I want the (cheap).
8. This pen is (good) than that one.
9. My car is (bad) than your car, but Henry's is the (bad) of the three.
10. Jean is ill, so she will be (comfortable) in bed than in the drawing-room.

Form questions for the following answers:

1. The Channel is 22 miles wide at Dover.
2. Spain is bigger than England.
3. We act a play once a year.

4. London is the largest town in the world.
5. The concert lasted about three hours.
6. This tea cost three shillings a pound.
7. Yes, Barcelona is farther from Paris than from Madrid.
8. London is 65 miles from Dover.
9. Betty is the tallest of the family.
10. My elder brother is twenty years old.

Complete the following sentences:

1. This house is not good — for me.
2. I met him — the way to St. Peter's Church.
3. This suit is not — expensive — the grey one.
4. If you turn — the left — the market place, you will see the school — the corner of St. Michael's Road and London Avenue.
5. The theatre is not — comfortable — the cinema, but it is — comfortable than the school hall.
6. How — does the journey to London from Birmingham take?
7. How — seats are there in the cinema?
8. How — do you go to church?
9. He is the — intelligent boy — the family.
10. I always go — work — foot.

Fórmense preguntas con las siguientes frases y contéstese a las preguntas:

How long?
How often?
How big?
How much?
How many?
How old?

Dictation:

From «Jimmy and Andrew...» to «...London Avenue.»

Translate into English:

La familia Jones quería ir a pasar las vacaciones de verano en la playa. «¿Cuál es el pueblo más agradable de (on) la costa sur?», preguntó el señor Jones a su esposa.

«A mucha gente le gusta Brighton o Eastbourne, porque son las ciudades más grandes de la costa, pero a mí me gusta un pueblo más pequeño, como Dawlish, por ejemplo, en Devonshire. Además, Brighton sería mucho más caro que Dawlish.»

«Me gusta mucho el Devonshire —dijo Pedro, el hijo—, porque no solamente hay el mar, sino* también las montañas que se llaman *moors,* como Dartmoor o Exmoor.»

«Sí, y Dawlish está muy cerca de Dartmoor», dijo la señora Jones.

«Unas setecientas millas. Por cierto, Brighton está mucho más cerca, pero es mejor ir más lejos de Londres. En Dawlish no habrá tanta gente como en Brighton. Además, si vamos a Dawlish estaremos muy cerca de Exeter, donde trabaja tu hermano mayor, y así él podrá venir a vernos los domingos.»

(* No se distingue en inglés entre *pero* y *sino.*)

LESSON FOUR

Vocabulary and Pronunciation

i: to gr*ee*t (saludar), gr*ee*ting (saludo, felicitación).

i   to d*i*stúrb (estorbar, molestar), *e*xcépt (excepto), *e*xáctly (exactamente), to *i*ntrodúce (presentar), nóis*y* (ruidoso), lángu*a*ge (idioma, lengua).

e   exc*e*pt, to st*e*p (pisar).

a   l*á*nguage, ex*á*ctly.

a: to l*a*ugh (reírse).

o: acc*o*rding to (según).

ə   to intr*o*dúce.

ə: to dist*ú*rb.

oi   n*ói*sy.

ou t*o*e (dedo del pie).

f   laug*h*.

Frase

as much as — tanto como

Grammar

Defective Auxiliary Verbs

1. THE VERB CAN (poder)

Affirmative		Negative		Interrogative	
Present	Preterite & Conditional	Present	Preterite & Conditional	Present	Preterite & Conditional
I can he can, etc.	I could he could, etc.	I cannot he cannot, etc.	I could not he could not, etc.	Can I? Can he?, etc.	Could I? Could he?, etc.

El verbo *can* traduce la idea de habilidad, posibilidad y permiso.

Por ej.: I can swim   Yo sé nadar.

I can speak English   Yo sé hablar inglés.

Can you come tomorrow? ¿Puede usted venir mañana?

Can I see you tomorrow? ¿Le podré ver mañana?

Se emplea muy a menudo en inglés delante de verbos de sensación.

Por ej.: I can see you. Ya le veo.

From the window you can hear the bells in the valley.
Desde la ventana se oyen las campanas abajo en el valle.

Contracciones

cannot se contrae en *can't* (ka:nt).
could not se contrae en *couldn't* (kúdənt).

2. THE VERB MUST (tener que, deber, deber de).
Sólo existe en presente de indicativo.

Affirmative	Negative	Interrogative
I must he must, etc.	I must not he must not, etc.	Must I? Must he?, etc.

Must traduce la idea de deber ineludible por obligación, necesidad, orden o consecuencia.

Por ej.: The children must be at school at nine o'clock.
Los niños deben estar en clase a las nueve.

Everybody must work if he wants to eat.
Todo el mundo tiene que trabajar, si quiere comer.

You must come home before nine o'clock.
Tenéis que regresar a casa antes de las nueve.

He must be upstairs. Debe de estar arriba.

Contracción

Must not se contrae en *mustn't* (mʌsənt).

3. THE VERB OUGHT (deber).

Sólo existe en presente de indicativo.

Affirmative	Negative	Interrogative
I ought to he ought to, etc.	I ought not to he ought not to, etc.	Ought I to? Ought he to?, etc.

Ought traduce la idea de deber moral o la del deber no ineludible.

Por. ej:. You ought to go home. Debes ir a casa.

Se traduce muchas veces al castellano por el condicional de deber.

Por ej.: I ought to learn English. Debería aprender inglés.

I ought to have gone yesterday. Debería haber ido ayer.

Contracción

ought not se contrae en *oughtn't* (ó:tǝnt).

Nótese bien que *ought* se construye siempre seguido de infinitivo con *to*, al contrario de los otros verbos defectivos.

4. THE VERB MAY (poder)

Affirmative		Negative		Interrogative	
Present	Preterite & Conditional	Present	Preterite & Conditional	Present	Preterite & Conditional
I may he may, etc.	I might he might, etc.	I might not he might not, etc.	I might not he might not, etc.	May I? May he?, etc.	Might I? Might he?, etc.

May traduce la idea de *poder* en el sentido de posibilidad o permiso.

Por ej.: May I come in?

¿Con permiso? ¿Se puede? (al entrar en una habitación).

You may smoke in this room.
Usted puede fumar en esta habitación.

He may come tomorrow. Puede venir mañana.

A menudo *may* se traduce por *quizá* con el subjuntivo.
Por ej.: He may come tomorrow. Quizá venga mañana.

Might se emplea para traducir la idea de posibilidad muy remota.
Por ej.: He might come tomorrow.
Es posible (pero poco probable) que venga mañana.

Contracciones

May not se contrae en *mayn't* (meint), y *might not* en *mightn't* (máitənt).

5. THE VERB SHOULD (deber)
   Tiene una sola forma, *should* (ʃud).

Affirmative	Negative	Interrogative
I should he should, etc.	I should not he should not, etc.	Should I? Should he?, etc.

Should tiene la misma significación que *ought to*.

Contracción

Should not se contrae en *shouldn't* (ʃúdənt).

PRACTICE TABLE

		Form answers
	speak only English in class?	
	come tomorrow?	
Can I	help them with their work?	Yes, you (he) ......
Can he	learn to swim?	No (he) you can't ...
Must I	learn to play the piano?	needn't .....
Must he	work harder?	may not ...
Should I	speak to the manager?	N. B. The negative
May I	give them more money?	answer to 'must'
Ought I to	buy a new suit?	'ought' and 'should'
	sell my house?	is **needn't**.

Observaciones importantes sobre los verbos defectivos

1. No añaden *s* a la tercera persona de singular del presente de indicativo.
2. No se construyen con el verbo auxiliar *to do* en formas negativa e interrogativa.
3. Van seguidos de infinitivo sin *to* (con excepción de *ought to*).

4. El pretérito pasado se emplea también como condicional (*could, might*).
5. No pueden estar seguidos de substantivos o de pronombres como complementos.

   Por ej.: I can't *do* this. No lo puedo.

6. Tiempos compuestos

Como los verbos defectivos no tienen participio pasado, no pueden formarse perfecto presente ni pluscuamperfecto de estos verbos. Sin embargo, existen formas equivalentes a estos tiempos. Se forman poniendo el infinitivo pasado a continuación del verbo defectivo en vez del infinitivo presente.

Presente:

I can come   Puedo venir.

Perfecto presente:

I can have come   He podido venir.

Pluscuamperfecto:

I could have come   Había podido venir.

Condicional pasado:

I could have come   Hubiera podido venir.

De la misma manera se dice:

He ought to have come	Hubiera debido venir.
We should have come	Hubiéramos debido venir.
They must have come	Han debido venir.
They may have come	Quizá hayan venido.
They might have come	Quizá hubieran venido.

Construcción con los verbos "teach", "learn" y "know".

El verbo *to know* se construye obligatoriamente con el infinitivo precedido de *how to*.

Por ej.: I know how to swim. Sé nadar.

Do you know how to play the piano?
¿Sabe usted tocar el piano?

Los verbos *teach* y *learn* se construyen o con *how to* o con *to* solo seguido de infinitivo.

{ Will you teach me how to swim?
{ Will you teach me to swim?
¿Quiere usted enseñarme a nadar?

{ I want to learn how to swim
{ I want to learn to swim.
Quiero aprender a nadar.

GREETINGS

Ramón, a young Spanish visitor to England, wants to learn as much English as he can while he is in England, so he is going to ask Mr. Brown some questions about the English language. Ramón is staying with Mr. Brown in London.

Ramón: May I come in, Mr. Brown, or am I disturbing you?

Mr. Brown: Not at all, Ramón, come in. What can I do for you?

Ramón: I should like to know how to say one or two things in English. Can you help me?

Mr. Brown: Of course, Ramón, with pleasure.

Ramón: First of all, when do I use «Goodbye»? Yesterday I met an English friend, and as I went past on my bicycle, I said «Goodbye», but he laughed. Why did he laugh?

Mr. Brown: Well, you ought not to say «Goodbye» except when you leave. If you want to greet somebody as you go past, you must say «Hullo», or «Good morning», «Good afternoon», or «Good evening», according to the time of the day. You mustn't use «Goodbye» exactly as you use «Adiós» in Spanish.

Ramón: When must I say «Good afternoon» and when must I say «Good evening»? That is another thing I ought to know.

Mr. Brown: Usually we use «Good afternoon» from lunch time until about six o'clock, and «Good evening» afterwards.

Ramón: Then, when do you say «Goodnight»?

Mr. Brown: «Goodnight» is generally used when you leave a house or person after dinner or late night. However, you may also use it when you meet somebody after dinner or late at night. Of course, you also say «Goodnight» when you go to bed.

Ramón: Another thing that I should like to know is what I ought to say when I am introduced to somebody and when somebody is introduced to me.

Mr. Brown: You both say «How do you do», which is not a question at all, but just a greeting, like «encantado» or «mucho gusto en conocerle». In good English you must never say «Pleased to meet you».

35

Ramón: And if I want to ask somebody how he is, what do I say?

Mr. Brown: Then you must say «How are you?». Now I shall ask you some questions, Ramón. See if you can answer. What do you say to a person on Christmas Day?

Ramón: «A merry Christmas and a happy New Year.»

Mr. Brown: And what should you say to a person on his birthday?

Ramón: I must have read that in Book I but I can't remember. Can you say «Happy Birthday»?

Mr. Brown: Yes, you can. But generally people say «Many happy returns of the day».

Ramón: Of course, I should have remembered that.

Mr. Brown: What would you say if you couldn't hear what somebody said to you in a noisy bus?

Ramón: «I beg your pardon.»

Mr. Brown: That's right. And what would you say if you had to get off the bus in a hurry and there were people in the way?

Ramón: «Excuse me, please.»

Mr. Brown: Excellent. And if you stepped on somebody's toe, as you got off the bus, what would you say?

Ramón: «Sorry» or «I'm sorry».

Mr. Brown: That's right. Or you could also say «I beg your pardon».

Exercises

A) **Answer the following questions:**

1. Who is Ramón?
2. What does Ramón want to do while he is in England?
3. Where is Ramón staying?
4. What does Ramón want to know?
5. What did Ramón say to his friend when he went past on his bicycle?
6. What should he have said?
7. What ought you to say when somebody is introduced to you?
8. What should you say to a person on his birthday?
9. What would you say if you couldn't hear what somebody said to you in a noisy bus?
10. What would you say if you met a friend in the street at 7.30 p.m.?

B) **Complete the following sentences:**
1. Mary wants to learn — much Spanish as she —, while she is in Spain.
2. — I smoke in this room, Mr. Brown?
3. As I went past — my bicycle, I said « —, Peter».
4. If you want to learn — to swim, you — go to the swimming lessons.
5. I — like to be introduced to the manager of the business.
6. You — say «Good afternoon» or «Good evening» — — the time of the day.
7. It is difficult to get — the bus because there are so many people — the way.
8. — is the best theatre in the town?
9. — — is Madrid from Barcelona?
10. — the beginning of his sermon he spoke about Aristotle and — the end about St. Paul.

C) **Form sentences using the following words:**

noisy, could, to step, wrong, ground floor, may, except, according to, ought, to disturb, might, to laugh, pleasure, should, language, afraid, must, spare room, to turn, can.

D) **Dictation:**

from «Ramón: Another thing that...» to «...say *How are you?»*

E) **Compongan un diálogo con los saludos apropiados:**
1. Una criada y un señor que ha llamado a un piso equivocado.
2. Un guardia y una señorita que le pregunta por la abadía de Westminster.
3. Dos amigos que no se han visto desde algún tiempo debido a la enfermedad de uno de ellos y que ahora se encuentran en la calle.
4. Una señora que presenta un señor a otro.
5. Un señor y un muchacho que le pregunta la hora.
6. Una madre que quiere enviar a su hija a la cama y la hija que no quiere ir.
7. Un padre y su hijo que le está pidiendo dinero para ir al fútbol.
8. La tendera y una señorita que entra en una tienda a comprar flores para enviar a una amiga por su santo.

Translate into English:

Ramón está escribiendo a un amigo en España que también quiere aprender el inglés, pero que no ha podido ir a Inglaterra como Ramón. Ramón ha pasado la tarde hablando con el señor Brown, que le ha enseñado los saludos en inglés.

«...Una de las muchas cosas — escribe Ramón — que no dicen en inglés como en español es *Adiós,* cuando encuentran a sus amigos en la calle. *Adiós* se traduce por *Goodbye,* pero sólo puedo decir *Goodbye* cuando salgo de casa, o cuando he hablado unos minutos con un amigo en la calle y le dejo. No puedo decir *Adiós* a un amigo a quien encuentro en la calle; tengo que decir en inglés *Hullo.*

»Otra equivocación que he hecho siempre hasta ahora es en el uso de *Good afternoon, Good evening* y *Goodnight.* Los ingleses dicen *Good afternoon* para *Buenas tardes,* solamente después del mediodía y hasta las seis o así de la tarde. Después dicen *Good evening. Goodnight* dicen cuando se van a la cama, o cuando salen de casa de sus amigos después de cenar, o cuando les dejan en la calle tarde a la noche, después del teatro, baile, o algo así.

»Aquí en Londres estoy divirtiéndome mucho. El señor Brown, en cuya casa estoy, me enseña mucho del idioma inglés y nos reímos mucho de mis equivocaciones. Pero ahora hablo mucho mejor. Él me presenta a mucha gente, y ahora yo sé decirles en inglés cosas como *encantado* — *How do you do* — y sé cómo saludarlos el día de sus cumpleaños y el día de Navidad. Pero todavía no sé hablar tanto como me gustaría. Quiero aprender a hablar bien y pronto.

»¿Cómo estás? ¿Y tu familia? ¿Y tus estudios, cómo van?»

LESSON FIVE

Vocabulary and Pronunciation

i: to bel*ie*ve (creer), sc*é*nery (decoraciones de teatro).

i   to enj*ó*y (disfrutar de, gozar de), bes*í*des (además), to des*í*gn (diseñar), reh*e*ársal (ensayo).

e   to sugg*é*st (sugerir), to perf*é*ct (perfeccionar).

a   to *a*ct (representar), *á*mateur (aficionado), dram*á*tic (dramático teatral).

o   j*o*b (tarea, empleo), f*ó*reign (extranjero).

o: dr*á*wing (dibujo).

ʌ   prod*ú*ction (obra, realización), cl*u*b (círculo).

ə   *á*mat*eur,* dr*a*mátic, *ó*ver (más de), to pr*o*d*ú*ce (realizar, poner en escena), pr*o*d*ú*ct*i*on, sc*é*n*e*ry, reh*e*árs*a*l, s*u*ggést, f*ó*r*e*ign, *o*cc*á*si*o*n*a*lly (de vez en cuando), to p*e*rféct.

ə: reh*e*ársal.

ei   to p*ai*nt (pintar), occ*á*sionally.

ai   bes*í*des, to des*í*gn.

oi   to enj*óy*.

ju: to prod*ú*ce.

ʃ   prod*ú*ct*i*on.

tʃ   ama*t*eur.

Consonante muda

g   muda en des*í*gn, f*ó*reign.

Frases

to act $\begin{cases} \text{a play} \\ \\ \text{plays} \end{cases}$ — representar $\begin{cases} \text{una comedia, una obra de} \\ \text{teatro.} \end{cases}$

spare time   — tiempo libre (véase *spare room,* Lesson I).

to hear about   — oír hablar de.

         Por ej.: I heard about you in London.
                 He oído hablar de usted en Londres.

to enjoy   — disfrutar de, gozar de (en inglés se construye con complemento directo).

         Por ej.: I enjoy the theatre very much.
                 Disfruto mucho en el teatro.

to be interested in — estar interesado en.

to take part in   — tomar parte en.

to call on (to visit) — visitar.

     Cuando se habla de Londres se añade muy a menudo *up* and *down* a los verbos de movimiento.

Por ej.: I am going *up* to London tomorrow.
          Voy a Londres mañana.

          He came *down* into the country yesterday.
          Vino al campo ayer.

to remember — acordarse. (Se construye con complemento directo.)

Por ej.: Did you remember my book?
¿Se acordó usted de mi libro?

Grammar

Traducción de "¿no es verdad?", "¿verdad?"

En inglés no existe una sola frase como *¿no es verdad?* que al añadirla cambie una afirmación en pregunta. Hay que repetir el verbo auxiliar de la frase afirmativa o negativa en la misma persona, pero repitiendo el verbo auxiliar en forma negativa después de una afirmación, y, al contrario, en forma afirmativa después de una negación.

Por ej.: *You are* coming with us, *aren't you?*
Usted viene con nosotros, ¿no es verdad?

You aren't coming with us, *are you?*
Usted no viene con nosotros, ¿no es verdad?

Si no hay un verbo auxiliar en la oración, se emplea el verbo auxiliar *to do* para formar la pregunta.

Por ej.: You go to work every day, don't you?
Usted va al trabajo cada día, ¿verdad?

Nótense bien los ejemplos de esta construcción en el trozo para la lectura y en el diálogo que sigue abajo.

Además, se repite el verbo auxiliar muchas veces (en inglés), donde en castellano se repite sólo el pronombre personal o sólo *sí* o *no,* por ejemplo, en contestaciones.

Por ej.: Have you received any news from your brother?
Yes, I have.

¿Ha recibido usted noticias de su hermano? Sí.

Did you come to England by air? Yes, I did.
¿Vino usted a Inglaterra por avión? Sí.

Who has taken my book? I have.
¿Quién ha cogido mi libro? Yo.

He has not lived in the East as long as I have.
No ha vivido en el Oriente tanto tiempo como yo.

Do you go to work on Sundays? No, I don't.
¿Va usted a su trabajo los domingos? No.

PRACTICE TABLE

In column 3 only use the form corresponding to column 1 — a with a, b with b, etc., but use *all* of column 2 with each.

	interested in the theatre	
You are	as intelligent as **Peter**	aren't you?
a	going to London	a
	working hard for your exam	
you aren't	learning to swim	are you
b	smoking too much	b
c	coming home soon	wasn't he?
he was	going to learn Persian	c
d	living at Cambridge	was he?
He wasn't	studying at Oxford	d

PRACTICE TABLE

In column 3 only use the form corresponding to column 1 (a) with (a); (b) with (b), etc., but use all of column 2 with each.

You will	pay for my ticket	won't you?
a	go to the country	a
You won't	travel by air	will you?
b	have lunch at a restaurant	b
He can	come home late	can't he?
c	act in that play	c
He can't	have a lot of spare time	can he?
d	paint the scenery	d
She didn't	take a job in England	did she?
e	cook the lunch	e
	paid for my ticket	
	went to the country	
	travelled by air	
	had lunch at a restaurant	
you	came home late	didn't you?
	acted in that play	
	had a lot of spare time	
	painted the scenery	
	took a job in England	
	cooked the lunch	

Construcción con "besides"

Besides se emplea sólo como adverbio, en el sentido de *además.*

Por ej.: You can't come in with your hat on: besides you haven't a ticket.

No puede entrar con el sombrero puesto; además no tiene entrada.

Además de seguido de infinitivo se traduce también por *besides,* pero en inglés va seguido no del infinitivo, sino de la forma en *-ing* (gerundio).

Por ej.: *Besides coming* home late, he always makes a noise and wakes me up.

Además de volver a casa tarde, siempre hace ruido y me despierta.

Besides being very clever, he works very hard.

Además de ser muy listo, trabaja mucho.

Reading

PLAYS AND ACTING

In many English towns and even in villages there are clubs of people who are interested in the theatre and who act plays during their spare time. These clubs are usually called Amateur Dramatic Societies and there are over 30,000 of them in Great Britain, besides the dramatic societies in the schools. Almost every school has its dramatic society and produces at least one play a year.

When Pedro arrived in Oxford to study he heard about the Oxford University Dramatic Society and went to see a production of Shakespeare's *Richard II* which he enjoyed very much. As he was very interested in the theatre he thought it would be pleasant to take part in a play and that it would be a good way to perfect his English. So he called on the secretary of the OUDS in his lodgings and asked if he could become a member.

«You would find it rather difficult to act in English, wouldn't you?» said the secretary.

«Yes, I should, but there are other jobs I could do besides acting, aren't there?»

«Certainly. What sort of job would you like?»

«I am very interested in designing costumes and painting scenery. You always design and make your scenery, don't you?»

«Of course. Perhaps then you could come to some rehearsals of our next play and prepare a drawing of the scenery you suggest. It will be Bernard Shaw's *St. Joan.*»

«The OUDS doesn't ever produce a play in a foreign language, does it?»

«No, we don't. But there are several societies or clubs in Oxford which act in different languages. The French Club, for example, often produces a play in French, and I believe the Spanish Club occasionally produces one in Spanish. That would probably interest you (Calling to a friend.) Peter, you ought to know. The Spanish Club produces plays in Spanish, doesn't it?»

«Yes, I saw the last one they did. Rather bad it was, too. Perhaps Pedro could help them to do the next one better.»

And so Pedro joined the Oxford University Dramatic Society and later acted in Spanish in a comedy by the Quintero Brothers which was produced by the Oxford University Spanish Club.

Exercises

A) Answer the following questions:

1. What do many people do in their spare time in English towns and villages?

2. About how many Dramatic Societies are there in England?

3. What did Pedro hear about when he arrived in Oxford to study?

4. What play did Pedro see in Oxford?

5. Did he enjoy it?

6. Why did Pedro call on the secretary of the OUDS?

7. Why did Pedro want to become a member of the OUDS?

8. In what was Pedro interested besides acting?

9. What did the secretary of the OUDS suggest to Pedro?

10. What societies in Oxford sometimes produce a play in a foreign language?

11. Was the last play the Spanish club produced good?

12. Did Pedro act while he was at Oxford?

B) Fórmense oraciones con las siguientes frases o palabras:

1. to act plays.
2. spare time.
3. to hear about.
4. to enjoy very much.

5. to be interested in.
6. to take part in.
7. to become.
8. besides.
9. occasionally.
10. to join.

C) **Complétense las siguientes oraciones con la frase inglesa que equivale a "no es verdad" en castellano, cambiando así la afirmación o negación en pregunta.**

1. You are going down to the country tomorrow, — —?
2. He isn't interested in the theatre, — —?
3. You wouldn't find it easy to act in English, — —?
4. You remember me, — —?
5. You are not taking him to Spain, — —?
6. You won't be late, — —?
7. He can speak Spanish, — —?
8. We didn't come this way, — —?
9. She couldn't call on you yesterday, — —?
10. There's no hurry, — —?

D) **Dictation:**

Plays and acting. From «In many English towns and even in the villages...» to «...a good way to perfect his English».

E) **Compositions:**

Write compositions of not more than 60 words on the following subjects:
1. An Amateur Dramatic Society.
2. A visit to the theatre.

Translate into English:

Pedro estaba muy interesado en el teatro, y, cuando fue a la Universidad de Oxford para estudiar, pensó que sería muy agradable — además de ayudarle en el idioma — tomar parte en alguna representación teatral. Había oído hablar mucho de los círculos de aficionados del teatro en Inglaterra que representan obras de teatro en su tiempo libre. Se acordó que hay más de 30.000 de estos Amateur Dramatic Societies en Gran Bretaña. En Oxford había oído hablar de la Oxford University Dramatic Society y quería ser socio.

«Desde luego yo no sé hablar inglés bastante bien para hacer un papel (to act), pero hay otras cosas que puedo hacer, ¿verdad? Sé diseñar y pintar las decoraciones de teatro y disfruto mucho con diseñar los vestidos también.»

«Es mejor — dijo el secretario —, porque ahora necesitamos a alguien para esas cosas más que actores. Tenemos siempre muchas personas que quieren tener papeles. Tienes tiempo para venir al próximo ensayo, ¿verdad? El sábado que viene, por la tarde. Entonces puedes ver la obra y darnos tus ideas para la decoración y también para los vestidos.»

«Otra cosa que creo que tú puedes decirme. Hay un círculo en Oxford que representa de vez en cuando obras de teatro en español, ¿verdad? Me gustaría ser socio de éste y tomar parte en las representaciones.»

«Sí, existe. Y creo que va a dar pronto una obra en español. Yo voy de vez en cuando a ver las producciones, y la última no estaba muy bien representada. Quizá tú puedes ayudarles, porque creo que necesitan españoles para hacer los papeles principales.»

Así Pedro en su tiempo libre tomó parte en producciones de teatro en inglés y en castellano.

LESSON SIX

Revisión

Pronunciación de los sonidos consonantes ʃ, tʃ, ʒ, dʒ.

ʃ	tʃ	ʒ	dʒ
cushion	furniture	revision	to enjoy
mention	lecture	pleasure	to suggest
production	picture	explosión	job
exhibition	century	to measure	luggage
position	temperature	measurement	village
pronunciation	teacher	occasión	manager

Nótese:

1. Que la terminación -*tion* se pronuncia -ʃən.
2. Que la terminación -*ture* se pronuncia -tʃə.
3. Que la terminación -*sion*, precedida de vocal, se pronuncia -ʒən.
4. Que la terminación -*age* se pronuncia -idʒ.
5. Que la letra *j* se pronuncia siempre dʒ, por ejemplo, *job, enjoy*.

Reading

CHARLES ARRIVES HOME

Mr. Armstrong: Betty, it's today that Charles is arriving, · isn't it?

Daughter: Yes. We ought to go and meet him at the station, oughtn't we?

Father: When does his train arrive?

Daughter: It comes in at 4.35 this afternoon at Paddington Station.

Father: Then you must go and meet him alone, Betty, because I can't be there in time. I've got to see the manager of the Furniture Hire Service. We have some very important business together and I'm certain I shan't leave his office before five. I may get an order to design furniture for his hire service, so I must stay there as long as he wants, mustn't I? But I hope the spare room is ready for Charles.

Daughter: Oh, yes. Mother and I have been painting it all the week and last night we put in the furniture, the curtains and the carpet. It is all ready. Only the electric stove doesn't work.

Father: Well, it will have to be mended. You should have taken it to the shop before.

Daughter: Last time we used it, it worked very well. It must have been broken since then.

Father: Well, I think the weather is becoming warmer, so perhaps he won't need it. Now I must be on my way to work. Good-bye, Betty.

Daughter: Good-bye, father.

At about half-past three in the afternoon Betty started off for Paddington Station to meet her elder brother, Charles. She should have gone to a piano recital at the musical society, but she thought this a much more important event, as she had not seen Charles for two years. She took a bus from her home to the station. The bus is slower than the underground (metro), but the underground is noisier and not so interesting, as you can't see anything. So Betty always goes by bus if she has time. She got to the station at a quarter past four.

«At what platform (andén) does the train from Plymouth come in?» she asked a porter.

«Platform No5,» he answered.

Betty bought a platform ticket and then sat down to wait for the train. Soon she saw her father who was coming towards platform No.5.

«Father,» she called.

«Hullo, Betty. I was able to get here after all. Have you been waiting long?»

Daughter: No, I've only been waiting for ten minutes. Let's go on to the platform and sit down there. When the train comes in, we shall be able to find Charles.

A few minutes later the train came in.

«Look, there's Charles getting out of the train. Hullo, Charles.»

Charles: Hullo, Betty. Hullo, Father. May I introduce my wife, Margaret? This is Betty, my sister, and my father.

Daughter: Charles, you're not married!

Charles: Yes, I am. I've been married for three weeks. Isn't that pleasant news?

Daughter: Of course, it is. Congratulations (felicidades), Charles.

Father: Now come along and get your luggage. Have you got a lot of *registered** luggage?

Charles: Only two large cases. (To a porter) Porter, will you take these cases and the two large registered cases to a taxi.

Porter: Yes, sir. I'll meet you with the luggage outside.

And so Charles arrived home, after two years in foreign countries, with his young wife Margaret.

Exercises

A) Answer the following questions:

1. When does Charles's train arrive at Paddington Station?
2. Why can't Mr. Armstrong go and meet Charles?
3. Who has been painting the spare room?
4. At what time did Betty start off for Paddington Station?
5. How long was it since Betty had seen Charles?
6. Why did Betty go by bus to the station?
7. At what time did she get to the station?

---

* Facturado. ¿Qué otro sentido tiene esta palabra?

8. How much registered luggage did Charles have?
9. What pleasant news did Charles bring?
10. How did the family go home from the station?

B) **Use the following words or phrases in sentences:**

week-end, the ground floor, on the left, to be afraid, to remember, in this way, puzzled, to amuse, to last, to reach, to laugh, to disturb, besides, job, production.

C) **Give the comparative and the superlative forms of the following adjectives:**

old, pleasant, comfortable, dull, absent-minded, good, bad, important, puzzled, wide, noisy, far.

D) **Form questions for the following answers:**

1. It comes in at 5.25 at Victoria Station.
2. No, it doesn't work.
3. I've been waiting ten minutes.
4. It will arrive at Platform No. 5.
5. Yes, I have two registered cases.
6. The hall has seats for 300 people.
7. I am 1 metre 80 centimetres tall.
8. The cinema is the most comfortable hall in the town.
9. Betty is the tallest of the family.
10. The river is about 20 metres wide.

E) **Substitution Table**

Form all the sentences possible and translate them into Spanish.

He	ought to have been must have been should have been could have been might have been can't have been may have been	well taught disturbed during the night introduced to the Mayor given the job amused by the story married in London told about the concert

F) **Accentuation**

Márquense las sílabas acentuadas en el trozo de lectura desde el principio hasta «...room is ready for Charles». Después léase el trozo tomando bien en cuenta la acentuación.

(Para las reglas de la acentuación en inglés véase *Inglés para Españoles,* Libro elemental, pág. 16).

LESSON SEVEN

Vocabulary and Pronunciation

i: to recéive, (recibir), to léave oút (omitir).

i to receíve, to nótice (observar), fígure (cifra), líterally (literalmente), relátion (pariente), Chrístian náme (nombre), íntimate (íntimo), to fínish (terminar), símply (sencillamente), prétentious (afectado), wísh (deseo, recuerdo).

e addréss (señas), to addréss (dirigir), corréct (correcto), mémber (socio, individuo), afféctionately (cariñosamente, con afecto), preténtious, hélpful (útil), réference (referencia), manageréss (directora), énding (terminación), esséntial (esencial).

a náturally (naturalmente), manageréss.

a: regárds (recuerdos).

o póssible (posible).

o: fórmula (fórmula).

u hélpful, in fúll (entero).

ə pérsonal, addréss, figure, corréct, líterally, fórmula, náturally, íntimate, mémber, afféctionately, relátion, preténtious, réference, manageréss, advíce (consejo), esséntial, énvelope (sobre).

ə: pérsonal (personal, particular).

ei látely (recientemente), Chrístian náme, relátion.

ai títle (título), advíce.

ou to nótice, to close (cerrar, terminar), énvelope.

ju: súitable, fórmula.

iə sincérely (sinceramente).

ʃ affectionately, relátion, finish, preténtious, essential, wísh.

tʃ náturally, Chrístian náme.

Frase

at the top = al principio de la página, en la parte superior.

Grammar

Pronombres y adjetivos indefinidos

Unidad	one	uno, una	He has only one arm.
Dualidad	both	ambos (as)	He took it with both hands.
	each	cada uno (de dos)	He has a ring on each hand.
	either	cualquiera (de dos)	Either boy can do it, but.
	neither	ninguno (de dos)	neither wants to.
Pluralidad	several	varios	I have several letters to write.
	most	la mayoría	Most of my relations live in England.
Totalidad	all	todo(s)	All the children have gone nome.
	each } every }	cada (uno) cada	Each boy has a ball. He goes to work every day.
	whole	entero	He has eaten the whole cake.
Cantidad — pequeña	some } any }	alguno (os)	I have some children but my brother hasn't any.
	a little	un poco de	I have a little money to spend.
	a few	algunos	The baby has a few toys.
Cantidad — grande	Much, many a great deal	mucho una gran cantidad	He hasn't much time. I have a great deal of work.
	a great many	una gran cantidad	I have a lot of work.
	a lot	una gran cantidad	I have a great many friends.
Cantidad — suficiente	enough	bastante	Have you enough sugar?
Cantidad — insuficiente	little	poco	I have little money to spend.
	few	pocos	The baby has few toys.
Ausencia	no } not any } none	ningún (adj.) ninguno (pronombre)	He has no servants. He hasn't any servants. He has none.
Adición	another	otro	Will you give me another glass?
	the other(s)	el otro, los otros	Have the others arrived yet?

Observaciones

1. Con *some, any, one, no* y *every* se forman las siguientes palabras compuestas que se emplean sólo como pronombres:

somebody anybody someone anyone	} alguien	something anything	} algo
nobody no-one	} nadie	nothing everything	nada todo
everybody everyone	} todo el mundo		

2. También se emplea sólo como pronombre *none*; y *no* y *every* se emplean sólo como adjetivos.

3. Nótese la posición de *all* y *both.* Se colocan después de un pronombre personal o después del verbo auxiliar en un tiempo compuesto.

   Por ej.: We all like to play tennis.
   They both went out.
   You have all made a mistake.
   You must both come this evening.

   Con un substantivo se colocan delante del artículo definido o después del substantivo.

   Por ej.: All the children came.
   Both the boys went home.
   The children all came.
   The boys both went home.

4. *Every* y *each* van seguidos de verbo singular. *Every* tiene sentido colectivo, y *each* un sentido más particular. *Each* se usa obligatoriamente hablando de dos personas o cosas.

   Por ej.: Every person in this house is a student.
   Cada persona en esta casa es estudiante.

   Each of the two boys was invited.
   Cada uno de los dos muchachos estaba invitado.

5. *Some, any, no.*

   Some y *any* se emplean cuando interviene la idea de cantidad.

Por ej.: The baker sells bread.
El panadero vende pan (en general).
I bought bread for tea.
Compré pan para el té (una cantidad).

6. *Not... any* no puede ser sujeto de la oración. Hay que emplear *no, o none.*

Por ej.:
They did not buy any bread. No bread $\Big\}$ was bought.
None

7. *Any* se emplea también en sentido muy indefinido para traducir *cualquier.*

Por ej.: Any person can do that.

8. *Either, neither.*
Either se traduce por *cualquiera de los dos* y *neither* por *ninguno de los dos.*
Neither, como *none,* va seguido de verbo en forma afirmativa.

9. *Most.*
Most se traduce por *la mayoría* y va seguido de verbo en plural. Puede ser pronombre o adjetivo.

Por ej.: Most people like sugar.
Most of the boys have come already.

PRACTICE TABLE

Both		
All	of them	
Several	of us	know how to do it
Most	of the children	
A few	children	
A great many	students	
Few		have come.
Some		

PRACTICE TABLE

Each person	is arriving tonight.
Every student	will pay for a ticket.
Everybody	can come to the concert.
Nobody	wrote a letter to the teacher.
Somebody	was invited.
Neither boy	was disturbed in the night.
Neither Tom nor Harry	went by bus to the station
Either Joan or Betty	lives on the ground floor.

10. *Other.*

Nótese el orden de las palabras en la frase *otros muchos — many others.*

Have you many other dresses? ¿Tiene usted otros muchos vestidos?

Reading

Mr. Brown: Good morning, Ramón. How is the English getting on?

Ramón: Very well, thank you. But there are a few things I should like to ask you. I have received a great many letters lately and I have no idea how to answer them in English.

Mr. Brown: What sort of letters are they, Ramón? Personal or business letters?

Ramón: Both. Some are from the friends I have met here in England, others from the manager of my bank and the bookshop in London where I ordered some books.

Mr. Brown: Well, let's begin with the personal letters. First of all, we put the address from which we are writing at the top of the page on the right.

12, St. Michael's Rd..
Bedford.

Notice that the number of the house is put before the name of the road or street. *Rd.* is a contraction for *road,* just as *St.* is a contraction for *Saint. St.* can also be a contraction for *street.*

24, Fleet St.,
London.

Under the address we put the date.

24, Fleet St.,
London.
February 1st, 1947.

We can also write the date in figures — 1/2/47. Either way is correct. Then we put the greeting. Nearly all letters in English, personal or business, begin with the greeting *Dear,* which, of course, is not always translated literally. It is only a formula. If you are writing to someone whom you call by his or her Christian name, you naturally say:

Dear Peter,

Dear Elizabeth, etc.

or if you want to be more intimate, you can say:

My dear Peter,
My dear Elizabeth, etc.

To close letters of this sort, there are several possible ways. *Yours ever,* is suitable for all. *Affectionately, Love,* is used between women, and between members of the same family. *Yours sincerely* can be used, but it is rather cold, as it is used for less intimate relations.

For all other personal letters most people begin *Dear Mr. Brown, Dear Mrs. Brown,* or *Dear Miss Brown,* and finish *Yours sincerely.*

If the person has a title, you address him by it. *Dear Sir Hubert, Dear Lady Maud, Dear Colonel Williams, Dear Professor Jones.*

A great many men who do not call one another by their Christian names but do not want to use *Mr.,* simply say *Dear Brown, Dear Jones, Dear Perrin* — leaving out *Mr.* Then they can finish with *Yours sincerely* or *Yours ever.* Women should not, of course, address men in this way without writing (sin escribir) *Mr.*

A great many people change *Yours sincerely* to *Sincerely yours,* but this is rather pretentious.

Ramón: That is very helpful, Mr. Brown. Now can you tell me how to answer these business letters?

Mr. Brown: Yes, it is very easy. The address and date you write at the top exactly as for personal letters. On the left you put the reference number, if there is one, and under that the name and address of the person or firm you are writing to. The normal opening is *Dear Sir,* or *Dear Madam,* if the firm has a manageress.

Ref.: ATW/BS.   12, St. Michael's Rd.,
The Manager,   Bedford.
Lloyd's Bank Ltd.,   Feb. 1st, 1946
24, High Street,
Bedford.
Dear Sir,

To close a business letter we nearly always use *Yours faithfully* though a few people use *Yours truly.*

Ramón: How do you address the envelope?

Mr. Brown: If you are writing to professional men you say
C. W. Brown, Esq.,
12, St. Michael's Rd.,
Bedford.

Esq. is a short form of *Esquire* which is never written in full. To a lady, if she is married, you say

Mrs. C. W. Brown,

If unmarried,

Miss Brown,

or   Miss Mary Brown.

Business letters are usually not addressed to a certain person, but to *The Manager,* or to the name of the firm:

B. H. Blackwell and Son, Ltd.,

Broad Street,

Oxford.

Now here is some advice for a Spaniard who is writing letters in English.

1. Do not translate the usual Spanish formula for the beginning or end of a letter in English. Such beginnings as *Muy señor mío* or *Distinguido señor* cannot be translated literally.

2. Do not use such endings as *I am* or *I remain* before *Yours sincerely.* They are only business endings and not essential, In personal letters, you can, of course, send *Best wishes* or *Kind regards.* For example:

«With best wishes to all your family,

Yours sincerely,

William Brown.»

or   «With kind regards to Mrs. — ,

Yours sincerely,

William Brown.»

3. Do not use Spanish terms like *Ilustrísimo* or *Excelencia* in the envelope. In English only Ambassadors are addressed *His Excellency...*, Cardinals *His Eminence,* and Bishops and Archibishops *His Grace...* Other titles are used without any formula:

The Vice-Chancellor,

Cambridge University,

Cambridge.

The Director,

The National Gallery,

London.

4. Do not use *Sir* to translate *Señor* on an envelope.

Señor don José Ramos becomes in English *José Ramos, Esq.* But when you talk to the person, you say *Mr. Ramos.*

Do not put *Mr.* as well as *Esq.*

Sir is used in front of a name as a title, like *marqués* or *conde.*

Sir William Brown.

5. Priests are addressed *Rev. Charles Brown* (Protestant) or *Rev. Father Brown* (Catholic).

Ramón: Well, that is certainly quite a lot to learn in one lesson. Thank you very much for your help, Mr. Brown.

Mr. Brown: Not at all, Ramón. I'm very pleased to be able to help you at any time.

Exercises

A) **Write the beginnings and endings of the following letters:**

1. A schoolboy (John Brown) to his Uncle Charles.
2. A doctor to the manager of a firm which makes medical instruments.
3. A student at a university (David Jones) to one of the professors (Professor Andrew Scott).
4. A young girl (Betty Howard) to her great friend (Mary Smith).
5. The secretary of a Football Club (Mr. C. H. Pickwick) to one of the members (Mr. A. E. Williams).

B) **Complete the following sentences with the suitable preposition:**

1. At what time do you get — in the morning?
2. How are you getting — with your Spanish?
3. You must get — the bus at Piccadilly Circus.
4. Put the address — the top of the page — the right.
5. Don't leave — the date on your letters.
6. We never write *Esquire* and *Mister* — full.
7. They have been living in Madrid — ten years.
8. — the beginning of a letter you put the address, and — the end you put the ending.
9. Go — the High Street and turn — the left at the bank.
10. Have you heard — the new play at the Piccadilly Theatre?

C) **Put in "some", "any" or "no" in each of these sentences:**

1. Did you see — one come into the room before lunch?
2. I must write — business letters this afternoon.
3. No, I have — idea how to answer these letters in English.
4. — Spaniard can tell you who Cisneros was.
5. I have never met — body like Dr. Spooner.
6. Did the postman give you — thing for me?
7. No, he gave me — thing at all for you.
8. — thing is burning in this room; — one must have left a cigarette burning.
9. Won't — body help me up the stairs with my box?
10. — house is better than — house.

D) **Put in one of the following words to complete these sentences - "most", "little", "few", "lot", "enough":**

1. — Englishmen know how to speak Greek.
2. Haven't you — money to buy a new suit?
3. This house is not big — for all my family.
4. Won't you have a — more tea?
5. He must have a — of money to be able to spend so much.
6. — people in England like to spend Christmas with their families.
7. I have received a parcel of new books: a — are interesting but — of them are dull.
8. He has only — money and — friends, but he is very happy.
9. Have you got — food? Yes, I've got a — more than I need, thank you.
10. — young men can be so intelligent as he is.

E) **Use the following words or phrases in sentences:**

several, suitable, to finish, to get on, whole, to address, Christian name, a great many, helpful, both, in full, none, to notice, nearly, either.

F) **Make the following sentences negative:**

1. Either room will be suitable.
2. You can have some more furniture for your bedroom.
3. Some of the curtains belong to my brother.
4. Both of them were late for the concert.
5. I could see somebody in the next-door garden.

G) **Write the following letters (of not more than 50 words each):**

1. Betty Brown to Mary Smith to invite her to a tea-party on her birthday.

2. Mr. Peter Jones to his Bank Manager asking for £25 credit (crédito) to finish his studies.

3. Mrs. Brown to Mrs. Smith, inviting the Smiths to spend the week-end with the Browns.

Ejercicio de construcción y de acentuación de la frase:

Se formarán todas las combinaciones de frases posibles con las palabras dadas, escogiendo la forma del verbo apropiada. Es de suma importancia preparar la frase escogida de antemano y decirla sin vacilación, acentuando sólo las sílabas accntuadas (marcadas así: *séveral*). Para las reglas de acentuación de la frase, véase libro I, pág. 16.

LESSON EIGHT

Vocabulary and Pronunciation

i:	to f*ee*l (sentir), wh*ee*l (rueda), wh*ea*t (trigo).
i	t*y*pical (típico, característico), v*í*ll*a*ger (aldeano), v*í*carage (vicaría), to h*i*t (golpear, pegar), to m*i*x (mezclar), to cons*í*st (consistir), f*í*ll*i*ng-st*á*tion (depósito de gasolina).
e	to l*e*t (dejar, permitir), f*e*lt (de *sentir*), to exp*é*ct (esperar), p*é*trol (gasolina), to el*é*ct (elegir).
a	*á*sp*e*ct (aspecto), *á*ccident (accidente), P*á*rish (parroquia), j*a*m (mermelada), bl*a*cksmith (herrero).
a:	f*a*st (rápido, rápidamente).
o	c*ó*ttage (casita campestre), to bl*o*ck (bloquear), auth*ó*rity (autoridad).
ʌ	p*ú*ncture (pinchazo).
u:	h*ó*rse-sh*oe* (herradura).
ə:	adv*é*rtisement (anuncio).
ai	to dr*i*ve (conducir, ir en coche).
ou	*ó*wner (propietario).
au	c*ou*ncil (consejo), h*ou*sekeeper (ama de llaves).
aiə	t*y*re (neumático).
eə	ch*ai*rman (director, presidente).
w	*w*heel, *w*heat.
tʃ	punc*t*ure.

Frase

> To have... left.   Quedarle a uno.

Por ej.: You haven't much petrol left.
> No le queda mucha gasolina.

Verbos irregulares

to feel — felt — felt	sentir, palpar.
to let — let — let	dejar, permitir.
to hit — hit — hit	golpear, pegar.

Grammar

The Infinitive

El infinitivo en inglés puede emplearse precedido de la preposición *to* o no, según el caso.

A) El infinitivo sin *to* se emplea:

1. Después de los verbos auxiliares defectivos (véase lección 4), con excepción de *ought*.

Por ej.: Can you come tomorrow?
> ¿Puede usted venir mañana?

> May I look at your newspaper?
> ¿Puedo ver su periódico?

Shall y *Will* son verdaderos verbos auxiliares defectivos que se usan así para formar el futuro :

Por ej.: We shall all bring you some books.
> They will not arrive tonight.

2. Después del verbo *to do,* cuando se emplea como verbo auxiliar para formar las formas negativas e interrogativas de los verbos regulares en presente y pretérito pasado.

Por ej.: Does he go to the club every day?
> ¿Va al círculo cada día?

> Do you know where my hat is?
> ¿Sabe usted dónde está mi sombrero?

> I didn't see him at the concert.
> No le he visto en el concierto.

59

3. Después de los verbos *to make* y *to let*.

Por ej.: I made him come.   Le hice venir.
       Let me go out.   Déjame salir.

Nótese bien la diferencia entre el verbo *to let* en sentido de *dejar, permitir,* y formando el imperativo en primera y tercera persona. Lleva la misma construcción en ambos casos.

Let us go)
Let's go   )   ¡Vámonos!
Let him come in.   ¡Que entre!
Let them go out.   ¡Que salgan!

También hay otro verbo *to let* en sentido de *alquiler, arrendar* (véase Book I).

4. Después de los verbos de sensación (véase Book I, Lesson 31), como *to see, to hear, to feel,* etc.

Por ej.: I saw the boy fall from the tree.
       He heard his father come in.

Nótese que se coloca el sujeto del verbo dependiente delante del mismo, al contrario del uso en castellano.

He heard *his father come in.* Oyó *entrar a su padre.*

PRACTICE TABLE

I saw	him	leave the house
I made		start off
We watched	her	drive the car away
They let		get in by the window
Did you hear	Mr. Brown	run away.
		go home
	Let's	

Sin embargo, si la acción dura algún tiempo se emplea la *forma progresiva* en *-ing* en vez del infinitivo sin *to*.

Por ej.: He saw his father coming down the street.
       Vio a su padre bajar la calle.

       I heard the rain falling on the roof.
       Oí caer la lluvia sobre el tejado.

B) El infinitivo con *to* se emplea:

1. Como sujeto de la oración:

Por ej.: To learn a foreign language is not always easy.

2. Después de la mayoría de los verbos, excluyendo los ya mencionados en *A*.

    to like, to decide, to want, to start, to hope, to **tell**, ought, etc.

Por ej.: It started to rain.

    He **wanted** to ask you a question.

    I **decided** to go home.

    We **ought** to help his brother.

3. Como calificativo:

Flat to let.	Piso para alquilar.
I've got a job to do.	Tengo una tarea que hacer.

Si se trata de un infinitivo con sentido pasivo, en inglés hay que emplear el infinitivo pasivo.

    There's a job to be done.   Hay una tarea que hacer.

    It was the last thing in my house that remained to be sold.

    Era lo último en mi casa que quedaba por vender.

4. Para formar la *construcción infinitiva* (acusativo e infinitivo) después de los verbos de deseo (*to want*, etcétera), de orden (*to order, to tell*, etc.), de ruego (*to ask*, etc.) y de expectación (*to expect*, etc.)

    I want you to come tomorrow.

    Quiero que usted venga mañana.

    He ordered the men to leave the town.

    Ordenó a los hombres que dejasen la ciudad.

    She told me to meet her at the tea-shop.

    Me dijo que le encontrara en el salón de té.

    They asked us to give them some books.

    Nos pidieron que les diéramos libros.

    We expect them to arrive tomorrow.

    Esperamos que lleguen mañana.

    He told her not to drive too fast.

    Le dijo que no condujese demasiado aprisa.

Nótese que se pone la negación *not* delante del infinitivo.

Traducción del subjuntivo castellano

Nótese bien que el subjuntivo castellano en las frases subordinantes introducidas por *que...* después de los verbos de *de-*

seo, orden, ruego y *expectación* no se traduce al inglés ni por subjuntivo ni por indicativo, sino por el infinitivo, y la conjunción *que* no se traduce al inglés.

Traducción del infinitivo castellano después de "pensar".

La construcción infinitiva después de *pensar,* como en la oración:

Por ej.: Pienso venir mañana,

no se puede traducir literalmente al inglés. Hay que emplear el futuro en inglés:

I think I shall come tomorrow.

Reading

Mr. Armstrong: Well, Conchita, would you like to go down to the country tomorrow and see a typical English village?

Conchita: Yes, very much. I should like you to show me all the different aspects of English life so that I can learn as much as possible about England and the English while I am on this short visit to your country.

Mr. Armstrong: I have seen an advertisement in the local paper which says that there is a cottage to let in the village of Oakshot, some twenty miles from here. As I want the children to spend their summer holidays in the fresh air, I thought we could drive down to Oakshot and look at the cottage and the village. If the cottage is suitable I shall take it for the summer.

So Mr. and Mrs. Armstrong and Conchita started off the next day in Mr. Armstrong's car. They had been going about half an hour and were in the country when Conchita said, «Will you let me drive now, Mr. Armstrong? The road is quite wide here.»

Mr. Armstrong: All right, Conchita. But don't drive too fast, and keep well to the left.

About two miles farther on, there had been an accident on the road and a policeman stopped the car and made them go round by a side road as the main road was blocked by the accident. He also told them to drive slowly as the side road was very bad. After a short time Conchita felt the back wheel on the left hitting the ground very hard and she said, «Mr. Armstrong, I think we have got a puncture.»

«Dear me», said Mr. Armstrong. «Stop the car and let's get out and see.»

When they got out of the car, they could hear the air coming out of the tyre. However, they soon changed the wheel
and were on their way again. They arrived at the village at
about half-past three.

Mr. Armstrong: I asked the owner to meet me at the cottage
at five o'clock so we have time to look around the village first and talk to some of the villagers. Last time
I was here I talked to old Archie Douglas who has a
farm at the end of the village. He expects me to
visit him every time I come to Oakshot. So let's go
there first. He's the chairman of the Parish Council.

Conchita: What's the Parish Council?

Mr. Armstrong: The Parish Council consists of about seven
or eight members of the village who are elected by the
other villagers to take care of all the village affairs
and help the other authorities, like the District Council. Of course, they are not paid for the work they do.

Conchita: What is that fine old building there, Mr. Armstrong?

Mr. Armstrong: That's the village school. It is nearly 350
years old, but it was not built as a school. It is a
typical English house of about the time of Shakespeare. In the same building the village Women's Institute meets. This is a sort of club for the ladies,
where they talk together and listen to lectures and
sometimes act plays. The women also bring their
fruit to the Institute to make jam and the Institute
gives help and advice to mothers and housekeepers.
Most villages have a Women's Institute, as they have
a Men's Club where the men meet to talk over a glass
of beer or play cards.

Conchita: Look at that fine church.

Mr. Armstrong: Yes, it is a fine building, isn't it?

Conchita: How old is it?

Mr. Armstrong: I should think it was built in about 1450. But
don't ask me to tell you its history because I know
very little about buildings. But I can tell you that
this house by the church is not old. It is the vicarage
where the vicar lives and where the church council meets
to discuss the affairs of the church. Besides this old
church there are two other churches, a Baptist chapel
and a small Roman Catholic chapel.

Conchita: Look, Mr. Armstrong, you haven't much petrol left.

Mr. Armstrong: No, I haven't. I must get some at the next filling station. There is one in the middle of the village.

Mr. and Mrs. Armstrong and Conchita drove to the filling station and got some more petrol. Then they got out of the car and told the man at the garage to mend the puncture. Then they walked along the main street of the village and saw the village shop which sells everything from bread to paint. Near it was *The Brown Cow,* one of the two inns or public-houses in the village. Farther down the street was the blacksmith, who was making a new shoe for a horse which was waiting. Then they visited Archie Douglas at his farm, which is a typical farm of this part of the country, a small mixed farm with cows and chickens, fields of vegetables and potatoes and fields of wheat. Quite a rich farm too.

Then they met the owner at the cottage and as it was near the river, where the children could bathe, Mr. Armstrong took it for summer. The owner ordered it to be painted so that it would be nice when Mr. Armstrong moved in.

Exercises

A) **Answer these questions:**

1. Who is on a visit to England?
2. Where is she staying?
3. What did the advertisement say which Mr. Armstrong read in the local paper?
4. Why did Mr. Armstrong want to take a cottage for the summer?
5. What did Conchita say to Mr. Armstrong after they had been driving about half an hour?
6. What did Mr. Armstrong tell Conchita to do when she started to drive?
7. Why was the main road blocked farther on?
8. What did the policeman make them do?
9. How did Conchita know they had a puncture?
10. At what time did they arrive at the village?
11. At what time had Mr. Armstrong asked the owner to meet him?
12. Who is Archie Douglas?
13. What is the Parish Council?
14. What is the Women's Institute?
15. How many churches are there in Oakshot?
16. What is a filling station?

17. What did Mr. Armstrong tell the man at the garage to do?
18. Why did the owner of the cottage order it to be painted?

B) **Substitution Table**

They
{ want / told / would like / will ask / expect / ordered }
{ him / us / Miss Brown }
{ to visit them in the country. / to mend the puncture. / to paint the house. / to let the cottage to them. / to meet them at the cottage. / to change the wheel. }

Form as many sentences as possible from the words given. There are more than 100 possible combinations.

C) **Put in the correct form of the verb which is given in brackets:**

1. I should like (to go) to the country by car.
2. May I (to drive) to London with you tomorrow?
3. I can hear the rain (to fall) on the roof.
4. Do you (to speak) English as easily as Spanish?
5. Did you hear Jimmie (to come in) late last night?
6. He wants the children (to spend) their holidays in the fresh air.
7. The policeman made us (to turn) into a side road.
8. Did you see the children (to bathe) in the river?
9. Let me (to help) you to paint the door.
10. Mr. Armstrong decided (to take) the cottage for the summer.
11. Will you (to have) another cup of tea?
12. You ought (to go) to the doctor's today.

D) **Dictation:**

From «Well, Conchita, would you like to go» to «... I shall take it for the summer.»

E) **Composition:** (To be done with the book shut.)

1. Describe Mr. Armstrong's drive to Oakshot.
2. Describe an English village.
3. Describe a village in Spain.
   Each composition should not be more than 120 words long.

F) **Put in the correct prepositions:**

1. I want the children to spend their holidays — the
   fresh air.
2. He was — a visit to his parents in London.
3. The Council consists — a chairman and six members.
4. They are well paid — the work they do.
5. I must get some petrol — the next filling station.
6. The village shop sells everything — butter — pencils.
7. As the cottage was — the river, we took it — the
   summer.
8. They talked about their farms — a glass of beer.
9. Have you heard — the accident on the main road?
10. Shall we drive — to the country this afternoon?

Translate into English:

Cuando Pedro estaba en la Universidad de Oxford, un
amigo le invitó a pasar una semana de las vacaciones de abril
en casa de sus padres, que viven en Devonshire.

Pedro estaba muy contento, porque quería conocer otras
partes de Inglaterra, y decidió ir con su amigo el primer día
de vacaciones. Su amigo John le dijo que llevase unos zapatos
fuertes y un traje viejo para andar por el campo. Así, fueron
en tren y llegaron allí por la tarde. La madre de John les
vio venir por la carretera, puso a hervir el agua para el té, y
fue a la puerta a encontrarles. Después del té había tiempo
para andar por el jardín, que estaba muy bonito con flores de
primavera y el nuevo verde de los árboles.

Mientras cenaron hablaron de lo que iban a hacer al
día siguiente. El padre de John tiene coche y John preguntó
a Pedro si le gustaría ir en coche para ver el campo y las aldeas
de esa parte de Inglaterra. Pedro dijo que le gustaría mucho,
y así, a la mañana siguiente, como parecía buen día, se fueron
en el coche a pasar el día en el campo. Las carreteras de Devonshire son muy estrechas y John había de tener cuidado
cuando veían otros coches venir hacia ellos. También pararon
muchas veces por perros que cruzaban la carretera y que parecía
que no tenían prisa por alcanzar el otro lado. Había muchas
vacas negras en los campos, y John dijo a Pedro que daban muy
buena leche. Pedro contestó que la leche que había tomado
para el desayuno por la mañana era la mejor que había tomado
nunca. Pasaron por muchas aldeas muy bonitas y se pararon
muchas veces para ver las viejas y hermosas iglesias, y una
vez para ver a un herrero herrar (poner una herradura) a un
caballo. A mediodía se pararon en una fonda para comer.

«¿Qué quieres tomar?» dijo John. «Tendrán buen jamón, huevos y queso y cerveza o sidra muy buena. Aquí se hace mucha sidra, porque Devonshire produce muchas manzanas, de las cuales sale (se hace) la sidra.» «Pienso probar la sidra y el jamón frío, con un poco de pan y queso después», dijo Pedro.

Acabada la comida, John continuó conduciendo el coche porque Pedro dijo que no sabía conducir. Cuando llegaron a casa, Pedro dijo que había disfrutado mucho del día y que pensaba volver muchas veces a Devonshire, porque le había gustado mucho.

LESSON NINE

Vocabulary and Pronunciation

i:	to feed (nutrir, alimentar, dar de comer), pléased (contento).
i	crícket (juego de pelota inglés), rib (costilla), búsy (ocupado), wílling (dispuesto).
e	to lend (prestar), chest (pecho), déntist (dentista), sécretary (secretario), head (cabeza).
a	to exámine (examinar, registrar), match (partido).
a:	gárage (garaje).
o	hóckey (hockey), to watch (vigilar, mirar, observar).
o:	sport (deporte), to score (marcar).
ə:	to prefér (preferir), to hurt (hacer daño, doler).
ai	to ride (montar a caballo), eye (ojo).
	to ride, rode, ridden (montar a caballo).
ou	rowing (remo), goal (tanto).
au	crowd (muchedumbre).
eiə	player (jugador).

Frases

It is said that...	Se dice que...
I have been told that...	Me han dicho que...
It is winter.	Es el invierno.
At present.	Actualmente, al presente.
At last.	Al final, finalmente.
To be willing.	Estar dispuesto.

Verbos irregulares

To feed,	fed,	fed:	alimentar, nutrir, dar de comer.
To lend,	lent,	lent:	prestar.
To hurt,	hurt,	hurt:	hacer daño, doler.

Verbos compuestos

to grow,	crecer.
to grow up,	hacerse persona mayor.
to call,	llamar.
to call in,	hacer venir.

Grammar

Adjetivos y pronombres posesivos y personales

		Pronombres personales		Posesivos	
		Nominativo (sujeto)	Acusativo y dativo (complemento)	Adjetivo	Pronombre
Singular	1.ª Persona (Yo)	I	me	my	mine
	2.ª Persona (Usted) (Tú)	you	you	your	yours
	3.ª Persona (Él)	he	him	his	his
	3.ª Persona (Ella)	she	her	her	hers
	3.ª Persona (Ello)	it	it	its	its*
Plural	1.ª Persona (Nosotros)	we	us	our	ours
	2.ª Persona (Ustedes) (Vosotros)	you	you	your	yours
	3.ª Persona (Ellos)	they	them	their	theirs

a) Para el uso de los *Pronombres personales,* véase *Libro Elemental,* pág. 46.

* Se emplea poco.

b) Para el uso de los *Adjetivos posesivos,* véase *Libro Elemental,* págs. 35 y 129.

c) Los *Pronombres posesivos* se traducen en español por los pronombres correspondientes, *mío, tuyo, suyo,* etc.

Nótese:

1. Que en inglés se usan siempre sin artículo.

Por ej.: Our baby is prettier than theirs.
Nuestro niño es más bonito que *el* suyo.

Your book is more interesting than mine.
Su (tu) libro es más interesante que *el* mío.

2. Que las frases españolas como
Un amigo mío,   Un libro tuyo, etc.
se traducen
A friend *of* mine,   A book *of* yours, etc.

This dog of yours is very intelligent.
Este perro suyo (tuyo) es muy inteligente.

Own

se traduce por el adjetivo español *propio,* y siempre va precedido de adjetivo posesivo.
John Stuart has his own car. John Stuart tiene su propio coche.

To say and to tell

DIFERENCIA DE SENTIDO

to say tiene el sentido de decir, recitar.
to tell tiene el sentido de decir, contar, ordenar.

Por lo tanto sólo se emplea *to say* para introducir oración directa.
«Can I have the car this afternoon?» he said.
«Our ground is better than theirs,» said one of the players.
Nótese que se puede poner el sujeto después del verbo *to say* en estos casos.
Sólo se emplea *to tell* para introducir una frase subordinada imperativa.
Tell him to come.   Dígale que venga.
He told the children to meet him at the station.
Dijo a sus hijos que le esperasen en la estación.

69

DIFERENCIA DE CONSTRUCCIÓN

To tell va seguido obligatoriamente de complemento de persona sin *to*.

To say puede emplearse con o sin complemento de persona que va precedido de *to*.

> He told his father that he was going out.
> He said to his father that he was going out.
> Dijo a su padre que iba a salir.

Pero   He said he was going out.   (Única forma posible.)
> Dijo que iba a salir.

Construcción con los verbos "to continue" y "to stop"

Estos verbos, como los verbos *to spend* y *to like* (véase *Libro Elemental,* pág. 130) van seguidos del verbo dependiente en gerundio.

He could not continue playing.   No pudo seguir jugando.
He stopped playing.   Cesó de jugar.

Reading

SPORTS

The English are very interested in sport and every English boy and girl learns to play several games at school, such as football, cricket or rowing for the boys, and tennis, cricket or hockey for the girls. When they grow up, they often belong to a sports club where they go at the week-ends. John Stuart, my young doctor friend, belongs to several sports clubs. In the winter he plays football, in the summer tennis and cricket, which is an English game, rather difficult to understand if you don't know how to play it. Occasionally he rides on Sundays but as there are few good horses in the town where he lives he prefers to do other things. At present, as it is winter, he goes to his football club every Saturday afternoon and plays a game of football. As he has a very busy morning and often comes home late for lunch, his father lends him his car to get to the football ground in time. As he is only a young doctor, he hasn't got his own car. On Saturday mornings, he has to visit the school where he is the school doctor and examine the children. This takes a long time. He often finds that some children have been hurt playing in the play-ground and have their legs and arms cut. Once he found that one of the bigger boys had broken a rib at football but had not realized that it was broken until the doctor told him. He said he felt something wrong, but that it did not hurt very much. Very often some of the boys have colds and he has to examine their chests and throats. He also looks at their teeth and calls in the dentist if necessary. Some of the poorer children often have bad eyes because they are not well fed. So you see he has a lot of work to do on Saturday mornings and he is very pleased to be free for his game of football in the afternoon.

Last Saturday the secretary of the Football Club told Dr. Stuart that there was an important match against another club and asked him to come and play. The match would begin at three o'clock, he said. That morning Dr. Stuart had a very busy time, however, as one of the boys had fallen and, cut his head badly, so that he did not leave the school until one o'clock. He had to go back home to fetch his football clothes and have lunch and then go out to the ground before three o'clock. He left the school with one of the teachers and they waited together for a bus. One arrived at last and the teacher said «Is this bus yours?» «No,» said Dr. Stuart, «it's not mine. I take a 45.» «Well, goodbye, then, I take this one» and he got into the bus. Dr. Stuart waited a few minutes more and then his came along. He got home at about half-past one.

«Can you lend me the car to go to the football ground this afternoon», he said to his father as he came in. «I'm afraid one of the back tyres has a puncture and it's at the garage. However, I told the man to have it ready for you at two o'clock, if possible. If it's not ready perhaps Mrs. Brown will lend you hers for the afternoon. I know she is not using it because she is coming to play bridge with your mother.» «That's a good idea. Besides, her car is much better than ours. I'll telephone and ask her.» Mrs. Brown was willing to lend John her car, so the Stuarts left theirs at the garage and sat down to lunch. Soon after two o'clock they had finished and started off for the football ground in Mrs. Brown's car, leaving the ladies to play bridge.

They arrived just in time. John Stuart changed into his football clothes and at three o'clock exactly the match began. «I'm glad we are playing on our ground,» said one of the members of the club. «Ours is much better than theirs.» «Yes, we always play better on our own ground,» said another. There was a big crowd of people watching the match and giving advice to the players. After about a quarter of an hour one of the players was hurt. His head was badly cut and John's father, who is also a doctor, looked at it. The player could not continue playing but sat down on the side of the football field and watched the others. After twenty minutes more they stopped playing to have a rest. This rest is called «half-time». When they had rested enough they started again and soon John's side scored a goal. No other goals were scored, however, by either side before the match finished. So John's side won.

After the match the players and their friends who had watched the game went into the club-house and drank tea or beer and talked about the game.

Exercises

A) **Answer the following questions:**

1. What games do English boys and girls play at school?
2. What games does John Stuart play?
3. On what days does John Stuart play football?
4. What does John Stuart do on Saturday mornings?
5. How does he often get to the football ground?
6. Why do some of the poorer children in the school have bad eyes?
7. Why was Dr. Stuart very busy last Saturday morning?
8. How did Dr. Stuart go home from the school?
9. At what time did he get home?
10. Why couldn't he use his father's car to go to the football ground?
11. How did he get to the football ground?
12. What did Mrs. Stuart do that Saturday afternoon?
13. At what time did the match begin?
14. What did the players do at «half-time»?
15. Whose side won?

B) **Complete the following sentences. The first is done to show you.**

1. I have a cottage: it is my cottage: it belongs to me: it is mine.
2. The farmer has a farm: it is — farm: it belongs to — : it is —.
3. The village has a filling station: it is — filling station: it belongs to —.
4. You have a car: it is — car: it belongs to — : it is —.
5. The manageress has a title: it is — title: it belongs to — : it is —.
6. We have a fine library: it is — library: it belongs to — : it is —.
7. The villagers have a football ground: it is — football ground: it belongs to — : it is —.

C) **Put in the suitable form of "to say" or "to tell" in the following sentences:**

1. «I always like playing on my own ground» — one of the players.
2. The doctor — the mother to feed her child better.
3. The secretary of the football club — that the match would begin at three o'clock.
4. The dentist — me that I had a bad tooth.
5. It is — that English people are very interested in sport.
6. He always — his daughter a story before she goes to bed.
7. «My English is getting on very well» — Ramón.
8. Why did he — you to go home?

D) **Put in the correct prepositions:**

1. When you go — — the room, shut the door.
2. He took the bus at the Town Hall and got — at the Post Office.
3. Does the milkman come — to your house?
4. He asked the owner — some more furniture.
5. Conchita looked — the tyre and saw that it had a puncture.
6. I had to stay behind and rest, but the others went — .
7. «Is Mr. Jones at home?» «No, I'm afraid he's not — .
8. Shall we go — foot or — bus?
9. Mr. Howard wants to speak to you — the 'phone.
10. The boys started — at six o'clock in the morning and came — home at ten o'clock — night.
11. Hurry —, Peter. We are all waiting — you.
12. — Saturday I heard a good concert — the radio.
13. I always listen — the radio — the evening.
14. The train arrived — London — half-past eight.
15. The chairman of the Church Council arrived — the vicarage when the vicar was out.
16. He has been looking — lodgings for — week and can't find any.
17. My young son wants to be a tailor when he grows — .
18. If your cold is not better tomorrow, I shall call — the doctor.
19. If you drive — that road, you will get a puncture.
20. I live — the ground floor of a big building.

E) **Put in the correct form of the verb in the following sentences:**

1. Besides (to drive) too fast, she did not keep to the left.
2. Dr. Stuart told the man at the garage (to mend) the puncture.
3. The player stopped (to play) because he had hurt his head.
4. The manager saw his secretary (to go) to the cinema when he should have been in the office.
5. Captain Hardy likes (to write) books about his journeys on foot in Spain.
6. The official at the aerodrome did not let the plane (to leave) as the weather was very bad.
7. The members of the dramatic society continued (to act) during the summer.
8. The maid spent her summer holidays (to visit) her relations.
9. He wanted his son (to become) famous.
10. She made her youngest son (to learn) English.

F) **Translate into English:**

A los ingleses les gusta mucho el deporte. Cada muchacho y cada muchacha aprenden varios juegos en la escuela, como el fútbol o el tenis, y más tarde, cuando son mayores, a menudo siguen jugando en los clubs de deportes. Generalmente cada club tiene su propio terreno, y los sábados los socios van a jugar o a ver un partido. Un amigo mío que es médico me llevó el sábado pasado a su club de fútbol. Para llegar al terreno tuvimos que ir en coche, porque mi amigo trabaja hasta muy tarde los sábados por la mañana. Como él no tiene coche propio, su tía estaba dispuesta a prestarle el suyo, pero le dijo que no lo condujese demasiado aprisa, porque tiene los neumáticos bastante viejos. Llegamos a tiempo al terreno, donde había una gran muchedumbre que presenciaba (miraba) el partido. Después de algún tiempo un jugador se hizo daño en la pierna y tuvo que cesar de jugar durante unos minutos. Estábamos muy contentos porque era un buen partido y nuestro equipo ganó. «No es tan agradable jugar en otros terrenos como en el nuestro», dijo mi amigo. Después del partido los jugadores y sus amigos fueron a tomar el té juntos. Me cité con mi amigo (hice una cita con) para montar a caballo al día siguiente, porque prefiero este deporte al fútbol.

LESSON TEN

Vocabulary and Pronunciation

i:	léader (jefe, caudillo).
i	actívity (actividad), díscipline (disciplina), indepéndent (independiente).
e	héalthy (saludable, sano), spécial (especial), test (prueba), séparately (separadamente), to depénd (depender).
a	ánimal (animal), to cárry (llevar, acarrear), axe (hacha).
o	óbject (objeto, fin), hónest (honrado), to prómise (prometer), to fóllow (seguir).
o:	organisátion (organización), law (ley), indoors (en casa), headquárters (cuartel general).
u:	móvement (movimiento), troop (tropa).
ə:	to retúrn (volver, regresar), to obsérve (observar).
ei	to obéy (obedecer), observátion (observación), aid (ayuda).
ai	guide (guía), kind (amable).
ou	patrol (patrulla).
au	scout (explorador).
ju:	úniform (uniforme), opportúnity (oportunidad, ocasión).
iə	chéerful (alegre, de buen humor).
s	díscipline.
ʃ	spécial.
tʃ	cheerful.

Consonante muda

h	muda en hónest.

Frases

In this way:	de esta manera.
In the same way:	de la misma manera.
first aid:	primeros auxilios.
in camp:	en campamento.
to make friends:	hacer amigos.
to ask questions:	hacer preguntas.

to consist in:	consistir en.
to write down:	apuntar, anotar.
to depend on:	depender de.
to look after:	cuidar, tener cuidado de.

Grammar

La forma verbal en "-ing"

Se forma añadiendo la terminación -ing al infinitivo del verbo.

to eat,   eating.
to hurry,   hurrying.

(Para las formas *to come, coming: to stop, stopping,* véase *Modificaciones gráficas,* libro I, págs. 84 y 90.)

Se emplea:

1. Para formar los tiempos continuos de los verbos:

   I am eating.
   We have been working.

2. Para traducir el participio pasado español en las frases:

to be sitting:	estar sentado.
to be standing:	estar de pie.
to be lying:	estar echado, tumbado.

3. Como adjetivo:

interesting:	interesante.
amusing:	divertido.

   an interesting story.
   an amusing book.

4. Como participio presente para una acción que ocurre al mismo tiempo que otra:

   Father is sitting by the fire *reading* a book.
   Padre está sentado al lado del fuego leyendo un libro.

5. Como sujeto o complemento de un verbo:

   Living at home is not so expensive as *living* in a hotel.
   Vivir en casa no es tan costoso como vivir en un hotel.

   They learn *cooking* and map *reading.*
   Aprenden a guisar y a leer el mapa.

Nótese que en castellano se emplea el *infinitivo* en estos casos.

6. Después de cualquier preposición, con excepción de *to* cuando forma el infinitivo, donde en castellano se usa el infinitivo:

He went out without *putting* his coat on.
Salió sin *ponerse* el abrigo.

He is tired of *working.*
Está cansado de *trabajar.*

After *having* tea he listened to the radio.
Después de *tomar* el té escuchó la radio.

Before *going* into the room he knocked at the door.
Antes de *entrar* en la habitación llamó a la puerta.

ON y BY seguido de la forma en *-ing* se emplea en vez de una frase subordinada de tiempo.

On seguido de la forma en *-ing* a veces se traduce por *al,* seguido de infinitivo en español.

On arriving he went upstairs.
Al llegar subió arriba.

On leaving the house he met his friend.
Al salir de casa encontró a su amigo.

By seguido de la forma en *-ing* se emplea para indicar la *manera* como se hace una cosa.

They learn things by playing games.
Aprenden cosas jugando.

By working hard he was able to pass his exam.
Trabajando mucho pudo aprobar su examen.

For seguido de la forma en *-ing.* Esta construcción se puede emplear para traducir *para* seguido de infinitivo, pero *sólo después de substantivos.*

An organisation for preparing boys to be scouts.
Una organización para preparar a los muchachos para ser exploradores.

A school for teaching foreign languages.
Una escuela para enseñar los idiomas extranjeros.

En otros casos *para* seguido del infinitivo se traduce sólo por el infinitivo inglés precedido de *to,* como ya hemos aprendido (véase *Libro Elemental,* pág. 41).

He took the bus to get there.
Tomó el autobús para llegar allí.

El verbo **"to obey"** (obedecer) se construye en inglés siempre con complemento directo.

He obeys his father.	Obedece a su padre.
He obeys the scout law.	Obedece a la ley scout.

Reading

BOY SCOUTS

There are several organisations for young people in England and one of the best known is the Boy Scout movement, which was started by Lord Baden-Powell at the beginning of this century. Boys from eleven to eighteen years of age can belong to this movement, but there is also an organisation for preparing younger boys to become scouts and one for older boys when they leave the scouts. There is also a movement for girls called the «Girl Guides», which was started by the wife of Lord Baden-Powell, Lady Baden-Powell, and which is run in the same way. The object of the two movements is to give young people a healthy occupation for their spare time. On becoming a scout, a boy has to learn the Scout Law, which says that a scout must be honest, must help other people, must obey orders, must be kind to animals, must be cheerful even under difficulties, must be clean and healthy, and he has to promise to obey this law. The Scouts or Guides wear a special uniform and meet every week at their own Headquarters which is perhaps a school-room or a church hall or even a garage. To become a scout a boy has to pass several tests, and when he is a member of a scout troop. he prepares for other tests under the direction of his Patrol Leader.

Each group of scouts is called a troop, which is divided into 'patrols' of about six boys. Sometimes the whole troop meet together or sometimes only the patrols separately. When the troop or patrol meets, the scouts learn observation, cooking, first aid, map reading and other useful things. They learn most of these things by playing games. For example, one game consists in sending the patrol down a certain street of a town and when the boys return the patrol leader asks them questions about what they saw in the street to see how much they have observed. The scout who answers the questions most correctly wins the game. Another game consists in putting on a table about twenty small things, such as a button, a piece of paper, a bus ticket, a glass, a fork, or a candle. The scouts look at them for one minute and then go into another room and write down as many things as they can remember. The scout who can remember most wins the game.

An important part of a scout's activities consists in taking exercise and playing games in the fresh air. This he does by walking across the fields with his patrol, observing the trees, the birds and the flowers and learning their names. Or the patrols may play games one against the other. In this way a scout learns discipline. He has to obey his patrol leader and the patrol leader has to obey the scout master, who is generally an older person. However, the scout is taught to be independent and not to depend on other people. Sometimes the patrol leader goes in front of the other scouts and leaves marks by the side of the road and in the fields and woods where he passes. The other scouts follow one after the other and each boy has to find the way alone. He carries a small tent, some food, a blanket, and so, if he cannot reach the end of the day's journey and find the patrol leader, because he has not seen some of the marks left by him, he can make a camp for the night, cook his own food and return home the next day. If he reaches the end of the journey he finds the other scouts of the patrol and they make a camp together for the night. The next day they may build a bridge across a river or play other games and return home in the evening.

Camping is, then, one of the most important parts of a scout's activities. It gives opportunities for doing things learned indoors, such as fire-lighting, cooking, using an axe or building a bridge. Camping in England begins at about Easter and lasts until September. There are camps for the weekends lasting two days only, such as we have already seen, but every troop likes to have a camp for a week or ten days in August. In camp each patrol has its own tent and does its own cooking and the boys learn to do things for themselves (para sí). They also learn to work together. One boy may cook, another may look after the fire, another may fetch the water or buy the food.

Scouts also learn to be useful to other people, by knowing how to give first aid or by knowing all the streets and buildings of their town. A scout should always help other people. During the winter, when camping is not possible, the troop sometimes prepares a concert or some other show. The boys who do not take part in the show acting or singing always help by building the stage or making the dresses, or in painting the scenery. So the scouts do everything without asking for help from other people.

The scout movement was started in England by a small group of boys forty years ago, but now there are scouts in

79

nearly every country in the world and they all belong to the same organisation. From time to time scouts from all countries meet together in a large camp which they call a 'Jamboree'. In this way a scout can learn about other countries and make friends with scouts from all parts of the world.

Exercises

A) **Answer the following questions:**

1. When was the Boy Scout movement started?
2. Who started it?
3. What movement for girls is run in the same way as the Boy Scout movement?
4. What is the object of the two movements?
5. What does the Scout Law say?
6. What does a boy have to do to become a scout?
7. Where do the scouts generally meet?
8. How do scouts learn observation?
9. How often do scouts go to camp?
10. What is a scout jamboree?
11. Have you got scouts in your country?
12. What organisations for young people are there in your country?

B) 1. **Describe a scout's activities.** *a)* Indoors. *b)* In the open air.

2. **Describe the youth movements of your country.**

C) **Complétense las oraciones siguientes:**

1. On arriving at the station ....
2. On seeing his brother ....
3. On hearing about the accident ....
4. On returning home ....
5. On receiving the news ....
6. On becoming a scout ....
7. On examining the packet ....
8. On stepping out of the bus ....
9. On reaching the filling-station ....
10. On leaving the aerodrome ....

D) Háganse todas las combinaciones posibles con arreglo al sentido:

By
{
playing games
passing tests
going to camp
taking exercise
observing the trees and flowers
building bridges
knowing how to give first aid
producing concerts) and shows
knowing map reading
}
the scouts learn
{
to do things for themselves.

to be useful to other people

to be healthy.

to enjoy life in the country.
}

E) Complétense las siguientes frases con la preposición apropiada:

1. We went to camp — Wednesday, August 8th, and returned home — Tuesday, August 14th.
2. How are you getting — with your English?
3. I like going for a holiday — the end of August or — September.
4. Have you paid — the boy's new uniform?
5. The ground floor is divided — two parts.
6. They walked — the village, looking — the cottages.
7. I must go to the tailor's to try — my new suit.
8. — last week the car has not been working very well.
9. The car has not been working well — some time.
10. The football mach could not begin — half past three, because the players had not all arrived.
11. — the crowd there were several famous men.
12. I don't like sleeping — the ground floor.

F) Put in the correct form of the verb in the following sentences-the infinitive is given:

1. He caught a cold because he went out without (to put on) his coat.
2. It is an organisation for (to help) poor people.
3. A scout promises (to obey) the scout law.
4. This game consists in (to see) some things on a table and (to remember) as many as possible in one minute.
5. I want the maid (to send) the curtains to the cleaner's.

6. I saw the absent-minded professor (to go) to the wrong house.
7. Instead of (to sell) your cottage, you should let it.
8. Besides (to act) the boys also build the stage and paint the scenery.
9. Before (to become) a scout a boy must pass several tests.
10. Before (to drive) to the country we had to mend the puncture.
11. John is (to sit) on the sofa (to read) a book.
12. After (to see) the advertisement in the paper, we wrote to the owner of the house.
13. We made the doctor (to drive) fast as there had been a bad accident.
14. They saw the player (to break) his leg at the football match.
15. After (to hurt) his head, he didn't play football again.

G) **Translate into English:**

En Inglaterra hay varias organizaciones para la juventud (gente joven) de las cuales quizá la mejor conocida es el movimiento «Boy Scout». Al hacerse explorador un muchacho tiene que aprobar varias pruebas, y después de aprobarlas tiene que prometer obedecer a la ley scout y ayudar a otras personas y serles útil. Los exploradores llevan un uniforme especial y se reúnen en su cuartel general cada semana, donde aprenden el primer socorro, observación y a leer el mapa, a guisar u otras cosas útiles.

Aprenden mucho jugando a diferentes juegos. Uno de estos juegos consiste en colocar varios objetos en una mesa que los muchachos miran durante un minuto. Después van a otra habitación y tratan de acordarse de todos los objetos. El muchacho que se acuerda de más, gana. En verano a los exploradores les gusta salir de las ciudades y hacer excursiones en el campo. A veces hacen un campamento y pasan la noche fuera (al aire libre). De esta manera tienen ocasiones para hacer cosas que han aprendido en casa, como encender el fuego, guisar, manejar el (un) hacha, o construir un puente. Los exploradores aprenden a ser independientes y a divertise sin depender de otras personas.

LESSON ELEVEN

Vocabulary and Pronunciation

i: be*a*n (alubia), French be*a*n (alubia verde), p*ea* (guisante).

i to d*i*g (cavar), létt*u*ce (lechuga), to p*i*ck (recoger).

e léttuce, ténder (tierno), to forgét (olvidar), héavy (pesado).

a to trável (viajar), fl*a*t (piso), c*á*bbage (col, repollo).

a: disadvántage (desventaja), to gárden (cultivar el jardín), hárdly (apenas), c*a*rnátion (clavel).

o cr*o*p (cosecha).

ʌ j*u*st (sólo, precisamente), ónion (cebolla), to l*o*ve (amar, encantar, gustar).

u: r*oo*t (raíz).

ə: to be w*o*rth (valer la pena).

ei fávourite (favorito).

ai to rem*í*nd (recordar), to m*i*nd (molestar).

ou to gr*ow* (cultivar), to suppóse (suponer), r*o*se (rosa).

oi to sp*oi*l (estropear), to av*ó*id (evitar).

Verbos irregulares

to dig,	dug,	dug:	cavar.
to spoil,	spoilt,	spoilt:	estropear.
to forget,	forgot,	forgotten:	olvidar.

Frases

all the same:	a pesar de todo.
It's all the same:	Es lo mismo. Es igual.
because of:	a causa de.
by the way:	a propósito.
That's very kind *of you*	Es muy amable *de su parte*.

Grammar

La forma verbal in "-ing" (continuación)

Se emplea:

7. En el verbo dependiente después de algunos verbos, que generalmente expresan la idea de *empezar, continuar* o *cesar.*

*to continue to go on	— seguir.
*to begin *to start	— empezar.
to stop	— parar, cesar.
to finish	— terminar, acabar.
*to like	— gustar.
to love	— gustar, encantar.
to keep	— no cesar, seguir.
to mind	— molestar.
to spend	— gastar, pasar (tiempo).
to enjoy	— gozar de, disfrutar de.
to avoid	— evitar.

Por ej.: I can't go on working today.
No puedo seguir trabajando hoy.

She enjoys meeting famous people.
Le gusta conocer gente famosa.

You must avoid reading too much or you will hurt your eyes.
Debe usted evitar leer demasiado o se estropeará los ojos.

* *to begin, to start, to continue* y *to like* se construyen también con infinitivo.

Por ej.: I like to go to the theatre.
A mí me gusta ir al teatro.
Etc.

8. Después de las frases:

it is no use it is no good	no sirve para nada, es inútil.
to be worth	valer la pena.
What's the use of?	¿De (para) qué sirve?

y de la palabra *besides*.

Por ej.: It is no use talking to him in Spanish; he doesn't undertand.
No sirve para nada hablarle en español; no lo entiende.

Is it worth buying new furniture for the spare room?
¿Vale la pena comprar muebles nuevos para el cuarto de huéspedes?

Besides acting and singing, they always build the stage and paint the scenery.

Además de actuar y de cantar, siempre construyen el escenario y pintan los decorados.

PRACTICE TABLE

He began	reading aloud
Do you like	learning English
Please go on	growing onions
Do you enjoy	studying Arabic
Please stop	working
Would you mind	playing the piano
Please continue	acting
Is it worth it	singing
What's the use of	taking exercise
It's no use	

9. Después del verbo *to need* (necesitar) en vez del **infinitivo** pasivo, que se puede también emplear.

Por ej.:

The house needs painting.	La casa necesita ser pintada.
The house need to be painted.	Hace falta pintar la casa.

....

TO REMIND y TO REMEMBER

To remind es el verbo activo (acordar, recordar) y se construye con el complemento directo de persona y la preposición *of* delante de la cosa.

He reminded his brother of the appointment.
Recordó la cita a su hermano.

To remember es el verbo pasivo (acordarse) y se construye con complemento directo de persona o cosa.

He *remembered his appointment* with me.
Se *acordó* de su cita conmigo.

TO LOVE

Se construye exactamente como *to like* en el sentido de gustar mucho, encantar.

He likes riding: le gusta montar a caballo.
He loves riding: le encanta montar a caballo.

To MIND

Verbo que se emplea personalmente para dar la idea de estorbar, molestar, no ir bien.

> Do you mind if we come home late?
> ¿Le importa que volvamos a casa tarde?
> Do you mind if I smoke?   ¿Le molesta si fumo?

La forma en condicional *Would you mind* se emplea para pedir algo cortésmente.

> Would you mind coming tomorrow?
> ¿Le importaría venir mañana?
> Would you mind painting the garage?
> ¿Le molestaría pintar el garaje?

JUST

La palabra *just* se emplea:
1. En sentido de sólo, solamente, nada más que.

> I don't grow vegetables, I just grow a few flowers.
> No cultivo verduras, sólo cultivo algunas flores.

2. En sentido de exactamente, justamente, precisamente.

> That's just why I came.
> Vine por eso precisamente.

3. Delante de imperativo, para darle más énfasis.

> Just leave it to me.   ¡Déjamelo a mí!

AT ALL

Se emplea para dar más énfasis a una negación.

> I have no books at all. No tengo libros, en absoluto.
> It's not bad at all. No es nada malo.

NOT AT ALL

Se emplea para *de nada*.

> «Thank you very much.» «Not at all.»
> «Muchísimas gracias.» «De nada».

To GROW

Se emplea como verbo transitivo en sentido de *cultivar,* y como verbo intransitivo en sentido de *crecer.*

> I grow tomatoes in my garden.
> Cultivo tomates en mi jardín.

This boy has grown a lot.
Este muchacho ha crecido mucho.

Reading

IN THE SUBURBS

Mr. Smith is looking over his garden wall and sees Mr. Jones next door working in his vegetable garden.

Mr. Jones: Good morning. How's the garden getting on, Mr. Smith?

Mr. Smith: Oh, not so badly, but of course, I don't get much time to work in it. Living so far from the office, I seem to have no time for anything besides travelling.

Mr. Jones: Yes, that's the great disadvantage of living in the suburbs. But, all the same, I shouldn't like living in a flat in the centre. There's nothing like having a garden, is there?

Mr. Smith: I don't know what the children would do without a garden. I'm afraid I can't keep a nice one like yours because of them. They enjoy playing cricket and football so much that I let them have the back garden and just grow a few flowers in the front garden.

Mr. Jones: Yes, it's no good trying to keep a nice garden with children. Before ours grew up, this one was just a playground. We had no flowers or vegetables at all. Now they are grown up they quite like gardening too, and often spend the summer evenings helping me.

Mr. Smith: I suppose you're pleased to have someone to do the heavy work for you.

Mr. Jones: Yes, I don't enjoy cutting the grass or digging much at my age.

Mr. Smith: I expect that if it goes on raining much more, your roses will all be spoilt.

Mr. Jones: Yes, and the tomatoes will be green if we don't get a little more sun. However, the lettuces will be nice and tender. Last year the sun was so hot that they were very dry and hardly worth eating.

Mr. Smith: Have you had a good crop of potatoes this year?

Mr. Jones: Not bad at all. I've only just started digging them up, but I've already found some big ones. I ought to have enough to last the whole winter without having to buy any. I always try to avoid buying po-

tatoes and vegetables. Home-grown ones are so much
better. Of course, we never have to buy flowers. By
the way, I see you've got a lot of fine carnations in
your front garden.

Mr. Smith: Yes, it's a good year for carnations. They're my
wife's favourite flower, you know, so we always grow
plenty. They remind her of Spain where she lived
when she was a young girl.

Mr. Jones: Would you mind giving me a few roots at the end
of the season? I should like to put some in the vegetable garden to give a little colour.

Mr. Smith: With pleasure. Remind me when the time comes,
however, or I may forget. Well, I must leave you now;
my dinner must be ready.

Mr. Jones: Just a minute. Would you like to take in some
French beans. We've got more than we need. I'll get
you some.

Mr. Smith: That's very kind of you. Thank you very much.

Mr. Jones goes into the house to fetch the French beans.
He returns with a basket of beans and some large onions.

Mr. Jones: Here you are. And I want you to look at these
onions.

Mr. Smith: By George! Those are fine onions. Did you grow
them in your garden?

Mr. Jones: Yes, they're the best onions I have ever grown.
Take a few.

Mr. Smith: Thank you very much. I must show them to my
wife. Good evening.

Mr. Jones: Good evening.

Mr. Jones continues to work in his garden. Mrs. Jones
comes out of the house.

Mrs. Jones: Haven't you finished picking the peas, Henry?
You have been a long time.

Mr. Jones: I've been talking to Mr. Smith, but I'll bring them
in in a minute.

Mrs. Jones: Bring in a cabbage at the same time. I'll need
one for tomorrow's lunch. Don't you think the garage
needs painting, Henry? I'm afraid the wood will be
spoilt if it isn't painted again soon.

Mr. Jones: Yes. I'll ask one of the boys to paint it. Peter loves
doing that sort of thing.

Mrs. Jones: Ask him to mend the doors at the same time.
They are very hard to open and shut. I could hardly
get in this morning.

Peter Jones comes out of the house into the garden.

Peter: Hullo, Dad. How's the garden? I hope there isn't any more digging to be done.

Mr. Jones: No, not for the moment. However, there's another job for you. Would you mind painting the garage in your spare time?

Peter: All right. I'll ask Betty to come and help me on Sunday. We ought to be able to finish it together in one day.

Mrs. Jones: The doors need mending too, Peter.

Peter: I'll look at the doors, mother. Just leave it all to me.

Mr. Jones: Here comes the rain again. Come along indoors. I can see we'll get no tomatoes this year.

Exercises

A) **Answer the following questions:**

1. What does Mr. Smith see over his garden wall?
2. How is Mr. Smith's garden getting on?
3. Why does Mr. Smith have little time for gardening?
4. What is the great disadvantage of living in the suburbs?
5. Why can't Mr. Smith keep a nice back garden?
6. What does Mr. Smith grow in his front garden?
7. Are Mr. Jones's children young?
8. How do Mr. Jones's children often spend the summer evenings?
9. Why doesn't Mr. Jones enjoy digging or cutting the grass?
10. What will happen (suceder, ocurrir) if it goes on raining?
11. How many potatoes will Mr. Jones get from his crop this year?
12. What flowers does Mr. Smith grow in his front garden?
13. Why does Mr. Smith always grow plenty of carnations?
14. What does Mr. Jones ask Mr. Smith to give him?
15. What does Mr. Jones give Mr. Smith?
16. What has Mr. Jones been doing in his garden?
17. Why does Mrs. Jones ask Mr. Jones to bring in a cabbage?
18. What is wrong with the garage?
19. Who is Peter going to ask to help him when he paints the garage?
20. Why does Mr. Jones think he will get no tomatoes this year?

B) **Form questions for the following answers:**

1. The garden? Oh, it's not getting on badly.
2. No, I shouldn't like to live in a flat.
3. No, I just grow a few flowers.
4. Yes, the children quite like gardening.
5. Yes, I should have enough to last the whole winter without buying any.
6. Because they remind her of Spain where she lived as a young girl.
7. With pleasure. I'll give you some tomorrow when I dig them up.
8. Yes, I grew them in my garden. They're the best onions I have ever grown.
9. Yes, I think it needs painting.
10. All right. I'll ask Betty to come and help me.

C) **Put the following sentences into the Past (Preterite):**

1. I don't get much time to work in my garden.
2. While the children are young, we just grow a few flowers in the front garden.
3. I see you've got some fine carnations in your garden.
4. Our roses are all spoilt this year because of the rain.
5. The absent-minded professor teaches me Greek in the morning, but often forgets to come.
6. My brother spends a lot of time playing football.
7. I buy a newspaper every evening to read the advertisements, as I want to buy a house.
8. He sleeps very well because he spends a lot of time every day walking.
9. The mothers of the children at this school feed them well.
10. My father lends me his car when I go to the football ground.

D) **Use the following words in sentences:**

journey, to travel, to suppose, just, because of, to mind, to avoid, disadvantage, heavy, to remind, to go on, to spoil, healthy, cheerful, opportunity, indoors. to be worth, law, to remember, honest.

E) **Composition:**

Describe life in an English suburb.

F) **Translate into English:**

Les gusta mucho a los ingleses trabajar en el jardín para pasar el tiempo de las vacaciones. Todas las casitas de los suburbios tienen un pequeño jardín donde se pueden cultivar legumbres y flores. Además hay muchas veces manzanas, peras y otras frutas. Cuando vuelve de su oficina, o de su trabajo en la ciudad, el padre de familia inglés goza de unas horas al aire libre, y sigue trabajando en su jardín hasta la hora de la cena. Los niños mayores le ayudan... Les encanta recoger las frutas y flores para la casa. Pero los pequeños prefieren jugar y jugando con pelotas estropean los guisantes y rompen las flores. Algunas veces el padre piensa que no vale la pena cultivar legumbres cuando los niños juegan en el jardín y piensa en cultivar solamente rosas y claveles y otras flores delante de su casa. Muchas personas no cultivan patatas y coles, que se pueden comprar muy barato en el mercado, y cultivan lechugas, cebollas, guisantes y judías, que son caros. Los años que hace mucho sol pueden recoger también una buena cosecha de tomates.

LESSON TWELVE

Revisión

La acentuación del inglés

La cuestión de saber dónde cae el acento en inglés es para los extranjeros sumamente difícil, y no se pueden dar reglas bien fijas de acentuación. Sin embargo, a pesar de las excepciones, los siguientes principios pueden ayudar.

1. En general, el acento cae sobre la raíz de la palabra. Los sufijos (*-er, -tion, -ary, -ate, -ing, -ant, -le*, etc.) y los prefijos (*re-, com-, de-, dis-, be-*, etc.) no llevan el acento de la palabra.

Por ej.: accórding, addréss, advértisement, afráid, **to** becóme, chéerful, déntist, depénd, desígn, distúrb, dráwing.

2. En palabras de tres o más sílabas el acento cae generalmente sobre la antepenúltima, sobre todo cuando la penúltima es breve.

Por ej.: fávourite, fúrniture, bícycle, íntimate, opportúnity, pérsonal, póssible.

Muchas veces la penúltima no se pronuncia siquiera.
Por ej.: hístory (hístri), búsiness (bíznis), séparate (séprət).

La terminación *-ary* cuenta como una sola sílaba, por ser la *a* muda.
Por ej.: sécretary, órdinary, mílitary.

3. El acento cae sobre la sílaba precedente a las siguientes terminaciones:

   a) *-tion* (español -ción):   representátion, pronun- ciátion, exhibítion, méntion.

   b) *-sion:*   revísion, excúrsion, ex- plósion, occásion.

   c) *-ic* (español -ico):   eléctric, públic, specí- fic.

   d) *-tious, -cious* (español -cioso):   preténtious, précious.

   e) *cial- -tial,* (español -cial):   spécial, substántial.

4. Algunas palabras de origen francés retienen la acentuación del francés.

Por ej.: enginéer, machíne, to suppóse, addréss.

Reading

The Evans family are sitting round the fire on a Sunday afternoon in autumn. As it is raining, they cannot go out, so Mr. Evans is reading the newspaper. Mrs. Evans is mending some stockings and the children, Owen and Margaret, are writing letters. Their Spanish friend Asunción is also writing letters.

Mrs. Evans: Owen, have you answered the letter you received from Uncle Charles last Thursday?

Owen: No, I haven't had much time for writing letters lately. I had to go to the football match yesterday and I have been preparing my scout tests in the evenings. Next week I have to pass my observation, fire-lighting, map reading and first aid tests.

Mrs. Evans: Well, I want you to write to Uncle Charles this afternoon. He's the kindest of all your relations and likes receiving letters from you. Ask him to come and see us soon.

Owen: All right, mother. I'll write to him now before going out.

Asún: Oh, what time does the post go on Sundays? I must write to my friend Brenda Johnson whom I met in London.

Mr. Evans: It goes at a quarter to six, so you will have to hurry.

Asún: How should I begin a letter to Brenda in English?

Mrs. Evans: Well, if you call her by her Christian name, then you simply say «Dear Brenda».

Asún: And how should I finish?

Mrs. Evans: You can put «Affectionately» or «Yours affectionately».

Margaret: Can you give me some stamps, Daddy? I didn't remember to buy any.

Owen: I spend my time reminding you to do things and you always forget. I expect you forgot the envelopes too.

Margaret: No, I bought some envelopes, but I didn't go near the Post Office.

Asún: Would you mind passing the ink, please, Owen. (Owen passes the ink.) Thank you.

Mr. Evans: If it goes on raining much more, there will be no football next week.

Asún: Do you enjoy watching football, Mr. Evans?

Mr. Evans: Certainly I do. Do you?

Asún: I don't like it at all. I prefer to stay indoors in winter in England. It's so cold and it rains so much.

Margaret: It doesn't rain so much as foreign people think. When I spent two months in Seville it rained all day every day.

Owen: Now, it's time to take the letters to the post. Who's coming with me?

Asún: I am. Are you coming, Margaret?

Margaret: No, I don't think it's worth going out in the rain. I'll stay at home by the fire and talk to father.

Asún: When will my letter reach Dulwich, Mr. Evans?

Mr. Evans: Tomorrow morning, Asún.

Asún: Oh, good. That's not long.

(Asún and Owen go out to the post.)

Margaret: It's quite good to take a letter all the way from Cambridge to London and across to Dulwich in one night.

Mr. Evans: Do you know how the letters go across London, Margaret?

Margaret: I suppose they are taken in cars or by the underground.

Mr. Evans: No, they travel all alone by a special underground train of which very few people have heard. This train runs between the main stations and the General Post Office, so that Asún's letter, on arriving at Paddington Station, will be taken at once by this special train to the other side of London. In this way the letters are not kept a long time in London, but continue their journey without stopping.

Mrs. Evans: Here come Owen and Asún back from the post. Let's have a game of cards, shall we?

Mr. Evans: Yes, that's a good idea.
(They start playing cards.)

Exercises

A) **Answer the following questions:**
1. Why hasn't Owen answered the letter from Uncle Charles?
2. What does Mrs. Evans want Owen to ask Uncle Charles in his letter?
3. Why must Asún hurry with her letter to Brenda?
4. Who forgot to buy some stamps?
5. Who enjoys watching football?
6. Does Asún enjoy watching football?
7. Who is going to the post with Owen?
8. Why isn't Margaret going to the post?
9. How are letters taken across London?
10. What does Mrs. Evans suggest when Owen and Asún return from the post?

B) 1. **Explain in English the following words or phrases.**

   2. **Use each word in a sentence. Do not translate.**

   a flat, first aid, football, garage, envelope, manageress, dining-room, butcher, architect, parents.

C) **Put the following sentences into** *a)* **The interrogative.** *b)* **The negative.**

1. The chairman always drives to the council in his car.
2. He looks at the advertisements in the paper every day.
3. You spend your spare time playing hockey.
4. I shall remind you to buy some stamps.

5. It is worth letting the house for the summer.
6. They like riding across the fields and through the woods.
7. We often forget to obey the laws of the country.
8. The back tyre got a puncture on the way to the football match.
9. Charles carried his case from the train to the taxi.
10. They avoided travelling in August because of the crowds.

D) **Complete the following sentences using the gerund form of the verb and any other words necessary:**

Example: He came in without...
He came in without ringing the bell.

1. I haven't much time for...
2. On ... they took a taxi home.
3. By ... she was able to pass her exam.
4. This year we have had no opportunity of ...
5. What's the use of ...
6. Besides ... we grow some flowers in the front garden.
7. That is the great advantage of ...
8. After ... we played a game of cards.
9. Before ... I always read the newspaper.
10. Instead of ... he stays at home with his family.

E) **Form all the sentences possible with the following words:**

| Asunción
I
Mr. and Mrs. Jones
You
It
We
Peter | am
is
are | going
willing | to rain this evening.
to lend you their car.
to become a scout next year.
to do the digging in the garden.
to let the house for the summer.
to go to the dentist's tomorrow. |

F) **Complete each of the following sentences, making them as long and as interesting as you can:**

I told him to ....
He wanted her to ....
You asked me to ....
We expected you to ....
He ordered them to ....
They invited us to ....

95

LESSON THIRTEEN

Vocabulary and Pronunciation

i: scénery (paisaje), to mean (significar, querer decir).

i Brítish (británico), Brítain (Gran Bretaña), Bríton (británico, subst.), rich (rico), dífference (diferencia), tradítion (tradición).

e to séparate (separar), Céltic (céltico).

a Spániard (español, subst.), uninhábited (inhabitado), flat (llano), cháracter (carácter).

o hóspital (hospital), populátion (población), Scótland (Escocia), to bórrow (tomar prestado), rock (roca, peñasco), órigin (origen).

o: poor (pobre), moor (páramo), northern (del norte).

ʌ úndulating (ondulante).

ai Wales (país de Gales), lake (lago). Isle (isla), varíety (variedad), wild (salvaje), to ísolate (aislar), díalect (dialecto).

ou low (bajo), stóny (pedregoso).

au mouth (boca, desembocadura), móuntain (montaña).

eiə área (área, superficie).

aiə Ireland (Irlanda), Irish (Irlandés).

k cháracter, Céltic.

s scénery.

Consonante muda

s en isle.

Frases

I should think:	me imagino, supongo.
On the other hand:	por otra parte.
To play a part:	desempeñar un papel
To be in use:	estar en uso.
I'll see you tomorrow:	hasta mañana.

Verbo irregular

to draw,	drew,	drawn:	dibujar, tirar.
to mean,	meant,	meant:	querer decir

Nombres gentilicios

País	Adjetivo	Substantivo	Idioma
Great Britain	British	Briton	English
England	English	Englishman	English
Wales	Welsh	Welshman	Welsh ⎫ and
Scotland	Scottish	Scotsman	Gaelic ⎬ English
Ireland	Irish	Irishman	Erse ⎭
France	French	Frenchman	French
Spain	Spanish	Spaniard	Spanish

Grammar

Possessive Case

Forma

Para formar el caso posesivo (o genitivo sajón) se añade *'s* a los substantivos en singular o en plural sin *s* (men, etc.) y *un apóstrofo solo* a los substantivos en plural con *s*.

Singular
- Mr. Brown's car. — El coche del señor Brown.
- Betty's book. — El libro de Isabel.
- The boy's father. — El padre del muchacho.
- A girl's handkerchief. — El pañuelo de una muchacha.

Plural
- 1. The children's toys. — Los juguetes de los niños.
- Those men's club. — El círculo de esos hombres.
- 2. These girls' house. — La casa de estas muchachas.
- Those boys' father. — El padre de esos muchachos.

Nótese: 1. Que el artículo definido del poseído queda suprimido cuando se emplea el caso posesivo delante.

Those boys' father. *El* padre de esos muchachos.

2. Los substantivos terminados en *-s* en singular añaden *'s* si son de una o dos sílabas y el apóstrofo solo si son de más de dos o de origen clásico.

St. James's church. La iglesia de Santiago.
Charles's book. El ligro de Carlos.
Cervantes' works. Las obras de Cervantes.

3. Si hay más de un poseedor para el mismo poseído, sólo el último poseedor se pone en caso posesivo.

Peter and Betty's father. El padre de Pedro e Isabel.

4. Si el poseedor se compone de una frase larga, sólo el último substantivo de la frase se pone en caso posesivo.

The Queen of England's country house.
La casa de campo de la reina de Inglaterra.

5. Muy a menudo se omiten las palabras *shop, church, house, college* y *hospital* después del caso posesivo.

I am going to the baker's.   Voy a la panadería.
We are going to Peter's.   Vamos a casa de Pedro.

6. También se pone el caso posesivo sin el poseído para evitar la repetición de éste en la misma oración.

This is my car and that is Mr. Brown's.
Éste es mi coche y aquél es el del señor Brown.

Is this your book?   ¿Es éste su libro?
No, it's Betty's.   No, es el de Isabel.

Cuando el poseedor no es una persona, se puede evitar la repetición de poseído, mediante el uso de *that of...* (el de, la de).

The area of Spain is greater than that of England.
El área de España es más grande que la de Inglaterra.

Uso del caso posesivo

1. En general se emplea sólo para seres. Para cosas se emplea la forma con la preposición of (de).

The horse's legs.   Las patas del caballo.
Peter's leg.   La pierna de Pedro.
pero   The leg of the table.   La pata de la mesa.

2. Se emplea con ciertos pronombres que representan a personas, como *somebody, someone, nobody,* etc.

This must be somebody's hat.
Tiene que ser el sombrero de alguien.

3. Se emplea también con expresiones de *tiempo, distancia, peso* y *valor.*

A week's rest.   Una semana de descanso.
A month's holiday.   Un mes de vacaciones.
Last year's crop.   La cosecha del año pasado.
An hour's walk.   Una hora a pie.
An hour's journey.   Un viaje de una hora.
Five pounds' weight of potatoes.   (El peso de) cinco libras de patatas.
Five shillings' worth of vegetables.   El valor de cinco chelines de verduras.

4. Se emplea en personificaciones, en el lenguaje poético y en ciertos modismos.

Britain's glory	La gloria de Gran Bretaña.
Night's dark mantle	El manto obscuro de la noche.
For heaven's sake.	Por el amor de Dios.

Modismos con el pronombre posesivo y el caso posesivo

Las frases españolas como *un amigo mío, un amigo tuyo,* etcétera, se traducen al inglés poniendo *of* entre el substantivo y el pronombre posesivo.

A friend of mine, a friend of yours, etc.

Are you a friend of his?   ¿Es usted amigo suyo?

Por analogía se forman frases de la misma construcción, poniendo el caso posesivo en vez del pronombre posesivo.

Are you a friend of Peter's?   ¿Es usted un amigo de Pedro?

He is a friend of my brother's.   Es amigo de mi hermano.

MORE THAN

Nótese que *más que* o *más de* en español se traduce indistintamente al inglés por *more than.*

Reading

THE BRITISH ISLES

Doctor García, who has been studying for few months at a big London hospital, is going to return to Spain soon. However, he wants to take a month's rest before going back to his work in his own country, and here he is talking to an English friend of his, Doctor Sutherland.

Dr. García: Well, I shall soon be leaving you now, but after all this time in London I feel I should like to see something of the rest of England before I go back to Spain.

Dr. Sutherland: Yes, you mustn't go back thinking that all England is like London and the country around the big city, and that all Englishmen are like Londoners, although nearly a quarter of the population of England lives in London.

Dr. García: What is the population of London at present?

Dr. Sutherland: About ten million, I think, including the suburbs.

99

Dr. García: Nearly half the population of the whole of Spain! And what is the population of England?

Dr. Sutherland: About 42 million, I should think. But don't forget Scotland, Wales and Ireland. Great Britain and Northern Ireland must have a population of some 47 million.

Dr. García: Yes, Spaniards often talk of England when they mean Great Britain or the British Isles. If I had time I should like to visit Scotland and Ireland, but I should need more than a month's holiday for that.

Dr. Sutherland: Couldn't you borrow somebody's car? Hiring one would cost you a lot of money, but if you had a car, in a month you could see a great deal of Great Britain and perhaps cross over to Ireland for a few days. There are no great distances in Britain like in Spain. Remember the area of Spain is twice that of the British Isles. However, you will find a greater variety of scenery in a small area of Britain than in large areas of other countries. But you must visit Highland Britain, not just Lowland Britain. If you don't visit Highland Britain you will never see the wilder side of English scenery.

Dr. García: What do you mean by *Highland* and *Lowland* Britain?

Dr. Sutherland: Well, if you draw a line from the mouth of the Tee on the north-east coast of England to the mouth of the Exe on the south-west coast, this line will divide Highland from Lowland Britain. The high land will be to the north and west of the line and the low land to the south and east. Highland Britain consists of older rocks which form poor, stony land, while the rocks of Lowland Britain are younger and form richer land. So only the better parts of Highland Britain are used, the valleys and the sea-coast, and the farms or villages are often separated by large areas of uninhabited mountains or moors. On the other hand in Lowland Britain the land is nearly all suitable for farming. It is mostly not flat, but undulating and the farms and villages are not often isolated. If you haven't time to go to Scotland you ought to visit the Lake District on the north-west coast. That has very fine scenery, typical of Highland Britain.

Dr. García: Is there any difference between the people of Highland and Lowland Britain?

Dr. Sutherland: Certainly. Although the population of Highland Britain is very small, the Highland people — the Scots, the Welsh, the Cornish and the Irish — play a large part in the life of the country and have their own traditions, dialect and character. They are more Celtic. In Wales, Ireland and the west of Scotland, Celtic dialects are spoken besides English. On the other hand the people of Lowland Britain are more Anglo-Saxon in origin and character.

Dr. García: Well, I must be going to St. Thomas's now, as I have an appointment there with Dr. Bird. Thank you for the interesting talk. I've learnt a lot about Britain I didn't know and now I must try to borrow a car.

Dr. Sutherland: Charles's car won't be in use next month: he's going to France for a few weeks' rest and I know he isn't taking it with him. When I see him tonight, I'll ask him if he is willing to lend it you.

Dr. García: That's very kind of you. Goodbye, I'll see you tomorrow.

Dr. Sutherland: Goodbye.

Exercises

A) **Answer the following questions:**

1. What has Doctor García been doing in London during the last few months?
2. What does he want to do before going back to Spain?
3. Who is Doctor Sutherland?
4. How many people live in London?
5. What is Great Britain?
6. What is the population of Great Britain and Northern Ireland?
7. Dr. García wants a car to visit Britain. How does Dr. Sutherland suggest that he gets one?
8. Which is bigger, the area of Spain or that of the British Isles?
9. Describe Highland Britain.
10. What difference is there between the people of Highland and Lowland Britain?

B) **Escríbanse en inglés:**

a) Seis partes del cuerpo.
b) Seis legumbres o frutas.

101

C) **Complétense las siguientes oraciones con la forma apropiada de una de estas palabras:**

St. James, hour, somebody, chairman of the parish council, Spaniard, women, men, this year, parents, doctor, Englishman.

1. A — character is different from that of an Englishman.
2. — crop will not be very good because of the rain.
3. The — authority is great among the villagers.
4. — clothes haven't as much variety as —
5. I should like to borrow — car.
6. Can you show me the way to — church?
7. It is about three — journey from London by train.
8. My — house is built on very poor, stony ground.
9. That old car of the — is not good enough to drive over the moors and mountains of northern England.
10. An — home has many traditions.

D) **Use the following words or phrases in sentences:**

variety, difference, scenery, poor, to isolate, origin, hospital, to separate, to borrow, character.
to play a part, to be in use.

E) **Complete the following sentences:**

1. — present the population of Ireland is about three million.
2. — arriving at the mountains we began to hear the people talking their own dialect.
3. I couldn't understand it — all.
4. It was very kind — him to take the boy to the hospital in his car.
5. I must write that — in my notebook.
6. The school dentist looks — the children's teeth.
7. The British Isles consist — England, Scotland, Wales and Ireland.
8. This game consists — putting several things — a table and trying to remember them all in one minute.
9. He has arrived — last.
10. I haven't much petrol: I must get some more — the garage — the middle of the village.
11. Put the address — the top of the page — the right.
12. Are you interested — watching football?

Composition:

An English friend is going to visit Spain in his car. Write a letter telling him where to go and describing the country to him.

Dictation:

In the passage *The British Isles,* from «Dr. Sutherland: Well, if you draw a line ...» to «... very fine scenery, typical of Highland Britain».

Translate into English:

El doctor está muy cansado. Ha trabajado todo el invierno sin tomar un día de vacaciones a causa de los muchos resfriados que ha habido. No ha podido descansar los domingos. Y además de su propio trabajo ha tenido que ayudar a un amigo suyo, el doctor Peters, en el hospital, porque uno de los médicos se rompió una pierna en un accidente. Empieza a creer que la vida de un médico no es muy agradable. «Deberías tomar un buen mes de descanso», le dice su mujer, «y así podríamos ir en coche a las montañas del país de Gales. El paisaje allí es salvaje y muy hermoso y podríamos vivir completamente aislados de la ciudad, sin oír llamar el teléfono todo el día. Además te gusta trepar por las rocas y podrías divertirte mucho.» «No es una mala idea. Podríamos quedarnos en la granja del tío Owen. Le escribiré esta noche. Me imagino que tendrá sitio para nosotros en su casa.» «Si no hay sitio en la casa de tu tío, podemos ir al pequeño hotel del señor Taffy, cerca del lago. No nos costará más de unos 10 chelines al día.» «Cuando ese galés me habla inglés yo no entiendo lo que (what) quiere decir.» «No importa. Yo le hablaré galés. Así estará muy contento.»

LESSON FOURTEEN

Vocabulary and Pronunciation

i: téa-spóon (cucharilla).

i líberty (libertad), skíll (destreza, habilidad), quíck (rápido), efféct (efecto), stíll (aún, todavía).

e efféct, dead (muerto), held (de to hold'), to offénd (ofender).

a	to h*a*ng (colgar, ahorcar), c*a*p (gorra), to th*a*nk (agradecer, dar gracias), to h*á*ndle (manejar), to spl*a*sh (salpicar), f*a*ct (hecho), unh*á*ppy (infeliz, desgraciado), f*a*t (gordo).
a:	y*a*rd (patio).
o	phen*ó*menon (fenómeno), c*ó*ntrary (contrario), h*ó*rrible (horrible), *ó*pposite (en frente), ch*o*p (chuleta).
o:	to p*o*ur (verter).
ʌ	l*ú*cky (afortunado), j*u*g (jarro), c*ó*ver (cubierta), to bl*u*sh (sonrojar).
ə:	to b*u*rst (estallar, reventar).
ei	l*á*dy (señora), str*a*nge (extraño), gr*á*vy (salsa), t*á*blesp*ó*on (cuchara sopera), s*a*fe (seguro), s*á*fely (a salvo).
ai	to surpr*í*se (sorprender), pol*í*te (cortés).
au	to d*ou*bt (dudar).
ou	b*ó*w-w*í*nd*ow* (mirador), p*ó*ultry (aves), to h*o*ld (tener en la mano, contener).
eə	r*ea*l (verdadero).
ju:	*u*sed (acostumbrado), *u*se (costumbre, uso).
u:	to l*o*se, perder.
f	*ph*enomenon.

Consonante muda

b	en dou*b*t.

Frases y modismos

to be hanging:	estar colgado (véase *to be sitting, standing,* etc.).
on which:	a lo cual, entonces.
to be used to:	estar acostumbrado a.
on the contrary:	al contrario.
Lord bless my soull	¡Dios me bendiga!
to take off:	quitarse.

Verbos irregulares

to hang,	hung,	hung:	colgar, ahorcar.
to hold,	held,	held:	tener en la mano.
to throw,	threw,	thrown:	echar, tirar.
to burst,	burst,	burst:	reventar, estallar.
to lose	lost,	lost:	perder.

Grammar

Los substantivos (nouns)

Formación

Los substantivos en inglés pueden ser de origen sajón, francés, latino o griego.

Pueden también formarse añadiendo sufijos o prefijos clásicos (*con-, com-, dis-, re-, -tion, -ary, -er*, etc.) o sajones (*mis-, un-, -or, -th, -dom*, etc.).

Pueden ser substantivos compuestos (*bedroom, tea-spoon*, etcétera).

Pueden ser gerundios (*reading, writing*, etc.).

Nótese que

1. Los sufijos anglosajones *-er* y *-or* indican un agente.

player:	jugador.
actor:	actor.
teacher:	profesor.
manager:	director.

2. Muchos substantivos en inglés tienen la misma forma que el verbo correspondiente.

to help:	ayudar.	help:	ayuda.
to walk:	pasear.	a walk:	paseo.
to answer:	contestar.	an answer:	contestación.
to change:	cambiar.	a change:	cambio. Etc.

Nótense las palabras de este tipo a medida que se encuentren en la lectura.

Substantivos compuestos (uso calificativo del substantivo)

El substantivo empleado como calificativo puede indicar las siguientes ideas:

1. *Lugar:* country people, the village church.
2. *Materia:* a silk handkerchief, a stone house.
3. *Uso:* a passport office, a coffee-room.
4. *Tiempo:* an evening paper, an afternoon class.

Nótese la diferencia entre:

an afternoon class:	una clase de la tarde.
an afternoon's work:	{ una tarde de trabajo. / el trabajo de una tarde.

105

5. *Contenido:* a picture paper, a flower garden.

6. *El complemento de un agente:* a bus - driver, a bank-manager.

Género de los substantivos

a) *Masculino:*
hombres y animales machos — the man, the boy, the horse.

b) *Femenino:*
mujeres y animales hembras — the lady, the maid, the cow.

c) *Común:*
substantivos que pueden indicar hombres o mujeres — the teacher, the doctor.

d) *Neutro:*
cosas y nombres abstractos — the spoon, the sun, the morning.

Nótese que

1. Un niño de pecho generalmente es neutro.
   The baby has a piece of paper in *its* mouth.

2. El substantivo colectivo *crowd* es neutro:
   The crowd was big: in fact it was too big.

3. Barcos, máquinas y países generalmente son de género femenino.
   She's a fine ship.
   Spain and her colonies.

4. Cuando no se especifica el sexo de un animal, se lo pone en neutro.
   The bird and its líttle ones.

Aunque el inglés prescinde generalmente de terminaciones distintas para masculino, femenino y neutro, existen, sin embargo, tres maneras de distinguir los géneros masculino y femenino.

a) Usando palabras distintas:

man — woman.
gentleman — lady.
boy — girl.
father — mother.

b) Mediante la terminación *-ess:*

actor	— actress:	actor.
master	— mistress:	dueño.
author	— authoress:	autor.
manager	— manageress:	director.
waiter	— waitress:	camarero.

c) Usando palabras compuestas:

man-servant
woman-servant (o maid-servant)
landlord
landlady

Añádanse otros ejemplos a medida que se encuentren **en** las lecturas.

Reading

DAVID COPPERFIELD HAS LUNCH AT THE INN

... I was thinking this when a lady looked out of a bow-window where some poultry and meat were hanging up, and said:
«Is that the little gentleman from Blunderstone?»
«Yes, ma'am» I said.
«What name?, asked the lady.
«Copperfield, ma'am» I said.
«That's not it,» answered the lady «Nobody's dinner is paid for here in that name.»
«Is it Murdstone, ma'am?» I said.
«If you are Mr. Murdstone,» said the lady, «why do you give another name first?»
I explained to the lady how it was*, who then rang a bell, and called out: «William! Show the coffee-room,» on which a waiter came running out of a kitchen on the opposite side of the yard to show it, and seemed a deal surprised when he found he was only to show it to me.
It was a large long room with some maps in it. I doubt if I could have felt much stranger if the maps had been real foreign countries and I lost in the middle of them. I felt I was taking a liberty to sit down, with my cap in my hand, on the corner of the chair nearest the door; and when the waiter put

---

* David Copperfield's mother had been married a second time to Mr. Murdstone.

a cloth on the table especially for me, I think I must have blushed to the roots of my hair.

He brought me some chops and vegetables and took the covers off in such a manner that I was afraid I must have offended him. But he put a chair for me at the table and said very politely: «Now, six-foot, come on!»

I thanked him and took my seat: but I found it very difficult to handle my knife and fork with skill, or to avoid splashing the gravy onto the table-cloth, while he was standing opposite, looking at me so hard and making me blush every time I caught his eye. After watching me into the second chop, he said «There's half a pint of beer for you. Will you have it now?» I thanked him and said «Yes.» On which he poured it out of a jug into a large glass and held it up against the light and made it look beautiful.

«My eye!» he said. «It seems a good deal, doesn't it?»

«It certainly seems a good deal,» I answered.

«There was a gentleman here yesterday,» he said. «A fat gentleman, by the name of Topsawyer — perhaps you know him?»

«No,» I said. «I haven't the pleasure...»

«He came in here» said the waiter, looking at the light through the glass, «ordered a glass of this beer — ordered it although I told him not to — drank it, and fell dead. It was too old for him. It oughtn't to be sold, that's the fact.»

I was very sorry to hear of this sad accident and said I'd have some water.

«You see,» said the waiter, still looking at the light through the glass, with one of his eyes shut, «our people don't like things being ordered and left. It offends them. But I'll drink it, if you like. I'm used to it, and use is everything. I don't think it will hurt me, if I throw my head back and drink it off quickly. Shall I?»

I answered that I should be pleased if he drank it, but only if he could do it safely, and when he threw his head back and drank it off quickly, I was horribly afraid of seeing him, like the unhappy Mr. Topsawyer, fall dead on the carpet. But it didn't hurt him. On the contrary, I thought he seemed fresher for it.

«What have we got here?» he said, putting a fork into my dish. «Not chops?»

«Chops,» I said.

«Lord bless my soul! I didn't know they were chops. Why, a chop's just the thing to take off the bad effects of that beer. Isn't it lucky?»

So he took a chop by the bone in one hand, and a potato in the other, and ate away with a very good appetite. He afterwards took another chop, and another potato. When he had finished, he brought me a pudding, and, having put it in front of me, seemed to be thinking of other things for some time. «How's the pudding?» he said, turning to me again.

«I think...»

«Why, it's my favourite pudding,» he continued, looking at it nearer and taking up a table-spoon. «Isn't that lucky? Come on, little 'un (one) and let's see who will get most.»

The waiter certainly got most. He more than once invited me to hurry and win the race, but with his table-spoon to my tea-spoon, and his appetite to my appetite, I was left far behind from the beginning. I never saw anyone enjoy a pudding so much, I think: and he laughed, when it was all finished, as if he was still enjoying it.

I was very surprised to find, on getting into the coach again, that I was supposed to have eaten all the dinner without help. I learnt this when I heard the lady in the bow-window say to the driver «Look after that child, George, or he'll burst!» and when I saw that all the women-servants came out to look at me as a young phenomenon and laugh. My friend the waiter did not seem to be disturbed by this, but also came out to admire me and to laugh with all the others.

(Adapted from *David Copperfield* by Charles Dickens.)

Exercises

A) **Answer the following questions:**

1. Who looked out of the bow-window where the poultry and meat were hanging?
2. Whose dinner was paid for at the inn?
3. What was the waiter's name?
4. What was there in the coffee-room?
5. What did the waiter bring David Copperfield?
6. Why did David find it difficult to handle his knife and fork with skill or to avoid splashing the gravy onto the table-cloth?
7. What was there for David to drink?
8. What did the waiter do with the beer after pouring it into a glass?

9. What happened (ocurrir) to Mr. Topsawyer?
10. Why did the waiter offer to drink the beer?
11. Why did the waiter say the beer wouldn't hurt him?
12. Did the waiter fall dead on the carpet after drinking the beer?
13. What did the waiter say was good to take off the bad effects of the beer?
14. What did the waiter bring after the chops and potatoes?
15. Whose favourite pudding was it?
16. Who won the pudding race?
17. Why did the women-servants come out and look at David as a young phenomenon?

B) 1. **Fórmense los substantivos correspondientes a los siguientes verbos, y**

2. **Empléese el substantivo en una oración.**

to address, to draw, to greet, to lecture, to manage, to move, to observe, to play, to produce, to teach, to work, to act, to arrive, to begin, to build.

C) 1. **Fórmense substantivos compuestos poniendo una palabra de la columna "A" delante de otra de la columna "B".**

2. **Empléese el substantivo compuesto en una oración.**

A	B
town	chair
flower	end
week	race

A	B
obstacle	garden
bank	hall
village	church
shop	shop
book	case
arm	manager
vegetable	window

D) **Put the following sentences into the Past Preterite:**

1. The doctor takes off his coat and hangs it up when he arrives at the hospital.
2. I often forget to buy an evening paper when I return from my work in the City.

3. When this waiter pours out my beer, he always holds the glass to the light to see if it is good.
4. He spoils the table-cloth by splashing gravy over it.
5. I find it difficult to handle my knife and fork with skill while he stands opposite looking at me so hard.
6. He orders a glass of beer, although I tell him not to, drinks it and falls dead.
7. After the chops and the vegetables he brings me a pudding.
8. I doubt if I could feel stranger if the maps were real foreign countries and I lost in the midle of them.
9. I think that he is used to drinking this beer.
10. The lady looking out of the bow-window seems very surprised.

E) **Composition:**

Write the story of *David Copperfield at the inn.* Do not use direct speech (oración directa). Write it in the Past and in the 3rd person and do not use more than 200 words.

F) **Translate into English:**

Carlos Dickens fue uno de los mejores autores del siglo pasado. Escribió muchos libros, de los cuales quizá el mejor conocido sea *La historia de David Copperfield,* en que cuenta hasta cierto punto la historia de su propia vida.

En el trozo de esta obra que acabamos de leer vemos al joven David camino de la escuela. Tiene un poco de miedo a la dueña de la fonda, que le llama desde el mirador. Como va a tomar el coche de la tarde para la escuela, tiene tiempo de almorzar en la fonda. Entra en el comedor, donde hay una camarera y un camarero. David se siente muy perdido, como si estuviera aislado en un país extranjero lejos de sus parientes y amigos. El camarero le trae unas chuletas con verduras y patatas, y le mira mientras come, de manera que David se sonroja y no puede manejar su tenedor y cuchillo sin salpicar la mesa de salsa. El camarero le sirve (vierte) un vaso de cerveza de un jarro, pero le cuenta la historia de un señor que bebió un vaso de esta cerveza y cayó muerto después. Así David prefiere beber agua y la cerveza se la bebe el camarero. No le hace daño, porque, como dice, está acostumbrado a ella. Al contrario, parece estar mejor que antes. Sin embargo, dice que las chuletas son buenas para quitar los malos efectos de la cerveza, y come las chuletas de David. Después de la comida

David quiere escribir una carta a un amigo y pide papel de escribir al camarero. Cuando va a salir al coche, David tiene que pagar el papel de escribir, pero el camarero dice que no le hará pagar la tinta.

LESSON FIFTEEN

Vocabulary and Pronunciation

i	perm*í*ssion (permiso).
e	ch*é*st of drawers (cómoda), to att*é*nd (asistir a).
a	undergr*á*duate (estudiante), gr*á*duate (licenciado), ch*á*pel (capilla).
o	c*ó*llege (colegio Mayor), p*ó*rter's l*ó*dge (portería), qu*á*drangle (cuadrángulo, patio).
o:	h*a*ll (comedor de colegio).
ʌ	c*ú*pboard (armario), unc*ó*mfortable (incómodo), tr*u*nk (baúl), c*ú*ltural (cultural), s*ú*bject (asunto, sujeto).
ə:	te*r*m (trimestre), to f*ú*rnish (amueblar).
ei	g*a*te (puerta exterior, cochera, verja), inform*á*tion (informes, información).
ai	f*í*nal (final), adv*í*ce (consejo).
au	g*ow*n (toga).
ou	pr*ó*gress (progreso), b*oa*t (bote, barco).
ju:	t*ú*tor (director de estudios).
eə	st*ai*rcase (escalera).

Frases

and so on: y así sucesivamente.
to attend, seguido de *complemento directo:* asistir a.
He attends a lecture: Asiste a una conferencia.
In College: En el Colegio.

Grammar

El substantivo (cont.)

Los números singular y plural

El plural del substantivo se forma añadiendo *s* al singular (o *-es* después de los sonidos *s, x, z, ch, sh*).

Pronunciación de la terminación del plural (-s o -es).

a) *s* precedida de vocal o sonidos consonantes sonoros (*b, d, g, l, m, n, r, v, ð*) se pronuncia *z:*

boys, beds, dogs, balls, arms, gloves, pans, bathes.

b) *s* precedida de sonido consonante sordo (*f, k, p, t, θ*) se pronuncia *s:*

handkerchiefs, marks, tops, visits, baths.

c) En las terminaciones del plural *-ces, -ses, zes, -xes, -ges, -ches, -shes,* la *es* se pronuncia *iz:*

faces, houses, sizes, boxes, ages, churches, dishes.

Plural irregular

1. Plurales anglosajones

man	— men:	hombre.
woman	— women:	mujer.
child	— children:	niño.
milkman	— milkmen:	lechero.
Englishmań	— Englishmen:	inglés.
foot	— feet:	pie.
tooth	— teeth:	diente.
mouse	— mice:	ratón.
goose	— geese:	ganso.
etc.		

2. Plural en "-ies" (*y* final precedida de consonante):

lady	— ladies:	señora.
family	— families:	familia.
etc.		

y final precedida de vocal añade *s* regularmente:

way	— ways:	camino.
day	— days:	día.

3. Plural en "-ves"

wife	— wives:	esposa.
knife	— knives:	cuchillo.
life	— lives:	vida.
leaf	— leaves:	hoja.
half	— halves.	mitad.
scarf	— scarves:	bufanda.
shelf	— shelves:	estante.
thief	— thieves:	ladrón.

113

Sin embargo, otros substantivos en -f siguen la regla general y añaden s:

roof	— roofs:	tejado.
proof	— proofs:	prueba.
chief	— chiefs:	jefe.
handkerchief	— handkerchiefs:	pañuelo.
grief	— griefs:	pena.
belief	— beliefs:	creencia.
relief .	— reliefs:	relieve, alivio.
cliff	— cliffs:	acantilado.

4. Plural en "-oes":

Las palabras terminadas en -o de uso corriente añaden -es:

potato	— potatoes:	patata.
tomato	— tomatoes:	tomate.
hero	— heroes:	héroe.

Sin embargo, algunas palabras de origen extranjero añaden s sola:

piano	— pianos:	piano.
radio	— radios:	radio.
cuckoo	— cuckoos:	cuclillo.
photo	— photos:	fotografía.

5. Ciertas palabras extranjeras retienen la forma original del plural:

series	— series:	serie.
crisis	— crises:	crisis.
bureau	— bureaux:	escritorio.
Mr.	— Messrs. (mesəz)	señor.

6. Ciertas palabras tienen la misma forma en singular y plural:

sheep:	oveja.
poultry:	aves.
cattle:	ganado.
fish:	pescado (*fish* en sentido de *pez* forma plural *fishes*).

Plural de los substantivos compuestos

La palabra principal solamente lleva la marca del plural (generalmente la segunda palabra):

Englishman	— Englishmen:	inglés.
bedroom	— bedrooms:	dormitorio.

El substantivo colectivo

En general los substantivos colectivos son de número singular o plural, según se consideren desde el punto de vista de la colectividad o de los elementos separados.

The crowd at the football match was very big.
The crowd were going home from the football match.
(cada uno a su casa).

Ciertos substantivos colectivos se emplean sólo en *singular*, aunque se traducen a veces al castellano por una forma en singular o plural,

advice:	consejos.
furniture:	muebles.
knowledge:	conocimiento(s)
progress:	progreso(s).
luggage:	equipaje.
nonsense:	tonterías(s).
news:	noticias(s).
information:	información, informe.
rubbish:	basura, desperdicios.

Por ej.: The news *is* good.

Para expresar la *unidad* de estas palabras se puede a veces emplear una perífrasis con *a piece of...*

a piece of furniture:	un mueble.
a piece of advice:	un consejo.
a piece of news:	una noticia.

Substantivos que se emplean sólo en plural

people:	gente. The people *have* all come.
trousers:	pantalones.
scissors:	tijeras.
goods:	mercancía.
wages:	sueldo.
customs:	aduanas.

Reading

AN ENGLISH UNIVERSITY

When an English boy leaves school to go to the university, he begins a new and very interesting life. Let us suppose that Derek is going to study at Oxford. On the day before term begins, he arrives at his college, Exeter College, which is one of the 30 colleges which together form the University of Oxford. He goes in by the main gate, where the porter's lodge is, and sees all the luggage of the undergraduates waiting to be taken to their rooms. He shows the porter which is his own piece of luggage and the porter shows him his rooms, which are on the first floor. He has two rooms; a sitting-room looking onto the quadrangle and a small bedroom looking onto the street. He is called an undergraduate at Oxford (and at Cambridge), not a student. When he passes his final examinations he becomes a graduate. The undergraduates live in their colleges at least some of the time they are at Oxford. The rest of the time they live in lodgings and go to the college for lectures, for dinner and for chapel. As Derek went past the porter's lodge he saw the Chapel on the left of the quadrangle and the Hall on the right. On the other two sides of he quadrangle there are staircases leading to the undergraduates' rooms. There is also a second quadrangle behind the chapel with more rooms and a garden called «the Fellows' Garden». A Fellow is the word used at Oxford for a tutor or professor. There are two «Common Rooms», one for the undergraduates and another for the Fellows which gives onto the Fellows' garden. Of course there is also a library.

When Derek had looked around the college he went back to his rooms. The rooms are generally let to the undergraduates furnished, but they can naturally add one or two pieces of their own furniture, if they want to. In the sitting-room Derek had two armchairs and a sofa, a desk for his work, some bookshelves, a cupboard for keeping his plates, knives, food and so on, and a fireplace. In the bedroom there was a rather uncomfortable bed, a chest of drawers, a wardrobe and a chair. The undergraduates generally add cushions, pictures and other small things to make their rooms more personal, but to have pianos or radios they have to ask permission from the college authorities.

Derek took his clothes and books out of his trunk and then it was time to go and have dinner in the Hall, or *in Hall,* as they say at Oxford. To have dinner in Hall and to go to lectures an undergraduate must wear his *gown.* The Hall was a fine old building of the fifteenth century, the oldest part of the college. At one end was the Fellows' table or the *High table* on a platform, where the Fellows have dinner. This was the first night on which all the undergraduates were in hall for dinner. After dinner, Derek talked to some of his new friends and then went to bed.

The next day he had to get up at half past seven and go

to the hall at eight o'clock and say good morning to the head of the college. An undergraduate has to do this four or five times a week to show that he is not spending all his mornings in bed. After that his servant brought him his breakfast in his room. There is generally one servant to look after all the men on one staircase. After breakfast all the new members of the college went to the hall where the head of the college gave them information and advice about their work. Each man was given a tutor and told to visit him at a certain time. Once a week the undergraduate will go to his tutor, alone or with one other man, to read him the work he has done during the week on a certain subject and to hear the tutor's advice. The student in this way can see the progress he is making and take advantage of the tutor's knowledge and advice. This «tutorial», as it is called, is the most important part of Oxford university life. The tutor will tell Derek which lectures to attend and which books to read.

After spending the morning seeing the head of the college and his tutor, Derek went back to his rooms for lunch. He invited a friend he had known at school, and who had also come to Oxford this term, to have lunch with him. During lunch, various undergraduates came to visit him and ask him if he wanted to become a member of one of the many student clubs or societies. These societies are run by the undergraduates without help from the authorities. Some societies are for the whole university, like the Oxford University Dramatic Society; others for one special college, such as the Exeter College Musical Society. There are sports clubs, like the football, rowing, cricket or hockey clubs, cultural societies, like the French Club, or the Spanish Club, musical societies, dramatic societies, and many others. Derek decided to be a member of the college rowing club and of the Spanish Club. The secretary of the rowing club told him to go down to the river that afternoon and see if a boat was going out. So after lunch Derek took out his rowing clothes and went down to the river. There were lots of undergraduates in their brightly-coloured college scarves by the river and several boats were already out. As Derek had learnt to row at school, the rowing club were very pleased to have him and he said he would come down to the river every afternoon. At about four o'clock the students all went back to their colleges. Derek had tea with the secretary of the rowing club and afterwards went to the college library to get out some books. He worked until dinner-time and after dinner went for a short walk in the town. However, he came

117

back early to do some more work in his rooms. At midnight he saw the porter shutting the gates of the college — all undergraduates must be in college before twelve — and went to bed.

Exercises

A) **Answer the following questions:**

1. Where is Derek going to study?
2. How many colleges are there in the University of Oxford?
3. How many pieces of luggage did Derek have?
4. Where are Derek's rooms?
5. What are the students called at Oxford before they pass their final exams?
6. What is a *Fellow* of an Oxford college?
7. Are their rooms let to the undergraduates furnished or unfurnished?
8. Can an undergraduate have a radio in his rooms?
9. Where did Derek have dinner on his first night at Oxford?
10. When does an undergraduate wear his gown?
11. What did Derek do the next day before breakfast and why did he have to do it?
12. Where did he have breakfast?
13. What did the new members of the college do after breakfast?
14. What does a *tutor* do at Oxford?
15. Who run the university and college societies and clubs?
16. Of which societies did Derek become a member?
17. What did Derek do after lunch?
18. Where had Derek learnt to row?
19. What did Derek do between tea and dinner?
20. At what time must all the undergraduates be in college?

B) **Form and read aloud (en voz alta) the plural of the following words** *(Plural en s, z, o iz):*

accident, address, animal, audience, axe, bank, bookcase, cabbage, club, cottage, crowd, dentist, desk, difference, advantage, dressing-table, eye, flat, garage, lecture, language, lettuce, manageress, reading-lamp, college, staircase, trunk, cupboard, boat, lodge.

C) **Write down the plural of the following words:**

university, common room, bookshelf, knife, chest of drawers, radio, society, scarf, library, leaf, way, Scotsman, tooth, handkerchief, tomato, fish, photo, postman, King of England, abbey.

D) **Translate into English:**

1. Voy a darte un consejo.
2. No hable usted tonterías.
3. Tengo una buena noticia para usted.
4. El estudiante está haciendo progresos en inglés.
5. Sus conocimientos de la lengua inglesa son pobres.
6. ¿No ha venido toda la gente?
7. Tenemos unos muebles muy bonitos.
8. Las noticias son muy malas.
9. Voy a asistir a un partido de fútbol esta tarde.
10. No estoy acostumbrado al frío.

E) **Composition:**

1. Describe an undergraduate's rooms at Oxford (60-70 words).
2. You are an undergraduate in his first term at Oxford. Write a letter home describing your life and activities (250-300 words).

F) **Translate into English:**

En las antiguas universidades inglesas, como Oxford o Cambridge, los estudiantes llevan (tienen) una vida muy interesante. Viven en uno de los colegios que forman parte de la universidad. Hay unos treinta colegios y cada uno tiene su capilla, su gran sala, donde los estudiantes cenan y donde se dan conferencias, sus salas de recreo para profesores y estudiantes, su biblioteca y las habitaciones donde viven y trabajan los estudiantes. Cada estudiante tiene dos habitaciones —un dormitorio y un salón de estar—, que el colegio le alquila amuebladas, pero puede también añadir cuadros, cojines y uno o dos muebles si quiere. Pero para tener pianos o radios en sus habitaciones los estudiantes tienen que pedir permiso al director del colegio. El portero del colegio es una persona muy útil para los nuevos estudiantes. Les da toda clase de consejos y da informes sobre la vida en el colegio. Cada estudiante tiene un director de estudios, que le dice a qué conferencias tiene que asistir y qué libros tiene que leer. Le dice también qué progresos hace y en general se ocupa del es-

119

tudiante. Los domingos todo el mundo va a la capilla del colegio. Por la tarde, entre las dos y las cuatro, muchos estudiantes salen a los campos de deportes para jugar al fútbol o a algún otro juego. Llevan corbatas y bufandas con los colores de su colegio. Hay muchas sociedades y círculos dirigidos por los estudiantes: por ejemplo, el círculo musical que da conciertos o el círculo dramático que representa obras de teatro en inglés, y a veces en idiomas extranjeros.

LESSON SIXTEEN

i: weak (débil), détail (detalle).
i   whip (látigo), difficulty (dificultad), difficult (difícil).
e   length (longitud).
a   cárriage (coche), báckwards (hacia atrás, de espaldas), báttleship (acorazado), dámage (daño, quebranto), back (espalda, lomo).
o   to drop (dejar caer).
o: fórward (adelante).
ʌ   mud (barro).
ei reins (riendas), tail (cola).
ai sídeways (de lado, de través), to cry (llorar, gritar, exclamar).
ou to contról (controlar).
ju: cúrious (curioso, extraño), huge (enorme), amúsement (diversión).
ie: to appéar (aparecer, parecer).
aiə quiet (quieto, tranquilo), desíre (deseo, desear).

Frases

on horseback:	a caballo (véase *on foot*).
in fact:	en efecto.
to think *of*:	pensar *en*.
to pick:	coger, recoger.
to pick up:	recoger (del suelo).
to run:	correr.
to run away:	escaparse.
either ... or:	o ... o.
to let go of:	soltar.
the more ... the more:	cuanto más ... más.

Pronombres y adjetivos interrogativos

		Personas		Cosas
Pronombres	who[1]	Who is that person?	what	What is that building?
	whom	Whom have you seen?	what	What have you seen?
	whose	Whose house is this?		
	which[1]	Which of you came yesterday?	which	Which of the pictures did you buy?
	what[1]	What is he? He's a farmer.		
Adjetivos	which	Which boy came yesterday?	which[2]	Which picture did you buy?
	what[1]	What man is that?	what[2]	What pictures do you like?

1. Nótese que *Who* pregunta la identidad: Who is that? That is Tom Brown. *What* pregunta la profesión: What are you? I am a tailor. *Which* se emplea en sentido selectivo: Which tailor do you go to? Johnson and Son.

2. Nótese que el adjetivo *which* se emplea en sentido selectivo, y el adjetivo *what* se emplea en sentido general.

Construcción

a) Un pronombre o adjetivo interrogativo cuando es *sujeto* de la oración va seguido de un verbo en forma *afirmativa*.

Cuando es *complemento* va seguido de un verbo en forma *interrogativa*.

Who *came* this morning?   Whom *did you see*?
Which book *was* the best?   Which house *did you buy*?

b) La preposición que rige un pronombre interrogativo se coloca muy a menudo al final de la oración, sobre todo en el estilo familiar. En este caso el pronombre *who* se emplea en vez de *whom*.

To whom are you writing   (estilo literario).
Who are you writing *to*?   (estilo familiar).

With whom are you going to the football match?
Who are you going the football match *with*?

Whose?

Se contesta por medio de un adjetivo o pronombre posesivo, (*my, mine*), o por un caso posesivo (*Peter's*):

Whose car is this? It is *my* car. It is *mine*. It is **Peter's.**

Which?

 a) Escogiendo entre dos cosas:
   Which book will you have? I shall have *this one.*
   I shall have *that one.*
   I shall have the *one about Spain.*
   I shall have *either* (cualquiera de los dos: no tiene importancia).
   I shall have *both* (ambos).
   I shall have *neither*
   I shan't have *either.* }(ninguno de los dos).

 b) Escogiendo entre más de dos cosas:
   Which book will you have?
   I shall have *this one, that one, the one about Spain.*
   I shall have *any one* (cualquiera).
   I shall have all (todos).
   I shan't have *any*
   I shall have *none* }(ninguno).

Adverbios interrogativos

How?	¿Cómo?
How much?	¿Cuánto?
How many?	¿Cuántos?
How far?	¿A qué distancia?
How wide?	¿Qué ancho?
How often?	¿Con qué frecuencia?
Why?	¿Por qué?
When?	¿Cuándo?
Where?	¿Dónde? ¿Adónde?
At what time?	¿A qué hora?
What ... for?	¿Para qué?
What ... like?	¿Cómo?
Etc.	

Where? se emplea también con las preposiciones *to* y *from* generalmente al final de la oración. (*To* no se puede poner delante de *where.*)

  Where is he going to? ¿A dónde va?
  Where has he come from? ¿De dónde ha venido?

What ... for (para qué) y *what ... like* (cómo) sólo se emplean con la preposición *for* o *like* al final de la oración.

  What has he come for? ¿Para qué ha venido?
  What is the road like? ¿Cómo está la carretera?

To come and To go

To come

1. Indica un movimiento de la persona a quien se habla hacia el sitio donde está o estará *la persona que habla.*

> Come here.   Venga aquí.
>
> You must come and see me in Oxford.
> Debe venir a verme en Oxford.

2. Indica un movimiento de la persona que habla hacia el sitio donde está o estará la persona a quien se habla.

> Waiter!   *Coming, sir.*
> ¡Camarero!   Voy, señor.
>
> I shall *come* and see you tomorrow morning.
> Iré a verle mañana por la mañana.

3. Se emplea en el sentido de acompañar.

> Will you come to the theatre with me tonight?
> ¿Quiere venir al teatro conmigo esta noche?

4. Se emplea en el sentido de llegar.

> He came half an hour late.
> Llegó con media hora de retraso.

To go

se emplea a veces en el sentido de partir.

> We must go at once.
> Tenemos que irnos ahora mismo.

Reading

A SCENE FROM THE PICKWICK PAPERS

«Now, about Manor Farm,» said Mr. Pickwick. «Is Winkle coming with us?»

«Yes,» said Mr. Snodgrass. «He's coming. How shall we go?»

«Let us ask the waiter,» said Mr. Tupman. «Waiter!»

«Coming, sir.»

«How can we go to Manor Farm from here?»

«Very nice four-wheeled carriage, sir — seat for two behind — one in front for the gentleman that drives. Oh, I beg your pardon, sir, that will only hold three.»

«What's to be done?» said Mr. Snodgrass.

«Perhaps one of the gentlemen would like to ride, sir?» suggested the waiter, looking towards Mr. Winkle. «Very good horses, sir. Any of Mr. Wardle's men coming to Rochester would bring them back, sir.»

«Just the thing,» said Mr. Pickwick. «Winkle, will you go on horseback?»

Mr. Winkle certainly doubted his skill at riding very much, but as he did not want his friends to know this, he answered, «Certainly. I enjoy riding a great deal.»

«Bring them to the door at eleven,» said Mr. Pickwick.

«Very well, sir,» said the waiter.

Mr. Pickwick was looking out the window of the coffee-room when the waiter came in and said that the carriage was ready. And in fact the carriage appeared at that moment in front of the coffee-room window. It was a curious little green box on four wheels, drawn by a huge brown horse. A man stood near holding another huge horse — which appeared to be a near relation of the animal in the carriage — ready for Mr. Winkle.

«Bless my soul!» said Mr. Pickwick. «Who's going to drive? I never thought of that.»

«Oh! you, of course,» said Mr. Tupman.

«Of course,» said Mr. Snodgrass.

«I!» said Mr. Pickwick

«No need to be afraid, sir,» said the man. «He's very quiet. A child in arms could drive him.»

So Mr. Tupman and Mr. Snodgrass took their seats at the back. Mr. Pickwick got up in front and the man put the reins in Mr. Pickwick's left hand and a whip into his right hand.

«Wo-o!» cried Mr. Pickwick, as the tall animal showed a decided desire to go backwards into the coffee-room window.

«Wo-o!» repeated Mr. Tupman and Mr. Snodgrass from the back.

Mr. Winkle climbed onto his horse with about as much difficulty as he would have had in getting up the side of a battleship.

«All right?» asked Mr. Pickwick, rather feeling that it was all wrong.

«All right,» answered Mr. Winkle, weakly.

Off went the carriage and the horse, with Mr. Pickwick driving one and Mr. Winkle on the back of the other, to the amusement of the whole inn yard.

«What makes him go sideways?» said Mr. Snodgrass in the carriage to Mr. Winkle on the horse.

«I can't imagine,» said Mr. Winkle.

His horse was going up the street in a most curious manner, side first, with his head towards one side of the road, and his tail towards the other. Mr. Pickwick had no time to observe either this or any other detail, being quite busy managing the animal drawing the carriage, who seemed very difficult to control. Sometimes he stopped completely, and then went on for some minutes so fast that it was impossible to manage him.

«What can he mean by this?» said Mr. Sondgrass.

Mr. Tupman was going to answer when Mr. Pickwick cried out:

«Wo-o! I have dropped my whip.»

«Winkle,» said Mr. Snodgrass, as the rider came up on the tall horse. «Pick up the whip, there's a good fellow.»

Mr. Winkle got down from the horse, gave the whip to Mr. Pickwick, and taking the reins prepared to get up again. However, as soon as Mr. Winkle had taken the reins, the horse went backwards to their full length.

«Poor fellow,» said Mr. Winkle. «Poor fellow, good old horse.»

But the more Mr. Winkle tried to get near «the poor fellow» the more he went back.

«What am I to do?» said Mr. Winkle. «What am I to do? I can't get on him. Please come and hold him.»

Mr. Pickwick threw the reins on his horse's back and got down from his seat and went to help Mr. Winkle. When Winkle's horse saw Mr. Pickwick coming towards him with the carriage whip in his hand, he went backwards in the direction from which they had just come rather more quickly. Mr Pickwick ran to help Mr. Winkle, but the more Mr. Pickwick ran forward the more the horse ran backwards, and at last Mr. Winkle let go of the reins. The horse turned round and quietly went home to Rochester. Mr. Winkle and Mr. Pickwick then heard a noise at a little distance.

«Bless my soul!» cried Mr. Pickwick. «There's the other horse running away.»

And in fact, it was so. The noise had made the animal afraid and the reins were on his back. He went off with the four-wheeled carriage behind him and Mr. Tupman and Mr. Snodgrass in the four-wheeled carriage. Mr. Tupman jumped into the mud on the side of the road and Mr. Snodgrass followed his example. The horse broke the four-wheeled carriage against a stone bridge and finally stopped a little further on to look at the damage he had done.

Adapted from CHARLES DICKENS.

Exercises

A) **Answer the following questions:**

1. Who wanted to go to Manor Farm?
2. Where were they starting from?
3. Whose advice did they ask about how to get to Manor Farm?
4. What did the waiter suggest?
5. Whom did Mr. Pickwick ask to go on horseback?
6. At what time did the carriage appear in front of the coffee-room window?
7. What was the carriage like?
8. What had Mr. Pickwick not thought of?
9. How was Mr. Winkle's horse going up the street?
10. Why had Mr. Pickwick no time to observe Mr. Winkle's horse?
11. What did Mr. Pickwick cry out?
12. Whom did Mr. Snodgrass ask to pick up the whip?
13. Why couldn't Mr. Winkle get back onto his horse?
14. Who went to help Mr. Winkle to get onto his horse?
15. What did Mr. Winkle's horse do when it saw Mr. Pickwick coming towards him?
16. Where did the horse go to when Mr. Winkle let go of the reins?
17. What had made the other horse afraid?
18. What did it do?
19. What did Mr. Snodgrass and Mr. Tupman do when the horse ran away with the carriage?
20. Have you ever driven a carriage?

B) **Complete the following sentences with the correct interrogative pronoun, adjective or adverb.**

1. — son are you?
2. — of these caps do your prefer?
3. «Is Mr. Brown a lawyer?» «No.» «— is he then?»
4. — is your tailor?
5. — do these oranges come from?
6. — is your house like?
7. — — is London from Madrid?
8. — are you thinking of?
9. — are you afraid of?
10. — — do you go to the theatre in summer?
11. — did Mr. Pickwick go to Manor Farms with?
12. — — — do you go to work in the morning?

C) **Explain in English and then use in a sentence the following words:**

university, chest of drawers, trunk, undergraduate, to blush, huge, a child in arms, a four-wheeled carriage, furnished, quietly.

D) **Complete the following sentences with the correct form of "to come" or "to go":**

1. *Mr. A.:* Doctor, I have a temperature: can you — and see me today?
   Doctor: Certainly. I'll — at about five o'clock.
2. How shall we — to London tomorrow from here?
3. When can I — to London to see you?
4. Will you — with me to the races today?
5. Where's Peter? Hasn't he — ? No, but I'm expecting him any minute.
6. No letters! Hasn't the postman — ?
7. When you were in London, did you — to Hyde Park?
8. When can I — and give you back the book you lent me?

E) **Composition:**

«Mr. Pickwick tells the story of the two horses.»
Not more than 225 words.

F) **Translate into English:**

Uno de los libros más conocidos de Dickens es la historia de Pickwick. El Sr. Pickwick es el presidente del círculo, y con tres amigos suyos hace un viaje por algunas ciudades del sur de Inglaterra.

Durante este viaje estaban en una fonda hablando de cómo podrían llegar a un sitio que se llamaba Manor Farm. Preguntaron al camarero la mejor manera de ir allí. «¿A dónde van, señores? ¿A Manor Farm? Hay un coche muy bonito con asientos para dos, detrás, y otro delante para el que lo conduce. Pero eso estaría bien para tres sólo, y ustedes son cuatro.» «Sí,» dijo el Sr. Snodgrass. «¿Qué podemos hacer?» El camarero preguntó si a uno de ellos le gustaría ir a caballo, porque en la fonda tenían muy buenos caballos y cualquiera de los hombres podría volver con el caballo a la fonda cuando vinieran a Rochester.

El Sr. Pickwick pensó que esto era buena idea, y preguntó a su amigo Winkle si iría él a caballo. El Sr. Winkle, que no quería que sus amigos supieran que no sabía montar bien a caballo, dijo que sí, que le gustaría mucho. «Entonces,

venga usted a la puerta, a las once, con el coche y los caballos»,
dijo el Sr. Pickwick al camarero.

A esa hora llegó el coche con un caballo enorme, y otro
también enorme para el Sr. Winkle.

«¿Quién va a conducir?», dijo el Sr. Pickwick.

Todos los amigos dijeron «tú, naturalmente». Como el
señor Pickwick parecía un poco asustado de esto, el camarero le
dijo que el caballo era muy tranquilo y que el señor no debía
tener miedo.

Así se fueron, el Sr. Pickwick conduciendo el coche, con
dos de sus amigos sentados detrás, y el Sr. Winkle montando
el otro enorme caballo. Los dos encontraban los caballos muy
difíciles de controlar. El caballo del Sr. Winkle subía la calle
de través, y el otro o se paraba completamente o iba muy de
prisa. El Sr. Pickwick dejó caer su látigo. «Iré a ayudarle»,
dijo el Sr. Winkle, y bajó del caballo y dio el látigo al Sr. Pickwick. Luego no podía subir otra vez, y el Sr. Pickwick bajó
del coche a ayudarle a él. Pero no podían controlar el caballo.
Por fin los dos caballos, dejando a los dos amigos en la carretera, volvieron tranquilamente a Rochester.

LESSON SEVENTEEN

Vocabulary and Pronunciation

i:	immédiate (inmediato), to steal (robar).
i	pig (cerdo), to milk (ordeñar), to insíst (insistir), to sing (cantar), bítter (amargo).
e	to rent (alquilar), step (paso), to spread (extender, esparcir).
a	shádow (sombra), sang (de to sing).
a:	párson (pastor).
o	to sob (sollozar), robin (petirrojo).
o:	cause (causa), stráwberry (fresa, fresón).
ʌ	búcket (cubo), sung (de to sing).
u:	fool (tonto-a, subst.), moon (luna).
ai	to lie (yacer, estar echado), píg-stye (zahúrda), to sigh (suspirar), to die (morir).
ou	stole, stólen (de to steal).

Frases y modismos

to take hold of: agarrar, coger (contrario de to let go).

He took hold of the reins: Cogió las riendas.
He let go of the reins: Soltó las riendas.

to laugh *at*:   reírse *de*

When I try to do it he always laughs at me
Cuando intento hacerlo siempre se ríe de mí.

to make mistakes: equivocarse.

His wife always makes mistakes.
Su esposa siempre se equivoca.

Own

Nótese el modismo:

A piece of land *of his own:*	Un trozo de tierra de su propiedad.
I have a car *of my own:*	Tengo coche propio.
She has a house *of her own:*	Tiene casa propia.

Verbos irregulares

to lie,	lay,	lain:	echarse, acostarse, yacer.
to steal,	stole,	stolen:	robar.
to spread,	spread,	spread:	extender, esparcir.
to sing,	sang,	sung:	cantar.

Grammar

Pronombres relativos

Singular y plural

	Personas	Cosas
Sujeto	who, that	which, that
Complemento	whom, that	which, that
Posesivo	whose	of which, whose
Después de preposición	whom	which
	what (lo que)	

Construcción

Sujeto: The man who went on horseback was late.
El hombre que fue a caballo llegó tarde.

The car which won the race was mine.
El coche que ganó la carrera era mío.

Complemento: The man whom I saw on horseback was late.
El hombre a quien vi a caballo llegó tarde.
The car which I bought in London won the race.
El coche que compré en Londres ganó la carrera.

Posesivo: The man whose son was at Oxford with Peter is a lawyer.
El hombre cuyo hijo estaba en la Universidad de Oxford con Pedro es abogado.

The carriage of which the horse fell belongs to a friend of mine.
El coche cuyo caballo cayó pertenece a un amigo mío.

The house whose gardens are very beautiful belongs to my father.
La casa cuyos jardines son muy hermosos pertenece a mi padre.

Después de preposición: The boy to whom the cap belongs has gone away.
El muchacho a quien pertenece el gorro se ha ido.
The house in which we live is very old.
La casa en que vivimos es muy vieja.

Muchas veces, sobre todo en el estilo familiar, la preposición se coloca *al final* de la oración relativa, en vez de delante del pronombre relativo.

The boy whom the cap belongs to has gone away.
El muchacho a quien pertenece el gorro se ha ido.

The house which we live in is very old.
La casa en que vivimos es muy vieja.

Empleo de "that", pronombre relativo.

Hay que emplear *that* en vez de *who, whom* o *which:*

a) Después de un adjetivo en grado superlativo y después de *first* y *last.*

London is the *largest* city *that* I have ever visited.
Londres es la ciudad más grande que he visitado jamás.

I was the *first* person *that* he saw on arriving.
Yo fui la primera persona que él vio al llegar.

b) Después de *all:*

He gave me *all* the books *that* he had brought from Spain.

Me dio todos los libros que había traído de España.

Nótese *all that* (todo lo que):

He did *all that* I wanted.

Hizo *todo lo que* quería yo.

c) Cuando el antecedente está compuesto de cosas y personas:

The *people* and the *carriages that* were going to the market blocked the road.

La gente y los coches que iban al mercado bloquearon la carretera.

Empleo facultativo pero preferible de "that"

That en contraste con *who, whom* y *which* se emplea en *sentido selectivo o restrictivo:*

My brother who is in America is a doctor.

Mi hermano es médico y está en América.

My brother that is in America is a doctor.

Mi hermano, el que está en América, es médico.

(Si hay sólo un hermano no se puede emplear that.)

Así no se puede decir:

My wife that is in America is ill.

Sino: My wife, who is in America, is ill.

Mi esposa, que está en América, está enferma.

(Porque sólo tiene una esposa).

No se puede colocar ninguna preposición delante de *that:* se colocan al final de la frase relativa.

The man *that* I gave it *to* has gone away.

El hombre a quien se lo di se ha ido.

Omisión del pronombre relativo.

a) El pronombre sujeto no se puede omitir.

b) El pronombre complemento *that* se puede omitir, pero *whom* y *which* no se omiten:

The man (that) I saw has gone away.

Pero: Parson Adams came to the house of Parson Trulliber *whom* he found with his coat off.

Parson Adams vino a la casa de Parson Trulliber, a quien encontró sin chaqueta.

c) Cualquier pronombre relativo regido por una preposición puede omitirse con tal que se coloque la preposición en posición final:

The boy (whom) the cap belongs to has gone away.
The house (which) we live in is very old.
The man (that) I gave it to has gone away.

d) La omisión del pronombre relativo es obligatoria si se coloca la preposición al final de una frase relativa formada con el *infinitivo.*

I have no place *in which* to keep my books.
No tengo sitio en donde guardar mis libros.

Pero: I have no place *to keep my books in.*

PRACTICE TABLE

This is the	house	I lent you
	money	I borrowed from you
	book	I gave to you
	pen	he gave to me
	knife	he lent to me
Where's the	pencil	I bought
		he borrowed from me.

PRACTICE TABLE

This is the	house	we drove to
	restaurant	I told you about
	building	we cycled to
	town	Tom walked to
	farm	you heard about
There's the	hotel	he works in
		we arrived at yesterday.

Traducción de "lo que"

Lo que generalmente se traduce por *what.*

What I don't understand is why he has come.
Lo que no entiendo es por qué ha venido.

I shall give you what you need for the journey.
Le daré lo que necesite usted para el viaje.

Orden de la oración

Nótese que en inglés el sujeto de la frase relativa se coloca delante del verbo, según la regla general (véase *Libro Elemental,* pág. 21). No se puede hacer la inversión del sujeto, como ocurre a menudo en español.

The house which *my father bought* is very fine.
La casa que compró mi padre es muy bonita.

Sin embargo, *whose* se construye como *cuyo* en español, poniendo el complemento al lado.

The man *whose house* we can see from here is very ill.
El hombre cuya casa vemos desde aquí está muy enfermo.

Reading

AN EIGHTEENTH-CENTURY PARSON

Parson Adams came to the house of Parson Trulliber whom he found with his coat off and a bucket in his hand, having just come from feeding his pigs; for Mr. Trulliber was a parson on Sundays, but all the other six might more exactly be called a farmer. He had a small piece of land of his own, besides which he rented a considerable deal more. His wife milked the cows and went to the markets with butter and eggs. The pigs fell mostly to his care, which he looked after at home and took to the markets, on which occasion he was often laughed at, his own size becoming with much beer little smaller than that of the animals he sold. He was indeed one of the largest men you could see and could have acted the part of Sir John Falstaff very well. Add to this, that he seemed much fatter because he was so short, his shadow being nearly as high when he lay on his back as when he stood on his legs.

Mr. Trulliber, hearing that somebody wanted to speak with him, immediately put on an old coat in which he always saw his visitors at home. His wife, who told him of Mr. Adams' arrival, had made a small mistake, for she had said to her husband that she thought a man had come for some of his pigs. This made Mr. Trulliber hurry out as fast as he could to meet his guest. As soon as he saw Adams, not doubting at all that the cause of his visit was what his wife had imagined, he said

133

to him that he had come just at the right time. They were all good and fat. Adams answered «I don't think you know me.» «Yes, yes,» cried Trulliber. «I have often seen you at the market. I have sold you some before. Yes, yes, I remember your face very well, but don't say a word more until you have seen them; I have never sold you such pigs as there are now in the pig-stye.» On which he took hold of Adams and pulled him into the pig-stye, which was indeed only two steps from his sitting-room window. When they were in the stye, he cried out «Feel them. Feel them, whether you buy or not (que compre o no compre).» With which words he opened the gate and pushed Adams into the pig-stye, insisting he feel them before he would talk one word with him.

Adams, who was always very polite, did what Trulliber wanted, and as he took hold of one of their tails the huge animal gave such a jump that he threw poor Adams on his back in the mud. Trulliber instead of helping him to get up burst out laughing and, coming into the stye, said to Adams: «Don't you know how to hold a pig» and was going to take hold of one to show Adams. But, Adams, who thought he had been quite polite enough, got up on his legs and, running away from the animals, cried out: «Nihil habeo cum porcis: I am a parson, Sir and have not come to buy pigs.» Trulliber said he was sorry for the mistake and added that his wife was a fool and always made mistakes.

Adapted from JOSEPH ANDREWS by Henry Fielding.

THE BABES [1] IN THE WOOD

My dear, do you know,
How a long time ago,
    Two poor little children,
    Whose names I don't know,
Were stolen away on a fine summer's day,
And left in a wood, as I've heard people say.

And when it was night,
So sad was their plight,[2]
    The sun it[3] went down,
    And the moon gave no light!
They sobbed and they sighed, and they bitterly cried,
And the poor little things, they lay down and died.

1. babe —forma de *baby.*
2. plight — estado, condición (póet.).
3. it — se omite en prosa.

And when they were dead,
The Robins so red,
    Brought strawberry leaves,
And over them spread:
    And all the day long,
    They sang them this song.
Poor babes in the wood! Poor babes in the wood!
And don't you remember the babes in the wood?

OLD SONG

Exercises

A) **Answer the following questions:**

1. What had Parson Trulliber just done when Parson Adams came to his house?
2. What was Parson Trulliber besides being a parson?
3. Was Parson Trulliber the owner of his land or did he rent it?
4. What did Mrs. Trulliber look after?
5. Who took the pigs to the market?
6. Why did people laugh at Parson Trulliber when he went to the market?
7. What did Mr. Trulliber do when he heard that somebody wanted to speak to him?
8. What mistake did Mrs. Trulliber make?
9. Why did Mr. Trulliber take hold of Parson Adams and pull him into the pig-stye?
10. Where was the pig-stye?
11. What did Mr. Trulliber tell Mr. Adams to do?
12. Why did Mr. Adams do what Mr. Trulliber wanted?
13. What did the pig do when Mr. Adams took hold of its tail?
14. Did Mr. Trulliber help Mr. Adams to get up?
15. What did Mr. Trulliber say about his wife?

The Babes in the Wood

1. How many babes were there in the wood?
2. What were they called?
3. At what time of the year were they left in a wood?
4. What did the robins do when the babes were dead?
5. Is this a sad or a happy song?

B) **Complete the following sentences with relative pronouns:**

1. I can remember a huge tree under — we stopped when it rained.

2. They are two little children — names I can't think of.
3. He called on his friend — he found mending his radio set.
4. He is one of the largest men — I have ever seen.
5. He put on an old coat — he always saw visitors in.
6. His wife — told him of the policeman's arrival had made a small mistake.
7. The cause of his visit was not — I imagined.
8. As he was very polite, he did all — I asked him to.
9. — surprises me is that he has not come to meet us.
10. His wife — is on a journey in France, never writes to him.
11. The last person — I lent my car to spoilt the paint.
12. This boy never does — he is told.

C) **Use the following words in sentences:**

to take hold, to let go, of my own, to laugh at,
inmediately, to steal, to lie, to sing, bitter,
step, to drop, to think of.

D) **Write the following sentences with the preposition in final position instead of in front of the relative pronoun:**

1. The car in which we drove to the races was lent to me by a friend.
2. The man to whom this boat belongs was an undergraduate with me at St. John's College, Oxford.
3. The dog of which the children were so afraid has died at last.
4. The shop-window at which we were looking had some very fine toys for the children.
5. We have no spare room in which to put visitors when they come to stay with us.
6. We give them the small one in which John generally sleeps.
7. That's the name of which I couldn't think when he asked me.
8. The pig of which he took hold threw him into the mud.
9. The old man at whom the children were laughing was very poor.
10. The dinner for which he paid so much money was not very good.

E) **Composition:**

a) Write the story of *The babes in the wood* in prose.

b) Write a letter to the Mayor of your town telling him that the bus services are very bad and asking him to make them better.

F) **Translate into English:**

En el siglo dieciocho había en Inglaterra, como también en otros países, pastores que no eran de los mejores, y de quienes se decía que eran más granjeros que párrocos. A veces, sin embargo, eran muy buenos, a pesar de ser muy pobres. Henry Fielding, que escribió varias novelas (novel), de las cuales quizá sea *Joseph Andrews* la mejor, describe la vida de la ciudad y del campo en ese siglo, y en esta novela, de la cual acabamos de leer un trozo, encontramos a dos pastores muy diferentes, a Parson Adams y a Parson Trulliber.

Parson Adams hace todo lo que debería hacer un buen párroco. Un día está viajando por el campo y encuentra que no tiene bastante dinero. Piensa que el párroco de la parroquia por la cual está viajando podrá prestarle alguno, y va hacia la vicaría, que no está muy lejos de la carretera. Al llegar a la vicaría, la esposa del párroco piensa que el pobre hombre que ha llegado debe de ser uno de los granjeros a quienes su marido vende cerdos. Por lo tanto, Trulliber sale de la casa en seguida y cogiendo al señor Adams por el brazo quiere enseñarle la zahúrda. Parson Adams, que es muy cortés, le acompaña y está dispuesto a palpar los gordos cerdos, aunque no sabe nada de (about) cerdos. Pero el cerdo que Adams coge por la cola le hace caer por el suelo, en el barro, y Parson Trulliber en vez de acudir (venir) para ayudarle a levantarse, se ríe de él. Entonces Adams explica quién es y por qué ha venido. Trulliber dice que su mujer es una tonta y siempre se equivoca, pero cuando Adams le pide dinero, no quiere prestarle ninguno.

LESSON EIGHTEEN

Revisión

Notes on Pronunciation

Pronunciación de las vocales "a, e, i, o, u"

Estas vocales se llaman en inglés:

A	E	I	O	U
ei	i:	ai	ou	ju:

y se pronuncian de la misma manera que se llaman **cuando**
llevan el acento de la palabra y van seguidas de una **consonante**
y de *e* muda al final de la sílaba o palabra.

Ejemplos:

A: to make, to take, page, face, gate, Wales, safe, **lately,**
etcétera.
Excepciones: a seguida de *re:*
care, square, rarely.

E: Complete, these, evening, scene, scenery.
Excepciones: e seguida de *re:*
sincerely, etc.

I: to decide, to divide, time, wine, fire, exercise, **white,** etc.
Excepciones: police, machine, to give, to live.

O: whole, to hope, nose, those, clothes, alone, to close, **stove,**
to suppose, etc.
Excepciones: o seguida de *re*;
before, etc.
y también: whose, to move, one, to love.

U: to use, huge, to amuse, to produce, to introduce, etc.
Excepciones: u seguida de *re:*
sure: seguro, etc.

Nótese que si se añade una terminación a estas palabras la **vocal**
retiene su valor original:

to take,	taking.
to decide,	decided.
to hope,	hoping.
to amuse,	amusing.

Sin embargo, cuando no lleva el acento la vocal se **pronuncia**
débil:

college, office, lettuce, luggage.

Vocabulary and Pronunciation

i	príson (cárcel).
e	ápopléxy (apoplejía).
a	ánger (ira, cólera).
ou	to *owe* (deber, tener deudas).
ɪə	sérious (serio).

THE MAN IN THE BROWN COAT

There was once a little man who was sent to prison because he could not pay some money which he owed. He was there a long, long time and he always looked the same, with a dirty face and a brown coat. He was a very quiet little man and always helping somebody, or playing cards and never winning. Everybody made friends with him, and after a time the keepers too liked to talk to him and he often went down to the keepers' lodge by the main gate and spent the evening with them.

One night he was in the lodge as usual, together with a very old friend of his who was watching the gate that evening, when he said: «Bill, I haven't seen the market outside» — for there was a market outside the prison at that time — «Bill, I haven't seen the market outside for seventeen years.» «I know you haven't», said the keeper, smoking his pipe. «I should like to see it for a minute, Bill», he said. «Very probably», said the keeper, smoking his pipe very hard. «Bill», said the little man, «I've got an idea. Let me see the public streets once more before I die; and if I don't fall down dead with apoplexy I'll be back in five minutes by the clock.» «And what would become of me if you fell down dead with apoplexy?» «Well, the person who found me would bring me home, for I've got my card in my pocket, Bill — Number 20, Coffee-room floor.» And that was right, for when he wanted to make friends with a new-comer, he pulled out a dirty visiting card on which these words and nothing more were written. And that was why he was always called Number Twenty. The keeper looked at him very hard and at last said in a very serious manner, «Twenty, you are an honest man, I don't doubt that; you won't make your old friend look a fool.» «No», said the little man. «I hope I should never do that.» He took the keeper by the hand, thanked him, and went out.

«And never came back again», said Mr. Pickwick. «Wrong for once, sir», said Mr. Weller, «for back he came, two minutes before the time, boiling with anger, saying how he had almost been hit by a carriage, as he was crossing the street, and that he wasn't used to it, and that he would write to the Lord Mayor of London about it. For five years after that, he never looked out of the lodge window.

«At the end of which time, he died, I suppose», said Mr. Pickwick.

«No, he didn't, sir», answered Sam Weller. «He got a desire to go and drink beer at a new public-house which had just been opened across the way. And it was such a nice place that he thought of going there every night. He did this for a long time, always coming back about a quarter of an hour before the gate shut. At last he began to have such a good time in the public-house that he forgot what the time was or didn't mind at all what it was, and he went on coming in later and later, until one night his old friend the keeper was just shutting the gate — had turned the key, in fact — when he arrived. «Wait a minute, Bill», he said. «What, are you still out, Twenty?», said the keeper. «I thought you were in long ago.» «No, I wasn't», said the little man, with a smile. «Well, then listen to what I have to say», said the keeper, opening the gate very slowly. «I think you have been making friends with bad people lately. Now, I don't want to make difficulties, but if you can't come back here in time, I'll shut the gate and leave you outside for ever.» The little man was so afraid when he heard this that he never went outside the prison walls afterwards.

(Adapted from *The Pickwick Papers* by Charles Dickens.)

Exercises

A) **Answer the following questions:**

1. Why was the little man in the brown coat sent to prison?
2. What did he do in prison?
3. Where did he often spend the evening?
4. What was the keeper's name?
5. How long was it since the little man had seen the market outside the prison?
6. Why was the little man always called Number Twenty?
7. Why was the little man boiling with anger when he returned to the prison?
8. Why did the little man start leaving the prison every evening?
9. Why did the little man start coming in later and later?
10. Why did the little man never go outside the prison walls again?

B) **Fórmese un substantivo compuesto con la misma significación que cada una de las siguientes frases:**

1. A room where people wait.
2. A cloth for covering the table.
3. A shop which sells books.

4. A man who comes round with the milk.
5. A man who pays taxes.
6. A man who brings the letters and parcels to your house.
7. Saturday and Sunday.
8. A man who manages a bank.
9. A small lamp for reading.
10. A newspaper that is sold in the evening.
11. A club where the members play football.
12. A place where a shop shows its goods to the public.

C) **Complétense las siguientes oraciones con preposiciones:**

1. The radio set we are listening — belongs — the owner of the flat.
2. Who are you waiting — ?
3. The little boy that the waiter was looking — was blushing and couldn't handle his knife and fork at all well.
4. The street which my bedroom looks — is very narrow and noisy.
5. What is the furniture in your sitting-room — ? It is rather old and dirty.
6. What are you laughing — ? I'm laughing at Mr. Pickwick.
7. I can never think — Sam Weller without laughing.
8. This isn't the shop that I'm looking —.
9. I expect you've forgotten all that I reminded you — this morning?
10. Did you pick — the handkerchief that I dropped in the street?
11. Have you got the information that I asked you — ?
12. It's the most amusing thing that I have ever heard —. this morning?

D) **Use the following words in sentences:**

door, gate, to attend, to put on, to take, off, lucky, to throw, bucket, to spread, immediately, progress, scissors, new-comer, anger, people.

E) **Composition:**

Tell the story of *The little man in the brown coat* as if you were the little man telling it to a friend in the prison.

LESSON NINETEEN

Vocabulary and Pronunciation

i: beef (carne de buey), sweet (postre, dulce), téa-cake (pasta de té).

i prínciple (principio), to fill (llenar), to kill (matar).

e shérry (jerez), yet (todavía).

a glad (contento, alegre), sálmon (salmón), sálad (ensalada), lamb (cordero), ángry (enfadado).

a: mármalade (mermelada de naranja).

o lóbster (langosta).

o: sure (seguro), hors d'oéuvres (entremeses), Yórkshire (condado de Inglaterra), to expórt (exportar).

ʌ crúmpet (especie de suizo tostado).

u: to choose (escoger).

ei steak (biftek), bácon (especie de jamón serrano), pátient (paciente).

ai ice (hielo, helado).

ou chose (de to choose), sole (lenguado), roast (asado), to toast (tostar), toast (pan tostado).

ju: fúture (futuro), ménu (menú, carta).

eə ánywhere (en cualquier sitio), mayonnaíse (mayonesa).

ʃ sure, pátient.

tʃ fúture.

Consonantes mudas

b muda en lamb.

l muda en sálmon.

Frases

in future: en el futuro, en el porvenir.
on principle: por principio.
not ... yet: no ... todavía.

Verbo irregular

to choose, chose, chosen: escoger

Grammar

Pronombres y adjetivos demostrativos

Adjetivos	Pronombres
	this — esto
this — este-a	this one — éste-a
these — estos-as	these — éstos-as
	that — eso, aquello
that — ese-a, aquel, aquella	that one — ése-a, aquél, aquélla
those — esos-as, aquellos-as	those — ésos-as, aquéllos-as

Examples

Adjetivos

Singular
> This meat is badly cooked.
> Esta carne está mal guisada.
> That house in the distance is my aunt's,
> Esa casa a lo lejos es de mi tía.

Plural
> These children are noisy. Can't they go to another room?
> Estos niños hacen mucho ruido. ¿No pueden irse a otra habitación?
> Those handkerchiefs at the back of the shop-window are quite cheap.
> Esos pañuelos del fondo del escaparate son bastante baratos.

Pronombres

This is very amusing. I'll read it to you.
Esto es muy divertido. Se lo leeré.
That's a good idea.   Ésa es una buena idea.
That's right.   Eso es.
Here are two dresses. Do you like this one or that one? I don't like either.

143

He aquí dos vestidos. ¿Le gusta éste o aquél? No me gusta ninguno de los dos.

Shall I wear these trousers or those?

¿Me pongo estos pantalones o aquéllos?

I prefer these. Me gustan más éstos.

El antecedente del pronombre relativo

He who... The one who... The one which...	el que... la que...
Those who... The ones who... Those which... The ones which	los (las) que
What	lo que

Examples

He who steals will finish in prison.

El que roba terminará en la cárcel.

(*He who, she who* se emplea poco y casi siempre en sentido muy general.)

Did they catch the thief? Which thief? *The one who* came yesterday to Mr. Jones's house.

¿Cogieron al ladrón? ¿Qué ladrón? El que vino ayer a casa del señor Jones.

Which station does the train leave from? *The one which* is near the river.

¿De cuál estación sale el tren? De la que está cerca del río.

Which doctors are the best? *Those who* (*the ones who*) live in Harley Street are the most expensive, but I don't know if they're the best.

¿Qué médicos son los mejores? Los que viven en Harley Street son los más caros, pero no sé si son los mejores.

What clothes shall I take? *Those which* (*the ones which*) you took to Italy last month.

¿Qué vestidos llevaré conmigo? Los que usted llevó a Italia el mes pasado.

ONE se emplea:
1. Como numeral:

He has only *one leg*. Tiene solamente una pierna.

2. Como pronombre impersonal, correspondiente al español *uno*:

> *One* likes to have *one's* own house.
> A uno le gusta tener su propia casa.

En este sentido *one* se emplea poco. Hay tendencia a emplear *you* o *they* como impersonal:

They drink wine in France.   Se bebe vino en Francia.
You can't go there by air.   No se puede ir allí por avión.
There's no service.   No hay servicio.

3. Como pronombre para evitar la repetición de un substantivo:

> There are many noisy streets and few quiet *ones* in London.
> Hay muchas calles ruidosas y pocas tranquilas en Londres.
>
> I don't like this flat much: I prefer *the one which* we saw yesterday.
> No me gusta mucho este piso: prefiero el que vimos ayer.
>
> Do you like this scarf?   ¿Le gusta esta bufanda?
> No, I prefer *that one*.   No, me gusta más aquélla (ésa).

Nótese que el adjetivo no se puede emplear solo en inglés, excepto en algunos casos excepcionales. Si se omite el substantivo se pone *one* como pronombre.

> Do you want a book?   ¿Quieres un libro?
> Here's a good *one*.   He aquí uno bueno.

Sólo *these* y *those* se pueden emplear como pronombres sin *one* (véase arriba *Pronombres demostrativos*.)

4. En el sentido de cierto:

> One day: un día, cierto día.

Reading

MEALS

George: Hullo, Pablo, where are you going to in such a hurry?
Pablo: Hullo, George, I'm just going to lunch.
George: Well, let's go together. Where do you usually have lunch?
Pablo: Oh, anywhere. Do you know a good restaurant?
George: Yes, I know a very good one in Soho, one which I'm sure you'll like.

Pablo: Good. I'm glad I met you because I never know what to eat in London. You can choose me a good English meal and tell me what to order in future.

George: Here we are. (To the waiter) A table for two, please.

Waiter: Yes, sir. Would you like this one or the one by the window?

George: I think the one by the window. Don't you, Pablo?

Pablo: Yes. That one is the better.

George: Now, let's have a good meal. You're not in any hurry, are you? Hors d'oeuvres to start with? Or would you like soup?

Pablo: Hors d'oeuvres, I think, thank you.

George: What fish is there today?

Waiter: There are some nice soles, or cold salmon, or lobster with mayonnaise and salad.

George: What would you like, Pablo?

Pablo: I should like to try those soles.

George: That's a good idea. I shall have the same. What meat is good today, waiter?

Waiter: The steak is very good and tender, sir. There are also lamb chops with peas and new potatoes, or if you prefer roast meat, sir, there is some good roast beef with vegetables and Yorkshire pudding. Or you could have roast chicken that is very young and tender.

Pablo: I think I must have the roast beef which I have always been told is so good in England. What are you going to have, George?

George: I should enjoy a good beef-steak. Shall we have new potatoes and peas, or would you prefer beans?

Pablo: Peas, I think George — and shall we have some salad?

George: Yes. And for the sweet, I suggest an ice. What do you think? Are there any strawberries yet, waiter?

Waiter: Yes, sir, the first ones we have had yet this summer. would you like strawberries with ice-cream?

So George and Pablo chose their meal, and ordered a glass of sherry each while they waited.

George: I expect this sherry is not so good as the ones which you are used to drinking in Spain, Pablo?

Pablo: Well, I find it is. Spain exports her best sherries, you know. This may be one of them.

George: How do you like English food?

Pablo: Not so bad, though there are many things I haven't tried yet. I don't have much breakfast, as I'm not used to it. I've not yet tried porridge or bacon and eggs for breakfast. I just have a cup of coffee and some toast and butter and marmalade. I find English people eat so often in the day. In Spain we only have two meals, lunch and dinner, and in the morning a cup of coffee and perhaps another cup at six o'clock in the evening.

George: Yes, but we don't eat very big meals. A business man often just has a glass of beer and some bread and cheese for lunch.

Pablo: And then a huge tea when he gets home with toasted tea-cakes, crumpets and all those things. By the way, what is a crumpet? It's so often on menu cards for tea.

George: Oh, it's a sort of tea-cake which you eat hot with butter on. Not bad. Try one one day. Have you read *Pickwick Papers?*

Pablo: No.

George: Well, you must. There's an amusing fellow called Sam Weller who is Mr. Pickwick's servant, and he's always telling stories. There's one about crumpets.

A doctor comes to see a patient and asks «What was the last thing you ate?» «Crumpets,» says the patient. «That's it,» says the doctor. «Don't you ever eat any more of them.» «Why?» says the patient, sitting up in bed, «I've eaten four crumpets every night for fifteen years, on principle.» «Well, then, you must stop eating them, on principle,» says the doctor. «Crumpets are good for you, sir,» says the patient. «Crumpets are *not* good for you, sir,» says the doctor, very angry. «But they're so cheap,» says the patient, becoming rather quiet and sad, «and they fill one so well for the money.» «They'd be dear to you at any price — dear if you were paid to eat them,» says the doctor. «Four crumpets a night will kill you off in six months.» The patient looks at the doctor hard, thinks about it for a long time and at last he says: «Are you sure of that, doctor?» «I'll never see another patient in my life if I'm wrong,» says the doctor. «How many crumpets eaten one after the other do you think would kill me?» «I don't know,» says the doctor. «Do you think half a crown's worth would do it?» says the patient. «I think it might,» says the doctor. «Three shillings worth would be sure to do it, I suppose?» says the patient. «Certainly,» says the doctor. «Very good,» says the patient, «Goodnight.» The next morning he gets up, lights a fire, orders three shillings worth of crumpets to be sent in, toasts them all, eats them all, and jumps head first out of the window.

«What did he do that for?» asks Mr. Pickwick. «What did he do it for, sir?» repeats Sam Weller. «Well, to show that crumpets were good for you and that he wouldn't be put out of his way for anybody!»

Pablo: Very amusing. I must meet Mr. Sam Weller.

George: Now for the fish. Just a minute, waiter, these plates are cold.

Waiter: Oh, I'm very sorry, sir. I'll fetch some hot ones.

George: I cannot understand how people can eat hot food on cold plates. Good food must be either boiling hot or quite cold, and you can't have hot food if you put it on a cold plate, can you?

Exercises

A) **Answer the following questions:**

1. Where was Pablo going to when he met George?
2. Where did Pablo usually have lunch?
3. Which table did Pablo and George choose?
4. What did they order to start with?
5. What fish was there on the menu?
6. What fish did they choose?
7. Do you ever eat soles?
8. What meat dishes were there on the menu?
9. Why did Pablo choose roast beef?
10. What meat did George choose?
11. What vegetables did they have with their meat?
12. What did they drink while they waited for the meal to be served?
13. Why didn't Pablo generally have much breakfast?
14. What did George say a business man often has for lunch?
15. Who is Sam Weller?
16. What did the patient tell the doctor he had eaten last?
17. How long had the patient been eating crumpets?
18. Why did the patient like crumpets?

19. How many crumpets eaten one after the other did the doctor say would kill the patient?
20. What did the patient do on the morning after he had seen the doctor?

B) **Evítese la repetición del substantivo en las siguientes oraciones mediante el uso de un pronombre:**

1. Do you prefer this table or the table by the window?
2. Will you have a hot dish or a cold dish?
3. Shall we go to a cheap restaurant or an expensive restaurant?
4. We shall need three glasses; bring another glass, please.
5. Do you like my furniture as much as your furniture?
6. These cliffs are not so high as those cliffs.
7. Our radio is better than their radio.
8. These photos are not as good as the photos which we took last summer.
9. The people we met in Yorkshire were not as polite as the people we met in London.
10. The old books are not as good or as interesting as the new books.

C) **Explain in English the meaning of the following words, then use them in sentences:**

patient, glad, restaurant, lunch, waiter.

D) **Name five articles of food and use each in a sentence.**

E) **Complete the following sentences with prepositions:**

1. I rent a lot — land and I have a small piece — my own.
2. — future I shall always choose roast beef.
3. This waiter always attends — me very well.
4. I insist — hot plates for hot food.
5. Hurry — or we shall arrive late — the station.
6. I never eat any meat except beef — principle.
7. Those who steal generally finish — prison.
8. I don't think this restaurant is expensive; — the contrary I find it quite cheap.
9. Shall we go — foot or — horseback?
10. Charles, someone is asking — you — the phone.

F) **Composition:**

a) Describe a visit to a restaurant.
b) Describe the meals in your home.

G) **Translate into English:**

LAS COMIDAS

Los que han visitado Inglaterra saben que la gente allí no come como en otros países. Lo que sorprende a muchos españoles es el desayuno inglés, que generalmente consiste en una sopa de avena seguida de (por) huevos fritos con jamón serrano frito o pescado frito. Para terminar, pan tostado con mermelada de naranja y café o té para beber. Pero hay algunos ingleses que prefieren un desayuno como el que toman los españoles. El almuerzo no es la comida principal como en España o Francia, y los hombres de negocios que no tienen tiempo para regresar a casa a mediodía a menudo toman sólo un poco de pan con queso y un vaso de cerveza. Si come en casa, el inglés tomará alguna carne asada o un biftek o unas chuletas con un plato de patatas y otro de verduras o ensalada, pero siempre toma las patatas y las verduras con salsa al mismo tiempo que la carne. Después habrá algún postre, y para terminar un poco de queso. Generalmente se bebe agua o cerveza. El vino se bebe sólo los días de cumpleaños, en Navidad o en alguna otra ocasión. El almuerzo se toma más temprano que en España, entre la una y la una y media. Entre las cuatro y las cinco se toma té, que consiste en pan tostado con mantequilla o *crumpets* o *tea-cakes,* también tostados, que son más o menos como los *suizos* en España. Después pasteles o un trozo de un pastel grande del tipo que en España se llama *plumcake.* Desde luego se bebe té. La cena se toma alrededor de las siete y media y no es muy diferente del almuerzo.

LESSON TWENTY

Vocabulary and Pronunciation

i:	to dr*ea*m (soñar), cr*éa*ture (criatura), st*ee*p (empinado), to cl*ea*n (limpiar), *éa*stwards (al este), sh*ee*t (sábana), asl*ée*p (dormido).
i	*i*ll (enfermo).
e	dr*ea*mt (*de to dream*), b*e*lt (cinturón), n*e*st (nido), to str*e*tch (extenderse), to s*e*t (ponerse -del sol), w*e*st (oeste).
a	r*a*t (rata), to att*á*ck (atacar), to h*á*ppen (ocurrir), g*á*llery (galería).
a:	l*a*rge (grande).

o:	p*aw* (pata), to*r*n (de *to tear*), fo*r*ge (fragua).
ʌ	to c*ó*ver (cubrir), r*ou*gh (áspero), st*ó*mach (vientre, estómago), bl*oo*d (sangre), bl*oó*dy (sangriento), d*ó*zen (docena), g*u*n (cañón).
u:	w*ou*nd (herida).
ə:	w*ór*kman (obrero).
ai	al*í*ve (vivo, con vida), to sm*i*le (sonreír), s*i*gn (signo, señal, seña), to r*i*se (salir el sol, levantarse).
ei	s*ai*l (vela), ash*á*med (avergonzado).
ou	*ó*cean (océano), s*ó*ldier (soldado), al*ó*ne (solo).
au	f*ó*untain (fuente, surtidor).
ju:	*ú*seless (inútil).
iə	f*ier*ce (feroz).
eə	to t*ea*r (despedazar, rasgar).
k	stóma*ch*.
ʃ	*ó*cean.
dʒ	s*ó*l*di*er, lar*g*e.

Consonante muda

g	en sign.

Frases

up and down	— arriba y abajo.
a dozen rooms	— una docena *de* habitaciones.
to rebuild	— volver a construir, *re*construir.

El prefijo *re* (ri:) se emplea a veces en inglés, como en español, en sentido de volver a hacer.

Verbos irregulares

to rise,	rose,	risen:	levantarse, salir el sol.
to set,	set,	set:	ponerse — del sol.
to dream,	dreamt,	dreamt:	soñar.
to tear,	tore,	torn:	despedazar, rasgar.

Grammar
El adjetivo

Formación

Terminaciones:

-*y*	anger (cólera)	angry	(colérico, irritado, enfadado).

-ful (lleno)	beauty	(hermosura)	beautiful	(hermoso).
	care	(cuidado)	careful	(cuidadoso).
	use	(uso)	useful	(útil).
-*less* (sin)	care		careless	(descuidado, negligente).
	use		useless	(inútil).
	hat		hatless	(sin sombrero).

-*ous* (corresponde a veces al castellano -*oso*)

		precious	(precioso).
		curious	(curioso).
		serious	(serio, grave).

-*ing* (participio presente)

| | amusing | (divertido). |
| | interesting | (interesante). |

Prefijos:

un- o *in-* (negación) comfortable (cómodo) uncomfortable (incómodo).

dependent (dependiente) independent (independiente).

a- afraid (medroso, temeroso)
alone (solo)

Adjetivos compuestos:

La primera parte modifica la segunda:
a) Adjetivo o substantivo delante de adjetivo.

dark-green:	verde obscuro.
light-blue:	azul claro.
grass-green:	verde hierba.

b) Adjetivo, adverbio o substantivo delante de participio presente.

dirty-looking:	que parece sucio.
hard-working:	trabajador.
wine-drinking:	que bebe vino.
fruit-growing:	que cultiva fruta.

c) Adjetivo, adverbio o substantivo delante de participio pasado (o imitación del participio pasado).

coffee-coloured:	de color de café.
well-dressed:	bien vestido.
sun-burnt:	tostado por el sol.
blue-eyed:	con ojos azules.

Construcción

1. El adjetivo en inglés es invariable.
2. El adjetivo atributivo *precede, por regla general,* al substantivo que califica.

> She is a kind, helpful, had-working and intelligent girl.
> Es una chica amable, útil, trabajadora e inteligente.

3. El adjetivo *sigue* al substantivo:
   a) Cuando se emplea como predicativo:

The girl is hard-working.   La muchacha es muy trabajadora.

Cierto número de adjetivos sólo se emplean como predicativos:

worth:	que vale.
well:	bien, sano.
ill:	enfermo.
to be ... left:	quedar.
to be ... missing:	faltar.

y los adjetivos con el prefijo *a-* (asleep, dormido; alone, solo; afraid, medroso; ashamed, avergonzado).

> This tea is not worth three shillings a pound.
> Este té no vale tres chelines la libra.

Are you well today?	¿Está usted bien, hoy?
No, I am rather ill.	No, estoy un poco enfermo.
He is asleep.	Está dormido.

b) En las expresiones de *medida.*

The street is a mile long.   La calle tiene una milla de largo.

c) Cuando califica a los pronombres en *-thing* y *-body.*

Have you heard anything new?	¿Ha oído usted algo nuevo?
I want somebody intelligent.	Deseo alguien inteligente.

d) Cuando está calificado por un complemento.
> She dropped a dish full of ices on to the floor.
> Dejó caer al suelo una fuente llena de helados.

Verbos compuestos

AWAY

1. Añadido al verbo da la idea de *alejamiento.*

To go:	ir.	to go away:	irse, marcharse.
to run:	correr.	to run away:	escaparse, irse corriendo.
to take:	llevar.	to take away:	llevar fuera, quitar.

153

2. A veces se emplea para expresar la *continuidad y el esfuerzo,*

> He ate away with a very good appetite.
> Comió con muy buen apetito.
> > Pull away! ¡Tira!

UP

1. Añadido al verbo da la idea de *levantamiento.*

to put:	poner.	to put up:	erigir.
to pick:	recoger.	to pick up:	recoger del suelo.
		to get up:	levantarse.

2. Se emplea para indicar que la acción del verbo se hace *por completo.*

> Hurry up! ¡Date prisa!
> Eat it up! ¡Cómalo todo!

Reading

GULLIVER IN BROBDINGNAG

When dinner was over, my master went out to his workmen, and, as I could tell by his voice and the movements of his hands, ordered his wife to take care of me. I was very tired and wanted to sleep, and, when my mistress saw this, she put me on her own bed, and covered me with a clean handkerchief, but larger and rougher than a boat sail.

I had been asleep about two hours and had dreamt I was at home with my wife and children, when I woke up and found that I was alone in a huge room, between two and three hundred feet wide and over two hundred high, lying in a bed twenty yards wide. I felt a little ill and wanted to get down. It was useless for me to call with such a voice as mine, at such a great distance from the room where I was lying to the kitchen where the family was. As I was thinking what to do, two rats climbed up the curtains and ran backwards and forwards on the bed. One of them came up almost to my face, on which I became very afraid and drew out my knife to kill it. These horrible animals attacked me on both sides and one of them put its front paws on my neck but I was lucky enough to open up its stomach with my knife before it could hurt me. It fell down at my feet; and the other seeing what happened to its friend ran away, but not without one good wound on the back which I gave it as it went off and which made the blood run. After this, I walked slowly up and down on the bed, waiting for someone to come in. These creatures were the size of a large dog but moved much faster and were much fiercer, so that if I had taken off my belt before I went to sleep, I should have been torn to pieces and eaten by them. I measured the tail of the dead rat and found it to be almost two yards long. But I could not pull the body off the bed, where it lay still bleeding. I saw it was still alive, but with a strong cut across the neck I killed it.

Soon after my mistress came into the room, and when she saw me all bloody ran and took me up in her hand. I showed her the dead rat, smiling and making other signs to tell her I was not hurt. She was very glad and called the maid to take up the dead rat and throw it out of the window. Then she put me on a table, where I showed her my knife all covered in blood, and cleaning it on my coat, I put it in my belt.

(Adapted from *Gulliver's Travels* by Jonathan Swift.)

The home of Henry Esmond

Father Holt took away Henry Esmond and showed him the great old house in which he had come to live.

It stood on a green hill, with woods behind it, in which were nests where the birds in the morning and returning home in the evening made a great noise. At the foot of the hill was a river, with a steep old bridge crossing it; and further on a pleasant green flat piece of ground where the village of Castlewood stood, and stands, with the church in the middle, the vicarage hard by it, the inn with the blacksmith's forge next to it, and the sign of *The Three Castles* hanging from a tree. The London road stretched away towards the risingsun, and to the west were undulating hills, behind which, on many occasions, Harry Esmond saw the same sun setting, that he now looks on thousands of miles across the great ocean — in a new Castlewood, by another river, that has, like the new country, the dear names of the land of his youth.

The house of Castlewood was built with two quadrangles or courts, of which one only, the fountain-court, was now inhabited, the other having been destroyed in the Cromwellian wars. In the fountain-court, still in good condition, was the great hall near to the kitchen, a dozen rooms, to the north, the little chapel that looked eastward and the buildings that stretched from there to the main gate. These and the hall looked into the court now destroyed. This court had been the more beautiful of the two, until Cromwell's guns broke down one side of it before the place was taken by his soldiers. They came in under the clock-tower, killing every man in the house and at their head my Lord's brother, Francis Esmond.

The Restoration did not bring enough money to Lord Castlewood to rebuild this destroyed part of the house where were the morning rooms, above them the long music gallery, and in front of which stretched the garden where, however, the flowers grew again under the care of the ladies.

(Adapted from *Henry Esmond* by Thackeray.)

Exercises

A) **Answer the following questions:**

Gulliver in Brobdingnag.

1. Who did Gulliver's master go out to see after dinner?
2. What did he order his wife to do?
3. How could Gulliver tell this?
4. Where did his mistress put him when she saw that he was tired?
5. How big was the handkerchief with which she covered him?
6. How long did he sleep?
7. Where did he find that he was when he woke up?
8. What did he see climbing up the curtains?
9. What did Gulliver do when the rats attacked him?
10. Did he kill them?
11. How large were they?
12. How long was the tail of the dead rat?
13. Who came into the room and what did she see?
14. What did Gulliver show her?
15. What did the maid do with the dead rat?

B) *The Home of Henry Esmond*

1. Where did the old house stand?
2. What was there in the woods?
3. What was there at the foot of the hill?
4. What buildings in the village of Castlewood are described?
5. What was the name of the inn and where did its sign hang?
6. What could one see to the west?
7. Was the house in good condition or had it been destroyed?
8. How many rooms were there?

9. Whose guns destroyed what had been the more beautiful court?
10. Why had Lord Castlewood not been able to rebuild the destroyed part of the house?
11. Who took care of the garden and what grew there?

C) **Form sentences with the following adjectives:**

well, hard-working, asleep, worth, useless, angry, ill, dark-green, careful, afraid, well-dressed, wide, long.

D) **Write the adjective opposite in meaning to the following adjectives:**

comfortable	dead	sorry
careful	sad	thin
well-dressed	rich	fast
useful	impolite	possible
intelligent	pleasant	insincere
ill	noisy	suitable
clean	unmarried	inhabited
unessential	left	weak
undulating	late	wide
interesting	dependent	wrong
difficult	huge	careless
unhappy	heavy	
different	healthy	

E) **Tell the above story from "Gulliver's Travels" in the third person.**

F) **Composition:**
1. Compare this old English country house with a Spanish one.
2. Describe a house you have lived in or visited.

G) **Complete the following sentences with adjectives:**
1. My husband did not go to work today as he was not —.
2. This girl is — but she is not very intelligent.
3. The rats were so — that they almost killed him.
4. The colour of my new dress is —.
5. This pen is — now, as it is broken.
6. The play I saw last night was very — and I laughed a lot.
7. The road was so — there that two cars could not pass.

157

8. The baby was in bed — so they did not disturb it when the visitor came.
9. His father was very — with him for breaking the window.
10. The grass and trees seemed very — after the rain.

Translate into English:

Gulliver durmió dos horas soñando que estaba en su casa con su esposa y sus niños, y cuando se despertó se encontró solo en una habitación enorme, de dos o trescientos pies de ancho, y de más de doscientos de altura, y echado en una cama de veinte metros de ancho. Por sábana tenía un pañuelo más grande y más áspero que una vela de barco. Sintiéndose un poco enfermo, pensó en lo que podría hacer para bajar de esta cama y salir de esta habitación, cuando vio dos ratas mayores que perros, con colas de casi dos metros de largo, y tan feroces, que casi le mataron. Pero Gulliver, por suerte, tenía un cuchillo en el cinturón y mató a una. La otra tuvo miedo de lo que había pasado a su amiga, y se fue corriendo. Cuando volvió el amo de la casa encontró a Gulliver con vida, pero todo cubierto de sangre. Afortunadamente sus heridas no eran graves y después de haberse limpiado la cara y las manos, Gulliver se dio cuenta de que le faltaba su pañuelo. Pensó que probablemente una de las ratas se lo había llevado, y en efecto recogió del suelo un trozo de pañuelo rasgado. Era todo lo que quedaba de su último pañuelo. Sentía mucho haberlo perdido, porque en ese país no encontraría tela bastante buena para hacer(se) unos nuevos. Después de este accidente, el amo de la casa no quiso dejarle nunca solo, y buscó a alguien bastante cuidadoso para quedarse todo el tiempo con él. Era una muchacha de unos veinte años con ojos azul obscuro, que siempre iba muy bien vestida. Le gustó mucho.

LESSONS TWENTY-ONE

Vocabulary and Pronunciation

i: to fr*ee*ze (helar, congelar), ind*ée*d (verdaderamente, de veras), *é*ven (aun), pr*ie*st (cura).

i   *í*nterest (interés), p*í*llow (almohada), ch*í*mney (chimenea).

e   br*ea*th (aliento), h*é*sitate (vacilar).

a	mátter (asunto), dámned (condenado), damp (húmedo), ágony (agonía).
a:	architéctural (arquitectónico), park (parque).
o	histórical (histórico), bódy (cuerpo).
o:	warm (caliente).
ʌ	úgly (feo), súffering (sufrimiento, pena, dolor), súddenly (súbitamente).
u:	truth (verdad).
ə	éffort (empeño, esfuerzo), to colléct (recoger), vícar (vicario), ínterval (intervalo), delícious (delicioso).
ə:	to presérve (preservar, conservar), pérfectly (perfectamente).
ei	preservátion (preservación, conservación), space (espacio), state (estado, condición), néighbouring (vecino, cercano).
oi	unspóilt (inmaculado, libre de).
ai	blínd (ciego).
ou	póet (poeta), to expóse (exponer), frózen (de *to freeze*).
eə	repáir (reparo, reparación), to repáir (reparar), to air (calentar), the air (el aire).
k	architéctural.
ʃ	preservátion, delicious.
tʃ	architéctural.

Consonante munda

n	en damned.

Frases

to be in need of: necesitar.
as well as: además de.

Verbos irregulares

to freeze, froze, frozen: helar, congelar.

Grammar

El adjetivo (cont.)

El adjetivo como substantivo

En general no se puede emplear el adjetivo como substantivo en inglés.

Have you seen that poor *man*?
¿Ha visto usted a aquel pobre?

The rich *people* of this town are very bad.
Los ricos de esta ciudad son muy malos.

a) Sin embargo, cuando se habla de una clase de gente
en conjunto y en general, se usa el adjetivo precedido del artículo definido como substantivo colectivo.

We must give a good education to the poor.
Tenemos que educar bien a los pobres.

The rich can eat good food.
Los ricos pueden comer bien.

The very old and the very young must be looked after.
Los muy viejos y los muy jóvenes deben ser cuidados.

The dead:	los muertos.
The dying:	los moribundos.
The blind:	los ciegos.
The wounded:	los heridos.
The good:	los buenos.
The bad:	los malos.
Etc.	

b) Un adjetivo de nacionalidad empleado para indicar *el idioma* se emplea como substantivo sin artículo.

He is learning Greek.
Está aprendiendo el griego.

He speaks English, French and Spanish.
Habla inglés, francés y español.

c) Se emplea a veces el adjetivo en singular precedido del artículo definido como substantivo abstracto.

The ideal and the real.   Lo ideal y lo real.

Do not go out in the cold and the wet.
No salga con tiempo frío y húmedo.

d) Ciertos adjetivos de uso corriente se emplean como substantivo.

the adult:	el adulto.
the patient:	el enfermo, paciente.
the noble:	el noble.
the public:	el público.

Nótese el uso del adjetivo en las siguientes frases:

En las expresiones que indican un estado o una condición, sea del tiempo, sea de la persona, cuando se emplean *hacer* y *tener* en español es preciso traducirlos por *to be* en inglés, que va seguido del adjetivo correspondiente.

It is fine today:	Hoy hace buen tiempo.
It is cold today:	Hoy hace frío.
It is warm today:	Hoy hace un poco de calor.
It is hot today:	Hoy hace calor.
I am one metre fifty tall:	tengo un metro cincuenta de altura.
I am fifteen years old:	tengo quince años.
I am afraid:	tengo miedo.
I am hungry:	tengo hambre.
I am thirsty:	tengo sed.
I am cold:	tengo frío.
I am hot:	tengo mucho calor.
I am warm:	tengo calor.
I am right:	tengo razón.
I am wrong:	estoy equivocado.
I am sleepy:	tengo sueño.

Nótese la diferencia entre:
It is cold: hace frío.
He is cold: tiene frío.

El adjetivo como adverbio

No se puede en inglés, como se hace en español, emplear el adjetivo como adverbio.

Sin embargo, hay unos adjetivos que tienen la misma forma que el adverbio correspondiente.

This is a *fast* train.	The train is travelling *fast*.
He came by the *early* train.	I must get up *early*.
This is a *hard* lesson.	Ésta es una lección difícil.
He works *hard*.	Trabaja mucho.

Reading

THE NATIONAL TRUST

At the end of the last century a society was formed in England with the object of preserving places of natural beauty or of historical interest. Like other great movements this society began its activities in a matter mainly of local interest. The great society of London was starting, at the end of the nineteenth century, to spread over the neighbouring country, and one of the first efforts of the new society was the preservation of the open space just outside London, called Wimbledon Common. Today Wimbledon Common is a public park both for the rich and the poor, and on Sundays many Londoners take a bus to the Common to ride on horseback or to walk.

The National Trust, having started by preserving Wimbledon Common for the people, decided to continue its work all over the country. The Trust is run by people who give their time and who are not paid for their help, like many other societies in England, such as St. Dunstan's Society for the Blind. Money is collected from people in all parts of the country. The rich are asked to help and some of them have given a lot of money to the Trust. But a great deal of the money collected is given by ordinary people who are sure that the Trust is doing fine work and spending its money for the good of everyone. The Trust is not in any way controlled by the State: it is an independent body, but it helps and works with the government in preserving buildings of historical interest or architectural beauty. In this way the National Trust is typical of many societies run by English men who give their services for the good of the whole people without receiving any personal advantage.

One of the second calls to the Trust for help was from a village in Sussex, Alfriston, where a fourteenth-century house called the «Priest's House» was very much in need of repair. The Vicar of Alfriston asked the Trust to preserve the house, the Trust asked the public for money, the house was bought and repaired, and it now stands for everybody to see, typical of the houses of its century, with its hall reaching up to the roof, as was usual at that time.

The preservation of Wimbledon Common and of the Priest's House at Alfriston is typical of the two sides of the Trust's work: the preservation of natural beauty for the use of all and of buildings of historical or architectural interest. Since those times, naturally, the Trust has become owner of much more land and many more houses. Large open spaces in the Lake District have been bought, as well as moorland in Surrey, not far from London. The coast of Cornwall has been preserved unspoilt by ugly houses or hotels. This land has been bought by money given by the public and this shows how the English love the natural beauty of their country and are willing to help to preserve it. Among the buildings of historical interest bought by the Trust or given to it, there is a fourteenth century castle, Bodiam Castle, and several sixteenth or seventeenth century houses.

Another part of the work of the Trust has been the preservation of land where certain birds made their homes, such as the Farne Islands near the coast of Northumberland. In this way the birds have not been killed and the people of the towns can come out and enjoy watching them. Once again the Englishman's love of nature is shown by his desire to preserve the birds of his island from being destroyed.

GETTING UP ON COLD MORNINGS

I have been warm all night and find my body in a state perfectly suitable to a warm-blooded animal. To get out of this state into the cold is so unnatural to such a creature that the poets, describing the sufferings of the damned, make one of the greatest of them consist in being suddenly carried from heat to cold — from fire to ice. On my first movement towards getting up I find that the parts of the sheets and pillows that are exposed to the air of the room are stone-cold. On opening my eyes, the first thing that meets them is my own breath coming out, as if in the open air, like smoke out of a chimney. Then I turn my eyes sideways and see the windows all frozen over. Think of that. Then the servant comes in. «It is very cold this morning, is it not?» «Very cold, sir.» «Very cold indeed, isn't it?» «Very cold indeed, sir.» «More than usually so, even for this time of the year?» (Here the servant hesitates and I lie in agony for some moments.) «Yes, sir, I think it is.» (Good creature! There is not a better or more truth-telling servant in the world.) «I must get up, however. Get me some hot water.» Here comes a long interval between the going away of the servant and the arrival of the hot water, during which, of course, it is «not worth» getting up. The hot water comes. «Is it quite hot?» «Yes, sir.» «Perhaps too hot for shaving? I must wait a little?» «No, sir, it is just right.» (Sometimes it is unnecessary to be quite so exact.) «Oh — the shirt — you must air my clean shirt; clothes become very damp this weather.» «Yes, sir.» Here another delicious five minutes. A knock at the door. «Oh, the shirt — very well. My socks — I think the socks need to be aired too.» «Very well, sir.» Here another interval. At last, everything is ready, except myself (yo mismo).

(Adapted from *Leigh Hunt.*)

Exercises

A) **Answer the following questions:**

THE NATIONAL TRUST

1. When was the National Trust started?
2. What is the object of the Trust?
3. What was one of the first efforts of the Trust?
4. Why do many Londoners go to Wimbledon Common?
5. Who runs the Trust?
6. How does the Trust get money?
7. Is the Trust part of the government of England?
8. What did the Trust preserve at Alfriston?
9. What sort of house is the «Priest's House» at Alfriston?
10. Where is the Lake District?
11. What buildings have been bought by the Trust or given to it?
12. How does the Trust preserve the bird life of England?

GETTING UP ON COLD MORNINGS

1. In what sort of state does the writer wake up?
2. What does he think is so unnatural?
3. What do poets often describe as one of the greatest sufferings of the damned?
4. In what state does the writer say he finds the parts of the sheets and pillows that have been exposed to the air of the room?
5. What is the first thing he sees as he opens his eyes?
6. What does his breath look like?
7. What has happened to the windows during the night?
8. What does he say to his servant when he comes into the room?
9. What does he ask the servant to get him?
10. What is the difference between the words *warm* and *hot*?
11. What does he want the hot water for?
12. What does he ask the servant to do to his shirt?
13. What happens to clothes in the winter?
14. What more does he give the servant to be aired?
15. Do you like getting up on cold mornings?

B) *a)* **Form sentences with the following words using them as adjectives:**

rich, blind, cold, wet, poor, Spanish, good, French, dead, young.

b) Form sentences using the same words as nouns.

C) Name some adjectives that have the same form as the corresponding adverb and form sentences with them.

D) Form all the sentences possible with the following words:

When you want to eat	you are warm
When you want to drink	you are sleepy
When you want to sleep	you are cold
If you don't wear a coat in the snow	you are hungry
If you wear a coat in summer	you are thirsty
If you think that Dublin is in Ireland	you are hot
If you think that Dublin is in England	you are right
If you wear a coat in winter	you are wrong.

E) Complete the following sentences:

1. Remember that you can always stay with us as — as you like.
2. How much luggage can I take with me? As — as you like.
3. As — as we reach the moors the villages become very isolated.
4. The basket didn't hold as — eggs as we hoped.
5. They went on horseback along the road as — as the mouth of the river.
6. After stealing the chops from the butcher's he ran away as — as he could.
7. The National Trust preserves buildings of historical interest as — as places of natural beauty.
8. I don't eat at restaurants as — as I eat at home.

F) Composition:

Going to bed on a cold night.

G) Translate into English:

Hoy día creemos todos que es necesario cuidar a los pobres y a los ciegos y en muchos países el Estado se ocupa de ellos. Pero, además del Estado, la Iglesia a menudo ayuda a los que tienen hambre o frío. En el invierno les da de comer (comida) y ropa cuando hace frío. Tampoco les deja en la calle con tiempo frío y húmedo, sino que construye asilos (traducción *hogares*), donde pueden tener calor cuando hace frío. Los ricos a veces ayudan a los pobres y a los desgraciados, pero los ricos de mi ciudad no quieren gastar su dinero. Además del Estado y de la Iglesia, hay en muchos países sociedades formadas para ayudar a los pobres o a los heridos, sobre todo después de las guerras. En Inglaterra, una de estas sociedades, que se llama la sociedad de San Dunstan, se cuida de los ciegos. Los que dirigen la sociedad piden dinero al público cada año, y con el dinero que reciben construyen hogares para los ciegos, donde aprenden a trabajar, a pesar de no poder ver. Así no se sienten inútiles y son mucho más felices, porque tienen interés por (en) la vida.

LESSON TWENTY-TWO

Vocabulary and Pronunciation

i: to le*a*n (apoyarse, asomarse).

i h*i*dden (de *to hide*), h*i*d (de *to hide*), sh*i*p (buque, barco), to *i*nténd (pensar, tener intención de).

e advénture (aventura), d*e*ck (cubierta).

a compánion (compañero), sávage (salvaje).

a: ch*a*nce (suerte, ventura; acaso, riesgo).

o: th*ou*gh*t* (pensamiento), on b*oa*rd (a bordo), on sh*o*re (a, en tierra), p*o*rt (puerto).

ʌ to w*ó*nder (preguntarse, maravillarse), tr*ó*uble (disturbio, congoja, turbación, pena).

u sh*oo*k (de *to shake*).

ə: mércy (misericordia).

ei to sh*a*ke (sacudir), sh*á*ken (de *to shake*), n*á*tive (nativo, indígena).

ai to h*i*de (esconder), s*i*gh*t* (vista), m*i*nd (mente).

oi v*ó*yage (viaje por mar).

eə b*ea*r (oso).

iə cl*ea*r (claro).

tʃ advén*t*ure.

dʒ sávage, vóyage.

Consonante muda

gh en thou*gh*t, si*gh*t.

Frases

leaning:	apoyado (véase *sitting, standing, lying, amusing,* etc.).
to shake hands:	estrechar la mano.
on board:	a bordo.
on shore:	en tierra, a tierra.
on leave:	de permiso.
on deck:	sobre cubierta.

The Lord have mercy on you.
Dios tenga misericordia de ti.
to get through: terminar, acabar.

Verbos irregulares

to hide,	hid,	hidden:	esconder.
to shake,	shook,	shaken:	sacudir.

Grammar

Concordancia de los tiempos

En un relato en pasado evítese el empleo del presente o futuro en oraciones subordinadas.

When they *came,* we all *went* to the cinema and John *said* he *would* drive us home in his car afterwards.

As they *came* near the gate of the house, one of the porters *told* them they *could* not go in then, as Her Majesty *was* just *going* to come out.

Estilo directo e indirecto

a) *Estilo directo*

Cuando se citan al pie de la letra palabras atribuidas a una persona determinada, esta narración se llama estilo directo. Las palabras citadas se ponen entre comillas.

«Will you come with me?», he said.
«How old is he?» I asked his father.

b) *Estilo indirecto*

Cuando una tercera persona relata una conversación pero sin citar las palabras mismas de los que hablan, se emplea el estilo indirecto. En inglés el estilo indirecto se introduce por la conjunción *that,* que, sin embargo, puede omitirse, o los pronombres y adverbios interrogativos *how, when, which, who,* etcétera. Se sustituye el imperativo en el estilo directo por la construcción infinitiva. Hay que observar la concordancia de los tiempos (véase arriba).

> He says, «I shall come.»
> He said (that) he would come.
> «Where is the Town Hall?» he asked.
> He asked where the Town Hall was.
> «Go to the hospital immediately» I said to him.
> I told him to go to the hospital immediately.

Whether

En el estilo indirecto puede emplearse *whether* en vez de *if*, para traducir *si*.

> «Will you come with me?» he asked me.
> He asked me whether (if) I wanted to go with him.

Naturalmente, como en el estilo indirecto se relata todo como ya pasado, no se puede emplear palabras como *now* (ahora). Las palabras que expresan cercanía de lugar o de tiempo se cambian por las que expresan distancia.

here	se transforma en	there
this »	»	» that
now »	»	» then
tomorrow »	»	» the next day
yesterday »	»	» the day before
Etc.		

Still, yet, already, again, even

Still expresa la continuidad de una acción o de un estado.

> Is he still asleep?   ¿Todavía está dormido?

Again expresa la repetición de una acción.

> Come and see me again tomorrow.
> Venga usted a verme otra vez mañana.

Already se traduce por *ya* en sentido de tiempo. No se emplea en sentido de *ya* enfático.

> I didn't expect him till later, but he has already come.
> No le esperaba hasta más tarde, pero ya ha venido.

Not yet se emplea generalmente en vez de *already* con la negación y se traduce por *no ... todavía*.

> He has not yet come.   No ha venido todavía.

Even se traduce por *aun, ni siquiera, hasta,* en sentido de encarecimiento.

Keep that in your mind, even if you forget all the rest.
No olviden eso, aunque olviden todo lo demás.
Not even half the people came.
No vino ni siquiera la mitad de la gente.
All the family have gone to Spain, even Peter.
Toda la familia se ha marchado a España, hasta Pedro.

Nótese: 1. La diferencia entre *still, adverbio* (aún, todavía), y *still, adjetivo* (quieto, tranquilo).

He is still ill : Aún está enfermo.
Keep still : ¡Estése quieto!

2. La diferencia entre el adverbio *not yet* (no ... todavía), y la conjunción *yet* (pero, sin embargo).

He has not yet come back. No ha vuelto todavía.

He was poor yet honest. Era pobre pero honrado.

He was poor, yet everyone liked him.
Era pobre; sin embargo todo el mundo le quería.

El verbo "to get":

1. Sentido general : conseguir, obtener, recibir, comprar.

The savages will get you into their valleys.
Los salvajes conseguirán que ustedes vayan a sus valles.

He always gets what he wants.
Siempre consigue lo que desea.
He got a letter this morning.
Recibió una carta esta mañana.
I got my new suit in London.
Compré mi traje nuevo en Londres.

2. En participio pasado para dar énfasis al verbo *to have.*
I've got a lot of work to do.
Tengo mucho trabajo que hacer.
I've got to go to London next week.
Tengo que ir a Londres la semana que viene.

3. Como verbo de movimiento : ir, llegar.
Get away from the fire. Aléjate del fuego.
Get up. ¡Levántate!

We got to the station just in time.
Llegamos a la estación justo a tiempo.

To get into trouble.
Caer en desgracia. Hacerse líos. Meterse en un jaleo.

4. Seguido de adjetivo equivale a *to become* (llegar a ser).

To get tired: cansarse.
To get ready: prepararse.
To get dressed: vestirse.
To get ill: ponerse enfermo.
Etc.

5. Modismos con *to get:*

to get through: terminar.

I got through this novel in one afternoon.
Leí esta novela en una tarde.

to get on: hacer progresos.

I am getting on well with my English.
Hago progresos en inglés.

Reading

AN ADVENTURE WITH THE NUKUHEVA NATIVES

When I saw Toby leaning, as I have mentioned, against the ropes and thinking hard, I imagined at once that the subject of his thoughts might be the same as my own. And if it is so, thought I, is he not just the one of all my companions whom I should like to choose to go with me on my adventure? And why should I not have some friend with me to make the journey easier? Perhaps I might have to lie hidden among the mountains for weeks. In such an event what a help would a friend be!

This all passed quickly through my mind and I wondered why I had not before thought of Toby. But it was still not too late. I woke him up from his dreams and found him ready for the adventure. A very few words were needed to settle the matter between us. In an hour's time we had already decided what we should take with us and where we should go. Then we shook hands and each went separately to his bed to spend the last night on board the Dolly.

The next day the group to which we both belonged was going on shore on leave, and we decided to take this opportunity to get off the ship and, as soon after reaching land as possible, to leave the rest of the men and start off at once for the mountains.

Our main object was to hide ourselves (nosotros mismos) from sight until the ship went away; then to take our chance and see how the Nukuheva natives would receive us; and, after staying on the island as long as we found our stay pleasant, to leave it on the first opportunity that was offered.

Early the next morning we were called on deck and our captain addressed us as follows:

«Now, men, as we have just finished a six months' voyage and have got through almost all our work in port here, I suppose you want to go on shore. Well, I intend to give you leave today, so you may get ready as soon as you like and go: but understand this, I am going to give you leave because I suppose you would be as angry as a lot of wild bears if I didn't: at the same time, if you'll take my advice, every mother's son of you will stay on board, and keep out of the way of the natives altogether. Ten chances to one, men, if you go on shore, you will get into some trouble, and that will be the end of you; for if these painted savages get you a little way back into their valleys, they'll catch you — that you may be certain of. Plenty of white men have gone on shore here and never been seen again. There was the old Dido — she came in here about two years ago, and sent some men off on leave; they weren't heard of again for a week — the natives insisted they didn't know where they were — and only three of them ever got back to the ship again, and one with his face damaged for life.

But I see it will be no use talking to you, for go you will, that I see clearly ; so all I have to say is, that you need not be angry with me if the islanders make a meal of you. You may have some chance of getting away from them, however, if you keep near the French camp, and are back at the ship again before sunset. Keep that in your mind, even if you forget all the rest I've been saying to you. There, go forward, get dressed, and be prepared for a call. At two bells the boat will be ready to take you off, and the Lord have mercy on you.»

(Adapted from *Typee* by Herman Melville.)

Exercises

A) **Answer the following questions:**

1. What was Toby doing when the writer saw him?
2. What did he imagine when he saw Toby?
3. What might he have to do for weeks?

4. What did he wonder?
5. What was decided between him and Toby in an hour's time?
6. What did they do after settling the matter?
7. Who was going on shore the next day?
8. What did Toby and he decide to do?
9. What was their main object?
10. What did they want to do when the ship went away?
11. What happened early the next morning?
12. How long had the voyage they had just finished lasted?
13. Had they got through all the work in port?
14. What did the captain intend to give the men?
15. When could they get ready?
16. What would happen if the captain didn't give the men leave?
17. What advice did the captain give the men?
18. What did the captain think, ten chances to one, the men would do on shore?
19. What had happened to plenty of white men there?
20. When did the ship Dido come in there?
21. How many of the men from the Dido ever got back to the ship again?
22. What had happened to one of those who got back?
23. Did the Captain think it was any use giving his men advice?
24. How would the men have some chance of getting away from the natives?
25. When would the boat be ready to take the men off?

B) **Translate the following sentences into English:**

a) Mi compañero estaba echado en la cubierta del buque.
b) El ciego estaba sentado delante de la portería.
c) Los ladrones estaban de pie detrás del muro, esperando el coche del director del Banco.
d) El chiquillo estaba apoyado en el escaparate y miraba los juguetes.
e) Esta novela es muy divertida pero un poco extraña.

C) a) **Explain in English the following words:**

voyage, companion, ice, ill, a dozen, ocean, to rebuild, sherry, a patient, anywhere.

b) **Use these words in sentences.**

D) **Complete these sentences with the appropriate word from the following:**

even, already, still, yet, again.

1. The house that was damaged in the war has not — been repaired.
2. All the windows are in need of repair, — the ones in the garage.
3. It was — raining in the evening so the two boys did not go for a walk in the woods, as they had wanted.
4. The first time we saw the Spanish play we didn't understand it very well, so we went to see it — last night.
5. He has only been learning to play the piano for a short time, but — he plays quite well.
6. John hasn't — got out of bed; he will be late for school.
7. It has only been freezing for two days, but the lake is frozen —
8. My watch — doesn't work well, although it has been repaired twice.
9. All the trees in the garden, — the large ones, have been spoilt by the strong wind.
10. Our car is very old, but it is — in good condition.

E) **Use another verb with the same meaning as the form of "to get" in each of the following sentences:**

1. I got two large parcels as well as a letter in this morning's post.
2. We got to the theatre just five minutes before the play began.
3. We got away from the house very early so that we were able to do the whole journey in one day.
4. My brother got through all his work in the morning so that he was able to go to the football match with me in the afternoon.
5. While I was in the town this morning I got some writing paper and some ink, as well as the socks you have been in need of for some time.

F) **Put into indirect speech:**

1. «What book did you choose for Peter's birthday present?» asked my father.
2. Mr. Brown said, «The pipes in my house freeze every year when it is very cold.»

3. «My baby brother tears up the newspaper every day if he has the chance,» said Mary.
4. «The sun sets in front of our sitting-room window, so we watch it every night», Isabel told her friend.
5. «Did you hide for a long time in the woods to get away from the natives?» Captain Armstrong asked his friend.
6. «What did you buy for lunch today?» Jean asked her mother.
7. «Did they sing well in last night's concert?» asked my mother, as I came in to breakfast.
8. «I usually lie in bed late on Sunday mornings as I haven't to go to work,» said Jimmie.
9. «Every summer the same boys steal apples from my garden,» said Mr. Jones angrily to his neighbour.
10. «Did you lend someone my book on architecture: I can't find it anywhere,» Paul said to his brother.
11. «Get some more petrol when you go past a filling station,» Mr. Brown said to his son.
12. «Have you chosen the steak or the chops?» George asked his friend as the waiter came up to their table.
13. «Which play shall we go to see when Pedro comes to stay next week-end?» he asked his brother.
14. «Come and see me tomorrow about 12 o'clock and we can talk about it,» my friend said to me.
15. «Tell me which day you would like me to go to the doctor with you and I'll keep it free,» Pablo's friend said to him.
16. «Which jug did you break — the green one or the old white one?» Mrs. Brown asked her maid.
17. «How shall we go to the moors tomorrow?» asked John, «On horseback or on foot?»
18. «Bring me some peas and a lettuce and a few tomatoes, as I shall need them for lunch,» Mrs. Jones said to her husband as he went out into the garden to dig.
19. «Shall we go on shore, or stay on board?» Toby asked his friend.
20. «Do you take milk or lemon in your tea?» asked Mrs. Hardy.

G) **Dictation:**

From «When I saw Toby...» to «...and where we should go.»

H) **Composition:**

Escríbase el discurso del capitán en estilo indirecto.

I) **Translate into English:**

Decidí dejar el buque en la primera ocasión propicia y salir de (en mi) aventura con mi compañero John. Me preguntaba si podríamos alcanzar las montañas y quedarnos escondidos allí hasta que el buque se marchara. Al día siguiente el capitán nos llamó sobre cubierta y nos dijo que podríamos ir a tierra de permiso. Hablé en seguida con John y decidimos aprovechar esta ocasión para escaparnos. Nos estrechamos la mano y fuimos a prepararnos. Ya habíamos decidido lo que llevaríamos con nosotros y adónde iríamos. Me habían dicho que los indígenas de las islas eran muy feroces y mataban a los blancos, pero no creímos todo lo que oímos y decidimos correr el riesgo* y ver cómo nos recibirían los indígenas. Preferimos correr cualquier riesgo y no quedarnos a bordo de este buque hasta el final del viaje. La vista del pequeño puerto de la isla tan cerca era un alivio muy grande para nosotros. Dejamos el buque a eso de las diez de la mañana y llegamos a tierra en unos minutos. Pasamos delante de un campamento francés, y un soldado que nos vio ir hacia las montañas nos dijo que era muy difícil escalar las rocas y que los indígenas, que eran muy salvajes, nos cogerían si entrábamos en los bosques. Lo más seguro sería seguir la carretera, nos dijo. Pero la carretera estaba a la (en) vista del buque, y por lo tanto decidimos intentar escalar las rocas.

LESSON TWENTY-THREE

Vocabulary and Pronunciation

i:	équal (igual), to agrée (estar, ponerse de acuerdo), speech (discurso).
i	bítter (amargo), to fíx (fijar), márriage (matrimonio, casamiento), reply (contestar, contestación).
e	to accépt (aceptar).
a	to stamp (patalear), sácrifice (sacrificar), márriage.
o	próperty (propiedad), upón (en), equálity (igualdad), óffer (ofrecer, oferta), philósopher (filósofo), hórror (horror), to stop (impedir, parar).

* Correr el riesgo (trad. *tomar* el riesgo).

o:	to be b*o*rn (nacer), úpro*a*r (tumulto).
ʌ	j*ú*stice (justicia) *ú*proar.
	true (verdadero, verídico).
ə	op*í*nion (opinión), néutr*a*l (neutral), *o*ccúr (ocurrir), up*ó*n, éqµ*a*l, *a*grée, *a*ccépt.
ə:	occ*ú*r.
ei	to h*a*te (odiar, detestar), to s*a*il (zarpar, navegar), to r*a*ise (levantar), str*á*nger (forastero, desconocido).
ai	hyp*ó*thesis (hipótesis).
oi	to app*ó*int (nombrar), ch*o*ice (elección).
ju:	né*u*tral, to ref*ú*se (rehusar, negarse).
eə	to decl*á*re (declarar)

Frases

upon:	otra forma de *on,* menos empleada.
at sea:	estar en el mar.
to sea:	hacerse a la mar, embarcarse.
	(véanse *at school, to school, at church, to church,* etc.)
in the first place:	en primer lugar.
on earth:	en el mundo.
to insist *on:*	insistir *en.*
to stamp one's foot:	patalear.
in reply:	en contestación.
in horror:	horrorizado.
to change one's mind:	cambiar de idea, de opinión.
to come to the point:	entrar en el grano.
Is it true?	¿Es verdad?

Grammar

Shall and Will

a) SHALL. Como ya hemos aprendido, el verbo auxiliar *shall* se emplea para formar el futuro en la primera persona.

I shall go to London tomorrow:	Iré a Londres mañana.
We shall go to London tomorrow:	Iremos a Londres mañana.

Sin embargo, se puede emplear *shall* como verbo auxiliar en la segunda y tercera persona, con lo cual se añade a la idea del futuro la de amenaza, orden, obligación o promesa.

You shall do it.   Sí, lo harás.

The enemy shall not pass.   ¡El enemigo no pasará!

El pasado *should* se emplea en sentido condicional (véase lección 2) y se traduce por *deber*.

I should go there, but I am too busy.

Debería ir allí, pero estoy demasiado ocupado.

b) WILL. *Will* se emplea para formar las segundas y terceras personas del futuro.

Will you stay at your father's house?

¿Se quedará usted en casa de su padre?

They will be at home this evening.

Estará en casa esta tarde.

Además *will* se emplea en su sentido original de *querer* (el substantivo *will = voluntad*) en todas las personas del futuro, incluso la primera, añadiendo así la idea de determinación o promesa al futuro.

I will do it.   Sí, lo haré.

He will not obey his parents.

No quiere obedecer a sus padres.

You will come tomorrow, won't you?

Usted vendrá mañana, ¿verdad?

El pasado de *will, would,* se emplea de la misma manera para dar la idea de deseo, determinación o promesa en oraciones en pasado.

Did you bring Anne?   ¿Has traído a Ana?

No, she wouldn't come.   No, no quiso venir.

Verbos compuestos

OFF

1. Se emplea en sentido de *away,* pero da generalmente la idea de un movimiento más repentino que *away.*

They went off together.   Se marcharon juntos.

We started off at six o'clock in the morning.

Nos pusimos en camino a las seis de la mañana.

He rode off on his father's horse.

Se fue montado en el caballo de su padre.

2. Se emplea en sentido contrario al de *on* (de encima de).

   We decided to get off the ship.

   Decidimos bajar del buque.

   I shall take off these gloves and put on some new ones.

   Me quitaré estos guantes y me pondré otros nuevos.

Modificaciones gráficas (cont.)

1. En los verbos monosílabos con vocal breve y una sola consonante al final, la consonante se dobla al añadir una terminación.

   Por ejemplo:

to cut:	cutting.
to run:	running.
to hit:	hitting.
to sit:	sitting.
Etc.	

2. Ocurre lo mismo en los verbos de dos sílabas, siempre que la última sílaba lleve el acento.

   Por ejemplo:

to occúr:	it occurred to me.
to prefér:	I preferred.

3. Los verbos que terminan en *-l* siempre doblan la *-l* al añadir una terminación.

   Por ejemplo:

to contról:	the controller.
trável:	the traveller, I travelled.

4. *-y, -ie.*

   Una *y* final nunca se cambia en *-ie* para formar el participio presente.

   Por ejemplo:

to try:	trying.
to cry:	crying.
to say:	saying.

   -ie final se cambia en *-y* para formar el participio presente de los verbos en *-ie*.

   Por ejemplo:

to lie:	lying.
to die:	dying.

   Para las demás modificaciones gráficas, véase *Libro Elemental*, págs. 84 y 90.

Reading

JACK EASY GOES TO SEA

«It has occurred to me,» said Jack, «that although the whole earth has been so wrongly divided among the few, the waters at least are the property of all. No man declares that the sea is his — everyone may there travel as he likes. Even war makes no difference; everyone may go on as he wants, and if they meet, it is nothing more than a neutral ground on which the two sides fight. It is, then, only upon the ocean that I may find that equality and the rights of man which we want so much to introduce on shore; and so I have decided not to go to school again, which I hate, but to go to sea and spread our opinions as much as I can.»

«I cannot listen to that, Jack. In the first place, you must return to school; in the next place, you shall not go to sea.»

«Then, father, all that I have to say is, that I declare I will not go back to school, and that I will go to sea. Who and what is going to stop me? Was I not born my own master? Has anyone a right to talk to me as if I were (subjuntivo-was) not equal to him? Have I not as much right to the sea as any other person on earth? I insist on perfect equality,» continued Jack, stamping his right foot on the floor.

What had Mr. Easy to offer in reply? He must either, as a philosopher, have sacrificed his hypothesis, or, as a father, have sacrificed his son. Like all philosophers, he preferred what he thought the less important of the two, he sacrificed his son; but we will do him justice — he did it with a sigh...

«Jack, you shall go to sea, if you want to.»

«That, of course,» replied Jack, with the air of one who has got what he wanted, «but the question is, with whom? Now it has occurred to me that Captain Wilson has just been appointed to a ship and I should like to sail with him.»

«I will write to him,» said Mr. Easy, sadly. And so the matter was settled.

The answer from Captain Wilson was, of course, that he would be glad to take Jack to sea with him, and promised to look after him as his own son.

Jack got onto his father's horse and rode off to Mr. Bonny-castle.

«I am going to sea, Mr. Bonnycastle.»

«Quite the best thing for you,» replied Mr. Bonnycastle. Jack met Dr. Middleton.

«I am going to sea, Dr. Middleton!»

«Quite the best thing for you,» replied the doctor.

«I am going to sea, mother,» said John.

«To sea, John, to sea? No, no, dear John, you are not going to sea,» replied Mrs. Easy in horror.

«Yes, I am; father has agreed, and he says he will make you change your mind and let me go.»

«Change my mind! Oh, my dear, dear boy!» and Mrs. Easy cried bitterly, as Rachel crying for her children.

(Adapted from *Mr. Midshipman Easy* by Captain Marryat.)

LIZZY REFUSES AN OFFER OF MARRIAGE

Mrs. Bennett would not give him time to answer, but hurrying immediately to her husband, called out as she came in the library.

«Oh, Mr. Bennett, you are wanted at once; we are all in an uproar. You must come and make Lizzy marry Mr. Collins, for she says she will not have him, and if you do not hurry he will change his mind and not have her.»

Mr. Bennett raised his eyes from his book as she entered and fixed them on her face with a quiet look.

«I have not the pleasure of understanding you,» said he, when she had finished her speech. «Of what are you talking?»

«Of Mr. Collins and Lizzy. Lizzy declares she will not have Mr. Collins, and Mr. Collins begins to say he will not have Lizzy.»

«And what am I to do on this occasion? It seems a hopeless business.»

«Speak to Lizzy about it yourself (tú mismo). Tell her that you insist on her marrying him.»

«Let her be called down. She shall hear my opinion.»

Mrs. Bennett rang the bell and Miss Elizabeth was called to the library.

«Come here, child,» cried her father as she appeared. «I have sent for you on a matter of importance. I understand that Mr. Collins has made you an offer of marriage. Is it true?» Elizabeth answered that it was. «Very well — and this offer of marriage you have refused?»

«I have, sir.»

«Very well. We now come to the point. Your mother insists that you accept it. Is it not so, Mrs. Bennett?»

«Yes, or I will never see her again.»

«An unhappy choice is before you. Elizabeth. From this day you must be a stranger to one of your parents. Your mother will never see you again if you do not marry Mr. Collins, and I will never see you again if you do.»

(Adapted from *Pride and Prejudice* by Jane Austen.)

Exercises

A) **Questions on "Jack goes to sea".**

1. What had occurred to Jack about the earth?
2. Who did he think the sea belonged to?
3. Why does war make no difference on the sea?
4. What did Mr. Easy and Jack want to introduce on shore?
5. What had Jack decided?
6. What did Mr. Easy at first reply to Jack when he said he was going to sea?
7. What did Jack declare when Mr. Easy tried to stop him from going to sea?
8. Why was Mr. Easy like all other philosophers?
9. Who did Jack want to go to sea with?
10. How did Mr. Easy settle the matter?
11. What answer did they get from Captain Wilson?
12. Where did Jack ride to on his father's horse?
13. What did Jack say to his mother?
14. Was Mrs. Easy pleased at what Jack told her?
15. What did Mrs. Easy do when Jack told her he was going to sea?

Questions on "Lizzy refuses an offer of marriage".

1. Where was Mr. Bennett when Mrs. Benett came to see him?
2. What did Mrs. Bennett want her husband to do?
3. Why did she want him to hurry?
4. What was Mr. Bennett doing when his wife came to see him?
5. What did Mr. Bennett reply to his wife?
6. Why did Mrs. Bennett ring the bell?
7. Was it true that Mr. Collins had made Lizzy an offer of marriage?
8. Had Lizzy refused it or accepted it?
9. What did Mrs. Bennett say she would do if Lizzy refused the offer?
10. What did Mr. Bennett say he would do if Lizzy accepted the offer?

B) **Complétense las siguientes oraciones con las palabras "shall" o "will" según expresen: 1) futuro sólo, 2) futuro con ideas de deseo, orden, amenaza, promesa, etc.:**

1. I — reach Spain in Captain Wilson's ship before next month.

2. I cannot let you do that; you — not go to sea.
3. If you marry Mr. Collins I — never see you again.
4. — you write to me when you are in Spain?
5. Of course, I — write to you: I — not forget.
6. — you lend me some money? I — give it back to you next week.
7. «I should like to sail with Captain Wilson», said Jack. «I — write to him», said Mr. Easy, sadly.
8. I declare that I — not marry Mr. Collins.
9. If you refuse his offer of marriage you — not stay in this house.
10. I — be at my office all morning tomorrow.

C) **Pónganse las oraciones del ejercicio precedente, una vez completadas, en estilo indirecto.**

D) **Complete the following sentences with prepositions:**

1. Lizzy insists — refusing the offer of marriage that Mr. Collins has made her.
2. Mr. Easy did not know what to say to Jack — reply.
3. «To sea, Jack? Never!» said Mrs. Easy — horror.
4. Jack rode — to see Mr. Bonnycastle.
5. Don't let the baby have the newspaper or he will tear it —.
6. Mr. Winkle fell — his horse and could not get — again.
7. Captain Wilson was walking — and — — deck.
8. Some of these buildings are very much — need of repair.
9. Hullo, George, where are you going — ?
10. You're not — any hurry, are you?
11. I don't have an English breakfast, as I'm not used — it.
12. He wanted to go — sea, but he stole some money and had to go — prison.
13. «Is Lizzy upstairs?» «Yes, she is.» «Let her be called — then.»
14. Have you got any property — your own?
15. — future I shall never have lunch anywhere except — home.
16. It is not nice to laugh — people when they make mistakes.
17. The more I think — Mr. Easy the more I find him a bad philosopher.

18. Mr. Trulliber wanted Mr. Adams to take hold — a pig.
19. When Mr. Pickwick let go — the reins, the horse ran —.
20. Either you must let Jack go — sea or you must change your mind about the rights of man.

E) **Use the following words in sentences:**

to freeze, to be born, to hate, to agree, speech, true, matter, damp, wet, ugly.

F) **Composition:**

a) Write the story of *Jack Easy goes to sea* in about 150 words without using any direct speech.

b) Write a letter to a friend telling him (or her) what happened when Lizzy refused to marry Mr. Collins.

G) **Translate into English:**

Cuando yo era joven, mi padre era filósofo y declaraba siempre que todos los hombres nacen con los mismos derechos. Pero cuando le nombraron alcalde de la ciudad cambió de opinión e hizo discursos contra la igualdad. Entonces se le ocurrió por primera vez que yo necesitaba ir a la escuela. Por lo tanto me envió a una escuela no lejos de nuestra casa, dirigida por un hombre feroz, a quien yo odiaba amargamente. Un día no quise ir a la escuela, y dije a mi padre que me marchaba al mar. «Irás a la escuela y no irás al mar», dijo. «No iré a la escuela; pero sí que iré al mar», le contesté, pataleando. Al fin nos pusimos de acuerdo y me embarqué (trad. navegué) con el capitán Wilson en un buque que se llamaba «El Dido». Encontré muy pronto que los hombres en un buque de guerra no son todos iguales, y la vida en el mar me pareció tan amarga como en la escuela, quizá aún peor. Cuando terminamos el viaje, no quise embarcarme otra vez en «El Dido»; preferí volver a casa. Allí encontré a una muchacha muy linda a quien hice una oferta de matrimonio. Ella me aceptó y ahora no pienso más en la igualdad ni en los derechos del hombre.

LESSON TWENTY-FOUR

Notes on Pronunciation

The letters "R" and "W"

A) *R* se pronuncia sólo cuando va seguida de vocal. Seguida de consonante o *e* muda es muda.

1) agree, true, sacrifice, breath, historical.
2) born, occur, port, warm, fierce, eastwards, sure, declare, anywhere, to tear, torn.

B) Sin embargo, *r* en posición final se pronuncia si la palabra siguiente empieza por vocal.

There are four oranges on the table.
Your adventures in South America were amusing.

C) La *r* vibrante del castellano no existe en inglés. La *r* inicial, la *rr* y la *r* simple se pronuncian todas de la misma manera.

rough, marriage, horror, roast, repair, raise, tomorrow, hurry.

A) *W* se pronuncia como la *u* en vergüenza al principio de palabra o de sílaba.

we, well, west, window, warm, watch, woman, warm, water, between, forwards, backwards.

B) Es muda:

1. Delante de *r* al principio de la palabra.

wrong, write.

2. Después de vocal al final de sílaba o con consonante sola después, pero cambia la vocal precedente en diptongo.

cow, how, blow, new, news, yellow, now, brown, town.
Exc. kno*w*ledge, con *o*.

3. Delante de *h* en las palabras

who, whom, whose, whole.

4. En answer, two, sword (espada, sable).

C) La combinación *wh* se pronuncia *w*, pero a veces se oye una ligera aspiración *delante* de la *w* (*hw*). Es mejor omitir esta aspiración que exagerarla, lo que resulta afectado.

when, where, what, while, why.

Exc. who, whose, whom, whole, como en *B* 3.

TO DO Y TO MAKE

To make se emplea en sentido más concreto que *to do*. Se traduce por *hacer,* en sentido de fabricar, crear, producir.

Nótense las frases:

to make a mistake:	equivocarse.
to make friends:	hacer amigos.
to make difficulties:	crear dificultades.
to make a speech:	hacer un discurso.
to make a plan (plans):	hacer un proyecto (planos).
to make progress:	hacer progresos.
to make money:	hacer dinero, ganar dinero.
to make an effort:	hacer un esfuerzo.
to make a fire:	encender fuego.

To do se emplea en sentido más abstracto y general. Se traduce a veces por *hacer* en sentido de ejecutar.

Nótense las frases:

to do something:	hacer algo.
to do nothing:	no hacer nada.
How do you do?	¿Cómo está usted?
to do an exercise:	hacer un ejercicio.
to do work:	hacer trabajo.
to do much, little:	hacer mucho, poco.
to do one's hair:	arreglarse el cabello, **peinarse.**

Vocabulary and Pronunciation

i	bú*sy* (ocupado), *i*nch (pulgada).
i:	mé*tre* (metro), k*i*lo (kilo).
a	gr*a*mme (gramo).
e	mé*a*surement (medida), mé*tric* (métrico).
ai	m*i*le (milla), p*i*nt (pinta).
au	p*ou*nd (libra), *ou*nce (onza).
oi	c*oi*n (moneda).
ʒ	mea*s*urement.
ə	metr*e*, m*e*asurem*e*nt.

Reading

VISITING ENGLAND

Jaime was thinking of making a journey to England in the summer holidays. So he went to see an English student he had made friends with in Madrid.

«Hullo, John. Are you busy?»

«Not very. I'm just doing an exercise for my Spanish class, but I haven't anything else to do.»

«I'm thinking of going to England this summer. I made quite a lot of money from my writing in the last few months, so I shall now take a holiday.»

«You are lucky to have had plenty of work to do. A lot of other people I know can't find much work and spend days doing nothing. But what about this journey you want to make to England?»

«Well, I should like to go by car. Is that easy?»

«Yes, all you need is the car papers. The customs will make no difficulties. But don't forget to drive on the left when you are in England, and you'll find distances still given in miles, although we now use metres for shorter measurements. For example we buy cloth by the metre. Many shops now put the measurements for clothes in both the old way in inches and in the new metric way in centimetres. This helps foreign visitors like you. So little by little we are changing to metric measurements.»

«Has the money changed?»

«Yes, that was the first to be made metric. We now have a hundred pence in the pound and new coins for fifty, ten, five, two, one and a half pence. But you may still find old coins marked 'Two shillings'. They are the same size as the ten pence coins and are worth ten pence. Others are marked 'One shilling' and these are worth five pence. So at present we have both kinds of measurements, the old English miles, pounds and ounces, and the new metres and kilos.»

«Oh, dear. I hope I don't make too many mistakes when I go shopping in England.»

«You'll find that many things are marked in both pounds and kilos, so it won't be difficult. But butter is still old by the old English half-pound, which is rather less than two hundred and fifty grammes, and tobacco is sold by the ounce, of which there are sixteen in a pound. But I think these too will soon be changed to metric measures. Milk and beer are still sold by the English pint and I don't think the beer drinkers will ever give up their pints.»

«Can I bring you back anything from England, John?»

«Yes, I should like some English tobacco. But buy it on the ferry as you come home; then it will be cheaper. You can also buy cheap brandy and whisky on the boat.»

«Well, I think it will be interesting to see England for the first time. I must make plans carefully so that I see as much as possible in the time I have for my holiday.»

«That's right; and I must make an effort to finish this exercise.»

«I'll say good-bye, then.»

«Good-bye.»

Exercices

A) **Answer the following questions:**

1. What was Jaime thinking of doing in the summer holidays?
2. Who had he made friends with in Madrid?
3. Was John busy when Jaime went to see him? What was he doing?
4. Why was Jaime able to take a holiday?
5. Why did John think Jaime was lucky?
6. How would Jaime like to travel to England?
7. How do people drive in England?
8. When are miles used and when are metres used now in England?
9. How do many shops in England help the foreign visitor?
10. How many pence are there in a pound?
11. What old coins are still used and what are they worth?
12. Give the names of two old English measurements?
13. How is butter sold in England? And tobacco?
14. What is sold by the pint?
15. What does John want Jaime to bring him back from England?
16. Where does John tell Jaime to buy it, and why?
17. Why must Jaime make plans carefully for his first visit to England?
18. What will John do when Jaime has left?

B) **In the Reading Passage find all the forms of the verbs "to make" and "to do" and notice how each verb is used.**

C) **Complete the following sentences with the correct form of "to do" or "to make".**

1. In January I shall have to — a journey to Madrid.
2. He goes to work at ten o'clock but just sits at his desk all morning — nothing.
3. As Charles is coming for the week-end it would be better to— a fire in the spare room.
4. He is — a lot of progress with his English.
5. Where's Betty? She's just coming: she's — her hair.
6. «The carriage will only hold three,» said Mr. Snodgrass. «What's to be — ?»
7. The noise — the animal afraid and he ran off towards Rochester.
8. His wife, who told him of Mr. Adams' arrival, had — a small mistake.
9. You won't — your old friend look a fool.
10. I don't want to — difficulties, but if you don't come back in time, I'll shut the gate and leave you outside for ever.
11. «Lizzy will not marry Mr. Collins and Mr. Collins begins to say he will not have Lizzy.» «Then what am I to — about it?»
12. We all hope that no nation will — war against any other nation in future.

D) **Use the following words in sentences:**

to fill, to get angry, to export, ill, dozen, ashamed, to run away, to freeze, state, effort, body, even, chance, ship, to wonder.

E) **Composition:**

Write conversations in English between:

a) a doctor and a patient. *b)* a shop assistant and a woman who looks at a lot of things but won't buy anything.

LESSON TWENTY-FIVE

Vocabulario and Pronunciation

i	wish (deseo, desear), to admít (admitir, conceder).
e	inténtion (intención), objéction (objeción), shépherd (pastor), lével (nivel), émperor (emperador).
a	cálendar (calendario), to wag (menear la cola), mánly (viril, varonil), to baptíse (bautizar), Báptist (Bautista).

o próper (propio, conveniente), diabólical (diabólico), cónsequence (consecuencia), cómmon (común), populárity (popularidad), Apóstle (apóstol).

o: stalk (tallo, tronco).

ʌ vúlgar (vulgar, ordinario), sómewhere (en algún sitio).

ei case (caso), ache (doler, dolor).

ai gíant (gigante), diabólical.

au cóunty (condado), sound (sonar, sonido).

ou pope (papa).

ʃ objéction, inténtion.

p shépherd.

k ache.

Consonantes mudas

l en stalk.

t en apostle.

h en shepherd.

Frases y modismos

Why!	se emplea como exclamación de sorpresa, además de en sentido de por qué.
what is the matter with:	qué pasa a, qué tiene.
in any case:	en todo caso.
to call someone *after* someone:	llamarle por alguien.
to have one's own way:	salirse con la suya, hacer su voluntad.
to have to do with:	tener que ver con.
What has that to do with me?	¿Qué tiene eso que ver conmigo?
It has nothing to do with you.	No tiene nada que ver con usted.
let me see: ⎱	⎰ veamos.
let us see: ⎰	⎱ vamos a ver.
just now:	ahora mismo.
to give up:	abandonar, renunciar.

Nótese la diferencia entre:

	somewhere:	en algún sitio.
	anywhere:	en cualquier sitio.
Ache:	My head aches:	Me duele la cabeza.
	I have a headache:	Tengo dolor de cabeza.

189

Grammar

Los adverbios

Formación del adverbio

a) El adverbio generalmente se forma del adjetivo añadiéndole la terminación -ly (véase *Libro Elemental*, página 145).
Además existen muchos adverbios de otra formación.

Nótese la terminación -ward(s) en sentido de hacia:

        forwards: hacia delante:
        backwards: hacia atrás.

b) Ciertos adverbios tienen la misma forma que el adjetivo correspondiente (véase lección 21).

Nótese la diferencia entre:

    hard: mucho (adv.) — hardly: apenas.
    late: tarde   — lately: recientemente.
    dear: costosamente — dearly: con cariño.

c) La mayoría de las preposiciones se emplean también como adverbios.

        Is Peter in?   No, he is out.

d) Nótense los adverbios compuestos:

        somehow: de alguna manera u otra.
        anyhow: de cualquier manera.
        somewhere: en algún sitio.
        anywhere: en cualquier sitio.
        everywhere: por todas partes.
        nowhere: en ningún sitio.
        elsewhere: en otro sitio.
        somewhat: algo.
    I am somewhat tired.   Estoy algo cansado.

e) Frases adverbiales.

        from time to time }
        now and then   } de vez en cuando.
        on purpose: a propósito.
        and so on: y así sucesivamente.
        of course: desde luego.
        this way: por aquí.

in this way:	de esta manera.
at once:	en seguida.
a long time:	mucho tiempo.
Etc.	

Posición del adverbio

a) El adverbio generalmente *precede* a la palabra que modifica (con excepción del verbo).

He is *very* clever.   Es muy listo.

b) El adverbio no debe separar el *verbo* del *complemento directo*.

He *speaks English* well.   Habla bien el inglés.

c) El verbo *to be* va generalmente seguido del adverbio.

She is always ill.   Siempre está enferma.
I am easily tired.   Me canso fácilmente.

En los tiempos compuestos después del verbo auxiliar.

She has always been ill.   Ha estado siempre enferma.

d) Con un *verbo transitivo* el adverbio se coloca o entre el sujeto y el verbo (en tiempos compuestos después del verbo auxiliar) o después del complemento directo.

He easily won the race.
He has easily won the race.
He won the race easily.
He has won the race easily.

He completely forgot the time.
He has completely forgotten the time.
He forgot the time completely.
He has forgotten the time completely.

e) Con un *verbo intransitivo* el adverbio se coloca inmediatamente después del verbo.

He smokes too much.
He drives very fast.
They have driven too fast from London.

Casos especiales

1. Los adverbios de *tiempo* indefinido se colocan entre el sujeto y el verbo (en tiempos compuestos después del verbo auxiliar). (Véase *Libro Elemental,* pág. 146).

I usually go to work at nine o'clock.
Generalmente voy a mi trabajo a las nueve.

Además, los siguientes adverbios se colocan en la misma posición.

almost (casi), also (también), first (en primer lugar, primero), once (una vez), nearly (casi), quite (completamente), hardly (apenas).

She almost (nearly) died.   Casi se murió.
I hardly understood what he said.
Apenas entendí lo que decía.

2. Los siguientes adverbios se colocan generalmente *en posición final.*

today   yesterday late   well   better very well
tonight   tomorrow   early badly   worse   very much

Peter reads badly, but Betty reads worse.
Pedro lee mal, pero Isabel lee peor.

3. *Enough* (bastante) se coloca *después* del *adjetivo, verbo* o *adverbio* que modifica.

He is not *careful enough.*
He doesn't *work enough.*
He doesn't work *hard enough.*

4. Si el adverbio modifica la oración entera, se coloca en posición *inicial.*

Luckily, we were able to get there in time.
Por suerte pudimos llegar a tiempo.

También se coloca en posición inicial para dar énfasis.

Comparación del adverbio

Los grados de comparación del adverbio se forman de la misma manera que para los adjetivos (véase lección 3).

Nótense: well   — better   — best: bien
             badly — worse   — worst: mal
             near   — nearer   — next: cerca
             far   — farther — farthest: lejos
             little — less   — least: poco
             much   — more   — most: mucho

Uso enfático del verbo "to do"

Se emplea el verbo auxiliar *to do* añadido a la forma afirmativa del presente, imperativo y pasado pretérito, para dar énfasis al verbo.

Forma normal	Forma enfática
I like it.	I *do* like it.
Come tomorrow.	*Do* come tomorrow.
He sold his car.	He *did* sell his car.

Reading

MRS. EASY, AS USUAL, HAS HER OWN WAY

It was the fourth day after the boy was born when Mr. Easy, who was sitting by his wife's bed in an arm-chair, began as follows, «I have been thinking, my dear Mrs. Easy, about the name I shall give this child.»

«Name, Mr. Easy! Why, what name should you give it except your own?»

«Not so, my dear,» replied Mr. Easy. «They call all names proper names, but I think that mine is not. It is quite the worst name in the calendar.»

«Why, what's the matter with it, Mr. Easy?»

«Nicodemus is a long name to write in full and Nick is vulgar. Besides, as there will be two Nicks, they will naturally call my boy young Nick, and of course I shall be called old Nick — and that will be diabolical.» [1]

«Well, Mr. Easy, in any case let me choose the name!»

«That you shall, my dear, and it was with this intention that I mentioned the subject so early.»

«I think, Mr. Easy, I will call the boy after my poor father — his name shall be Robert.»

«Very well, my dear, if you wish it, it shall be Robert. You shall have your own way. But I imagine, my dear, that, after a little thought, you will admit that there is a great objection.»

«An objection, Mr. Easy?»

«Yes, my dear; Robert may be very well, but you must think of the consequences; he will certainly be called Bob.»

«Well, my dear, and suppose they do call him Bob?»

«I cannot listen to that, my dear. You forget the county in which, we are living, the hills covered with sheep.»

---

1. diabolical: En inglés el diablo se llama «Old Nick».

«Why, Mr. Easy, what can sheep have to do with a Christian name?»

«There you are; women never think of the consequences. My dear, they have a great deal to do with the name of Bob. Ask any farmer in the county if ninety-nine shepherds' dogs out of a hundred are not called Bob. Now, your child is out of doors somewhere in the fields, you want him and you call him. Instead of your child, what do you find? Why, a dozen dogs at least, who come running up to you, all answering to the name of Bob and wagging their tails. You bring your son down to the level of an animal by giving him a Christian name, which, because it is so short. has been used for all the dogs in the county. Any other name you like, my dear, but in this one case I really must refuse to accept Robert.»

«Well, then, let me see — but I'll think of it later, Mr. Easy: my head aches very much just now.»

«I will think for you, my dear. What do you say to John?»

«Oh, no, Mr. Easy, such a common name.»

«A proof of its popularity, my dear. We have the Apostle and the Baptist — we have a dozen Popes who were all Johns. We have plenty of kings who were Johns — and besides, it is short, and sounds honest and manly.»

«Yes, very true, my dear; but they will call him Jack.»

«Well, we have had several famous characters who were Jacks. There was — let me see — Jack the Giant Killer, [1] and Jack of the Bean Stalk — and Jack — Jack ...»

«Jack Spratt,» [2] replied Mrs. Easy.

«And Jack Falstaff, above all, Jack Falstaff — honest Jack Falstaff.»

«I thought, Mr. Easy, that I was going to choose the name!»

«Well, so you shall, my dear; I leave it to you. Do just as you like; but remember, John is the right name. Isn't it now, my dear?»

«That's what you always do, Mr. Easy; you say you leave it to me, and that I shall have my own way, but I never do have it. I am sure that the child will be called John.»

---

1. Jack the Giant Killer y Jack of the Bean Stalk son dos personajes de cuentos para niños, en Inglaterra.

2. Jack Spratt: Otro personaje que aparece en los siguientes versos para niños:

> Jack Spratt would eat no fat,
> And his wife would eat no lean,
> And so betwixt between them both
> They licked the platter clean.

«No, my dear, we shall do just what you like. Now that I remember, there were several Greek emperors who were Johns: but you decide, my dear.»

«No, no,» replied Mrs. Easy, who was ill and not able to make any more objections, «I give it up, Mr. Easy. I know how it will be, as it always is; you give me my own way as people give money to children; it's their own money, but they must not spend it. Yes, call him John.»

«There, my dear, didn't I tell you you would be of my opinion you your own way and you tell me to call him John; so now we're both of the same opinion, and that point is settled.»

«I should like to go to sleep, Mr. Easy; I don't feel well.»

«You shall always do just as you like, my dear,» replied the husband, «and have your own way in everything. It is the greatest pleasure I have, when I do what you wish. I will walk in the garden. Good-bye, my dear.»

Mrs. Easy made no reply, and the philosopher left the room. As may easily be imagined, on the following day the boy was baptised John.

(Adapted from *Mr. Midshipman Easy* by Captain Marryat.)

Exercises

A) **Answer the following questions:**

1. How long after the boy was born was Mr. Easy sitting by his wife's bed?
2. What had Mr. Easy been thinking about?
3. What name did Mrs. Easy first suggest for the boy?
4. Why did Mr. Easy think his name was the worst in the calendar?
5. What would happen if they called the boy Nicodemus?
6. Why did Mrs Easy want to call the boy Robert?
7. What is the short form of Robert?
8. What were the hills covered with in the county in which Mr. and Mrs. Easy were living?
9. What are shepherds' dogs generally called in that county?
10. Does Mr. Easy agree to call his son Robert?
11. Why does Mrs. Easy want to think of a name later?
12. What name does Mr. Easy suggest to Mrs. Easy?
13. Why does Mrs. Easy not like this name?
14. Which people called John does Mr. Easy mention to show the popularity of the name?

15. What is the other form of John which Mrs. Easy says they will call him?
16. Which famous characters called by this other form of John does Mr. Easy mention?
17. Does Mrs Easy always have her own way?
18. Why was Mrs. Easy unable to make any more objections?
19. What is the greatest pleasure that Mr. Easy says he has?
20. What happened on the following day?

B) **Write the following sentences with the adverb in the correct place:**

1. Early: It was my intention to get up this morning, but I didn't wake up until ten.
2. Fast: He drove the car because he was late.
3. Well: The new maid can't cook.
4. Easily: We reached home in time for dinner as the roads were empty.
5. Always: He wore a brown suit.
6. Never: He reads novels; he hasn't time.
7. Hard: He has worked for this exam.
8. Completely: The view is spoilt by the new flats.
9. Quite: The dinner was cold as we arrived so late.
10. Better: At first he could not speak much Spanish, but now he speaks.
11. Almost: Get ready; it is time to go.
12. Today: I insist on going there.

C) **Form adverbs from the following words:**

easy, bad, good, fast, lucky, early, certain, equal, horrible, true, possible, cheerful.

D) *a)* **Explain the meaning of the following words in English:**

Usually, armchair, shepherd, yesterday, out of doors, garden, giant, calendar, battleship, philosopher, pigstye, first-aid.

b) **Use these words in sentences.**

E) **Complete the following sentences with an appropriate adverb:**

1. We had — begun our walk when it started to rain.
2. He arrived — at the restaurant and his friends had — begun their lunch.

3. Was Toby — when you went to his house this afternoon?
4. When we finished shopping the basket was — full.
5. The tailor promised to have my suit ready a fortnight — but it isn't ready —
6. I usually have lunch at home but — and — I go to a restaurant.
7. I must have left my watch — but I can't find it —
8. When I met Betty — she was not very well dressed, but today she was wearing a beautiful new suit.
9. When I call my dog he comes — —, wagging his tail.
10. I should never marry Mr. Collins — if he had a lot of money.

F) **Composition:**

Tell the story of *Mrs. Easy as usual has her own way* in about 200 words without using any direct speech.

G) **Put the verbs in the following sentences in the emphatic form by using the auxiliary verb "to do".**

1. Come and play bridge with us tomorrow evening.
2. You drove fast to arrive here so early.
3. Let's go on horseback onto the moors this afternoon.
4. I like your new dark-green dress.
5. I think the food in this restaurant is well cooked.
6. Let me have my own way this time, Mr. Easy, and call him Robert.
7. Accept Mr. Collins, Lizzie, or I will never see you again.
8. I want to get away from this ship, even if we get caught by the natives on shore.
9. Pick up my whip, Mr. Winkle, before this horse runs away.
10. Come to the pig-stye to see my pigs; they are very fine just now.

Translate into English:

La historia de Mr. Midshipman Easy es un libro que siempre ha gustado al público inglés desde su aparición en 1836. Fue escrito por el capitán Marryat, que se hizo a la mar cuando (era) joven y pasó una gran parte de su vida en la mar.

Jack Easy es el hijo de Mr. Easy, que es un filósofo un poco extraño. Está siempre hablando de los derechos del hombre, y su hijo empieza a hacer lo mismo. Pero pronto encuentra que la igualdad apenas la entienden los chicos en la escuela. Al maestro no le gustan mucho las ideas de Jack, y no deja a Jack siempre hacer su voluntad, como le gustaría. De vez en cuando le pega con un bastón (stick) cuando no trabaja bastante bien, y al final Jack no quiere volver a la escuela. Quiere hacerse a la mar. Pero una vez a bordo se da cuenta inmediatamente que la vida en la mar también puede ser dura. Después de los primeros días en el buque ya está dispuesto a admitir que los hombres no son todos iguales, y después de haber navegado unos meses olvida completamente los derechos del hombre. Así cuando vuelve a casa de permiso se enfada contra su padre que aún habla todo el día de los derechos del hombre y de la igualdad.

LESSON TWENTY-SIX

Vocabulario and Pronunciation

i:	f*ee*ling (sentimiento).
i	ind*i*gnant (indignado), rágg*e*d (andrajoso), *I*ndian (indio).
e	w*e*lcome (bienvenida), *e*lse (otro, más), pr*e*sence (presencia).
a	r*a*gged.
o	ast*o*nished (atónico), G*o*d (Dios), sh*o*t (de *to shoot*).
o:	acc*o*rd (acuerdo, convenio).
ʌ	c*o*mpany (compañía), str*u*cture (estructura).
u:	to sh*oo*t (matar de un tiro, disparar).
ei	prepar*a*tion (preparación), l*a*zy (perezoso), to cont*ai*n (contener), n*ei*ghbour (vecino, subs).
ai	to t*i*e (atar, liar), *ei*ther (tampoco), *i*déntity (identidad).
au	to cr*ow*d (apretarse, apiñar).
eə	to comp*are* (comparar).
iə	b*ear*d (barba).
ʃ	prepar*a*tion, astóni*sh*ed.
*t*ʃ	str*u*cture.
ð	ei*th*er.

Consonantes mudas

gh	en neig*h*bour.

Frases y modismos

in the presence of:	delante de, ante.
of one's own accord:	de su propia voluntad.
over there:	por allí.
to fall asleep:	dormirse.

"Else":

Else se emplea en sentido de *otro* o *más:*

1. Después de los pronombres indefinidos compuestos de *some, any-, no-,* y *where.*

Do you want anything else? ¿Quiere usted algo más?

Nobody else will come now. No vendrá nadie más ahora.

Don't put the piano here; put it somewhere else.
No ponga usted el piano aquí, póngalo en algún otro sitio.

2. Después de los pronombres interrogativos *what, where, how.*

What else did you see in Spain?
¿Qué más vio usted en España?

Where else did you go in Spain?
¿A qué otro sitio fue usted en España?

"Either":

En oraciones negativas se emplea *either* en sentido de *tampoco,* colocándose siempre en posición final.

If you don't go. I won't go either.
Si no va usted, no iré yo tampoco.

No se confunda either, tampoco (adv.), con either, cualquiera de dos (pron. o adj.), ni con either ... or (o ... o).

Either book is good.
Cualquiera de los dos libros es bueno.

Come and see me either today or tomorrow.
Venga usted a verme hoy o mañana.

Verbo irregular

to shoot, shot, shot: matar con un tiro, disparar.

Grammar
Pronombres reflexivos y enfáticos

Pronombre personal	Adjetivo personal	Pronombre reflexivo y enfático
I (yo)	my (mi)	myself (me, yo mismo)
you	your	yourself
he	his	himself
she	her	herself
it	its	itself
one	one's	oneself
we	our	ourselves
you	your	yourselves
they	their	themselves

El *pronombre reflexivo* se emplea para formar los verbos reflexivos, poniéndose en inglés *después del verbo.*

Me lavo:	I wash *myself.*
Se ha cortado:	he has cut *himself.*

Oneself se emplea para el pronombre reflexivo impersonal.

It is necessary to wash oneself every day.
Hay que lavarse cada día.

Nótese que: 1. En inglés sólo son verbos reflexivos aquellos en que la acción verdaderamente recae sobre la persona que la ejecuta. Por lo tanto, existen muchos menos que en español.

Por ej.:

to wash oneself:	lavarse.
to enjoy oneself:	divertirse.
to amuse oneself:	divertirse.
to dress oneself:	vestirse.

to hurt oneself:	hacerse daño.
to cut oneself:	cortarse.
to kill oneself:	matarse.
Etc.	

2. Muchos verbos que son reflexivos en español no lo son en inglés.

to get up:	levantarse.
to remember:	acordarse.
to turn:	volverse.
to make a mistake:	equivocarse.
Etc.	

3. Muchos verbos reflexivos del castellano que tienen un sujeto inanimado son intransitivos en inglés.

He pulled so hard that he *broke the rope.*
Tiró con tanta fuerza, que *rompió la cuerda.*
He pulled so hard that *the rope broke.*
Tiró con tanta fuerza, que *la cuerda se rompió.*

4. Muchos verbos se emplean en forma reflexiva en español en vez de en voz pasiva. Éstos se ponen siempre en voz pasiva en inglés. No se puede emplear la forma reflexiva en vez de la voz pasiva en inglés. (Véase *Libro Elemental,* pág. 133.)

Se dice que...	It is said that...
Me llamo Pedro.	I am called Peter.
En Inglaterra se habla inglés.	English is spoken in England.

5. Algunos verbos que en español expresan el cambio de un estado a otro se traducen al inglés por *to become* o *to get* seguido del adjetivo apropiado.

to become tired:	cansarse.
to get used to:	acostumbrarse a.
to get ready:	prepararse.
to get ill:	ponerse enfermo.
to get worse:	empeorar.
to get dressed:	vestirse.
to become old:	envejecer.

6. Nótese el modismo formado por el pronombre reflexivo precedido de *by.*

by myself, by yourself, by himself, etc.: a solas.

El pronombre enfático

Los mismos pronombres reflexivos se emplean como pronombres enfáticos y corresponden a las formas *yo mismo, nosotros mismos,* etc., en español.

> She herself gave it to me (o She gave it to me herself.)
> Me lo dio ella misma.
> Give me the letter itself, not the copy.
> Déme la carta misma, no la copia.

El pronombre recíproco

One another sólo se emplea cuando se trata de *más de dos personas...*
Each other se emplea cuando se trata de *dos personas.* Sin embargo, puede emplearse en vez de *one another,* pero *one another* no se puede emplear en vez de *each other.*
Each other y *one another* son invariables e inseparables.

They loved each other.	Se amaron el uno al otro.
Let us help one another.	Ayudémonos unos a otros.
Don't speak to one another.	No hablen unos con otros.
Football players often hurt one another.	
Los jugadores de fútbol a menudo se hacen daño.	

Pueden emplearse en el caso posesivo.

> The two girls wore each other's dresses.
> Las dos muchachas llevaron los vestidos la una de la otra.

Nótese, sobre todo, que en inglés es imposible emplear el pronombre reflexivo como pronombre recíproco.

They hurt themselves.	Se hacen daño (a sí).
They hurt each other.	Se hacen daño el uno al otro.

Reading

MR. LILLYWICK GETS MARRIED

«Now then,» said Crummles, who had been helping Mrs. Grudden with the preparations, of which there were many more than Mr. Lillywick quite liked. «Breakfast, breakfast.»*

---

* The reception after a marriage is called a «Breakfast».

No second invitation was needed. The company crowded themselves at the table as well as they could and began eating immediately: Miss Petowker blushing very much when anybody was looking, and eating very much when anybody was *not* looking; and Mr. Lillywick himself going to work as if he had decided that, as the good things must be paid for by him, he would leave as little as possible for the Crummleses to eat up afterwards.

«It's very soon finished, sir, isn't it?» Mr. Folair asked Mr. Lillywick, leaning over the table to speak to him.

«What is soon finished, sir?» replied Mr. Lillywick.

«The tying up, the fixing oneself with a wife,» answered Mr. Folair. «It doesn't take long, does it?»

«No, sir,» answered Mr. Lillywick. «It does not take long. And what then, sir?»

«Oh, nothing,» said the actor. «It doesn't take a man long to hang himself, either, eh? Ha, ha!»

Mr. Lillywick put down his knife and fork and looked round the table, indignant and astonished.

«To hang himself,» repeated Mr. Lillywick.

Everyone stopped talking.

«To hang himself,» cried Mr. Lillywick again. «Is anyone in this company trying to compare marriage and hanging?»

«The rope, you know,» said Mr. Folair, a little ashamed.

«The rope, sir,» answered Mr. Lillywick. «Does any man dare to speak to me of a rope, and Henrietta Petowker —.»

«Lillywick», suggested Mr. Crummles.

« — and Henrietta Lillywick in the same breath?» said Mr. Lillywick. «In this house, in the presence of Mr. and Mrs. Crummles.»

«Folair,» said Mr. Crummles, «I'm astonished at you.»

«What are you getting angry with me in this way for?» said the unhappy actor. «What have I done?»

«Done, sir,» cried Mr. Lillywick. «What have you done, sir! You have attacked the whole structure of society. Rope! As if a man were caught by leg and tied instead of going into marriage of his own accord.»

«I didn't mean to say you were caught by the leg and tied,» answered the actor. «I'm sorry; I can't say any more.»

«So you ought to be, sir,» said Mr. Lillywick. «And I'm glad to hear that you have enough feeling left to be so.»

(Adapted from *Nicolas Nickleby* by Charles Dickens.)

Rip Van Winkle returns home

«Oh, Rip Van Winkle,» they cried out. «Oh, yes, that's Rip Van Winkle over there, leaning against the tree.»

Rip looked and saw a person exactly like himself, when he went up the mountain: he appeared as lazy, and was certainly as ragged. The poor fellow was now completely puzzled. He doubted his own identity and whether he was himself or another man. In the middle of this, the man in the curious hat asked who he was and what his name was.

«God knows,» he said, «I'm not myself — I'm somebody else — that's me over there — no — that's somebody else got into my shoes — I was myself last night, but I fell asleep on the mountain, and they've changed my gun, and everything's changed, and I'm changed, and I can't tell what my name is, or who I am!»

The people standing around began now to look and make signs at each other. There was some talk, also, about taking the gun, and stopping the old fellow from doing any damage to himself or to anybody else. When the man in the curious hat heard them talk like this, he was afraid and ran away rather fast. At this moment a fine woman pushed her way through the crowd to get a look at the grey-bearded man. She had a healthy, fat, little child in her arms, which was afraid of him and began to cry. «Be quiet, Rip», cried she, «be quiet, you little fool; the old man won't hurt you.» The name of the child, the air of the mother, the sound of her voice, all reminded him of something.

«What is your name, my good woman?» he asked.

«Judith Gardenier.»

«And your father's name?»

«Ah, poor man, Rip Van Winkle was his name, but it's twenty years since he went away from home with his gun, and never has been heard of since — his dog came home without him; but whether he shot himself, or was carried away by the Indians, nobody can tell. I was then only a little girl.»

Rip had only one question more to ask; but he asked it with a hesitating voice.

«Where's your mother?»

She too had died, only a short time ago; she had got so angry with her lazy son that she had suddenly fallen down dead. That, at least, was a relief.

The honest man could contain himself no longer. He caught his daughter and her child in his arms. «I am your father,» cried he — «Young Rip Van Winkle once — old Rip

Van Winkle now! — Does nobody know poor Rip Van Winkle?»

All stood astonished, until an old woman, coming out from among the crowd, put her hand to her eyes and, looking under it in his face for a moment, said, «It's true! It's Rip Van Winkle — it is himself! Welcome home again, old neighbour — Why, where have you been these twenty long years?»

Rip's story was soon told, for the whole twenty years had been to him just one night.

(Adapted from *Rip Van Winkle* by Washington Irving.)

Exercises

A) **Question on Mr. Lillywick gets married.**

1. Who had been helping Mrs. Grudden with the preparations for the breakfast?
2. Why did Mr. Lillywick not quite like so many preparations?
3. Was there plenty of room at the table?
4. What did Miss Petowker do when anybody was looking?
5. What did she do when nobody was looking?
6. What did Mr. Lillywick appear to have decided?
7. What did Mr. Folair say did not take long?
8. What did he say which made Mr. Lillywick indignant and astonished?
9. Why was Mr. Folair a little ashamed?
10. What was Mr. Folair by profession?
11. What was Mrs. Lillywick's name before the marriage?
12. What did Mr. Lillywick say Mr. Folair had done?
13. Did Mr. Lillywick think that a man went into marriage of his own accord or did he think he was caught and tied?
14. Was Mr. Folair sorry for what he had said?
15. Who wrote the story of Nicolas Nickleby?

Questions on Rip Van Winkle returns home.

1. Whom did Rip see leaning against a tree?
2. Was the person he saw well-dressed and hard-working?
3. Why was Rip completely puzzled?
4. What happened to Rip on the mountain the night before?

5. Why did the people standing around begin to look and make signs at each other? (loco=mad).
6. Why did they want to take the gun away from Rip?
7. Why did the man in the curious hat run away?
8. .Had Rip got a beard?
9. Why did the child in the woman's arms begin to cry?
10. What did the mother of the child think had happened to Rip twenty years before?
11. What had happened to Rip's wife?
12. Was Rip sorry that his wife was dead?
13. Who was the woman with the child in her arms?
14. What did the old woman who came out of the crowd say to Rip?
15. Why was Rip's story soon told?

B) **Complete the following sentences with the correct form of the reflexive, reciprocal or emphatic pronoun:**

1. The neighbours, who had all been invited, crowded — around the table.
2. Mr. Folair said that it didn't take long for a man to hang —.
3. I think Miss Petowker was enjoying — very much.
4. The people in the crowd began to make signs to — —.
5. Don't help me: I want to see if I can do it by —.
6. I was so careless with the gun that I almost shot —.
7. Be careful how you pick the fruit at the top of the tree or you'll fall and hurt —.
8. It is not very easy to dress — in the dark.
9. We can't come down to breakfast yet; we haven't washed — .
10. Did you repair the garage door —; yes, I repaired it —

C) **Háganse todas las combinaciones posibles con las siguientes palabras:**

I	saw	myself	at the party.
Mr. Lillywick	looked at	yourself	in the mirror (espejo).
Mrs. Grudden	enjoyed	himself	in the wood.
You	hurt	herself	with a knife.
The neighbours	lost	ourselves	in a car accident.
We	cut	yourselves	
		themselves	

D) **Háganse todas las combinaciones posibles con las siguientes palabras:**

Mr. Lillywick	looked after the preparations	himself.
I	paid for the meal	themselves.
My aunt	designed the house	ourselves.
You	chose the menu	myself.
We	painted the spare room	herself.
The workmen	bought the property	yourself.

E) **Explain the following words or phrases in English and use them in sentences:**

to have one's own way, to stamp one's foot.
to shake hands, to get through, neighbour,
shepherd, lazy, grey-bearded. somewhere,
somewhat.

F) **Composition:**

a) Write a letter to a friend describing Mr. Lillywick's marriage and the breakfast that followed (150 words.)

b) Describe the return of Rip Van Winkle as if you were one of the crowd telling it to a friend afterwards.

G) **Translate into English:**

Ahora hemos llegado al final del segundo libro de *Inglés para Españoles,* y espero que los estudiantes tengan ya una idea de la estructura de la lengua inglesa. Porque lo (que es) difícil en el inglés no es tanto el vocabulario como la manera de emplear las palabras. Un estudiante a solas puede aprender muchas palabras sin ser capaz de decir dos frases en inglés. Por lo tanto, tiene que acostumbrarse a aprender frases enteras, además de palabras. Desde luego, tiene que saber la gramática, pero no sirve para nada tampoco saber gramática si no sabe emplear su conocimiento para hablar o escribir en inglés. Sabiendo la gramática y cierto número de palabras y frases, el estudiante puede aprender a construir oraciones y pequeñas conversaciones leyendo trozos de inglés y copiando (to copy) las oraciones que encuentre allí. Los estudiantes pueden entretenerse en las clases de inglés haciéndose preguntas el uno al otro en inglés. Una persona puede hacer el papel del camarero, otra el del cliente (client); una, el papel del dentista; otra, el del paciente; y así sucesivamente. Desde luego se harán muchas faltas al principio, pero poco a poco el inglés de los estudiantes mejorará. Pueden hacer otro ejercicio muy bueno, cambiando el sujeto de la oración varias veces y formando así muchas oraciones de la misma especie. Después pueden cambiar los complementos. Así el estudiante se acostumbra a la estructura de estas oraciones y aprende a formar él mismo otras de la misma especie. Sobre todo nadie debería aprender una palabra del inglés sin emplearla formando una oración que la contenga.

VERBOS IRREGULARES

to become	became	become :	*llegar a ser.*
to burst	burst	burst :	*reventar, estallar.*
to choose	chose	chosen :	*escoger.*
to dig	dug	dug :	*cavar.*
to draw	drew	drawn :	*dibujar, tirar.*
to dream	dreamt	dreamt :	*soñar.*
to drive	drove	driven :	*conducir.*
to feed	fed	fed :	*alimentar, nutrir, dar de comer.*
to feel	felt	felt :	*sentir, palpar.*
to forget	forgot	forgotten :	*olvidar.*
to freeze	froze	frozen :	*helar, congelar.*
to grow	grew	grown :	*crecer, cultivar.*
to hang	hung	hung :	*colgar, ahorcar.*
to hide	hid	hidden :	*esconder.*
to hit	hit	hit :	*golpear, pegar.*
to hold	held	held :	*tener en la mano, tener, contener.*
to hurt	hurt	hurt :	*hacer daño, doler.*
to lean	leant	leant :	*apoyarse, asomarse.*
to lend	lent	lent :	*prestar.*
to let	let	let :	*dejar, permitir, alquilar.*
to lie	lay	lain :	*yacer.*
to lose	lost	lost :	*perder.*
to mean	meant	meant :	*significar, querer decir.*
to ride	rode	ridden :	*montar a caballo.*
to rise	rose	risen :	*levantarse, salir del sol.*
to set	set	set :	*ponerse, del sol.*
to shake	shook	shaken :	*sacudir.*
to shoot	shot	shot :	*disparar.*
to sing	sang	sung :	*cantar.*
to spoil	spoilt	spoilt :	*estropear.*
to spread	spread	spread :	*extender, esparcir.*
to steal	stole	stolen :	*robar.*
to teach	taught	taught :	*enseñar.*
to tear	tore	torn :	*despedazar, rasgar.*
to tell	told	told :	*decir, contar.*
to think	thought	thought :	*pensar.*
to throw	threw	thrown :	*echar, tirar.*

VOCABULARIO

(*Verbos irregulares)

A. INGLÉS-ESPAÑOL.

absent-minded	distraído
to accept	aceptar
accident	accidente
accord	acuerdo
according to	según
ache	dolor
to ache	doler
to act	representar, hacer
activity	actividad [un papel
to address	dirigir (una carta)
address	señas, dirección
to admit	admitir, conceder
adventure	aventura
advertisement	anuncio
advice	consejo
affectionately	afectuosamente
to be afraid	temer
agony	agonía
to agree	estar, ponerse de acuerdo
aid	ayuda, auxilio, so-
air	aire [corro
to air	calentar
alive	vivo, en vida
amateur	aficionado
to amuse	divertir, entretener
amusement	diversión
anger	ira, cólera
angry	enfadado
animal	animal
anywhere	en cualquier sitio
apostle	apóstol
to appear	aparecer, parecer
to appoint	nombrar
architectural	arquitectónico
area	área, superficie
as long as	tanto tiempo como
as much ... as	tanto ... como
aspect	aspecto
astonished	atónito
to attack	atacar
to attend	asistir
audience	auditorio, público
authority	autoridad
to avoid	evitar
axe	hacha
back	espalda, lomo
backwards	hacia atrás
bacon	especie de jamón serrano, tocino
bank	banco

to baptise	bautizar
Baptist	Bautista
battleship	acorazado
bean	judía
bear	oso
beard	barba
to become*	hacerse, llegar a ser
bedside-table	mesita de noche
beef	carne de buey
to believe	creer
belt	cinturón
besides	además (de)
bitter	amargo
blacksmith	herrero
blind	ciego
to block	bloquear
blood	sangre
bloody	sangriento
to blush	sonrojar
on board	a bordo
boat	bote, barca
body	cuerpo
to boil	hervir
bookcase	estante, estantería
to be born	nacer
to borrow	tomar prestado
bow-window	mirador
brass	latón
breath	aliento
Britain, Great Britain	Gran Bretaña
British	británico (adj.)
Briton	Británico (subst.)
bucket	cubo
to burst*	estallar, reventar
busy	ocupado
cabbage	col
calendar	calendario
cap	gorra
carnation	clavel
carpet	alfombra
carriage	coche
to carry	llevar, portear
case	caso
cause	causa
Celtic	céltico
chairman	director, presidente
chapel	capilla
chance	suerte, ventura; acaso, riesgo
character	carácter

cheerful	alegre, de buen hu-	delicious	delicioso
chest	pecho [mor	dentist	dentista
chest of drawers	cómoda	to depend on	depender de
chicken	pollo	to design	diseñar
chimney	chimenea	desire	deseo
choice	elección	to desire	desear
to choose*	escoger	desk	escritorio
chop	chuleta	detail	detalle
Christian name	nombre de pila	diabolical	diabólico
to clean	limpiar	dialect	dialecto
the cleaners'	tintorería	difference	diferencia
clear	claro	difficult	difícil
to close	cerrar, terminar	difficulty	dificultad
club	club, círculo	to dig*	cavar
coach	coche, diligencia	disadvantage	desventaja
coin	moneda	discipline	disciplina
to collect	recoger	to disturb	estorbar, molestar
college	colegio mayor	to doubt	dudar
comfortable	confortable, cómodo	dozen	docena
common	común	to draw*	dibujar, tirar
common room	sala de recreo	drawing	dibujo
companion	compañero	dramatic	dramático
company	compañía	to dream*	soñar
to compare	comparar	dressing-table	peinadora, tocador
congratulations	felicidades	to drive*	conducir, ir en c
consequence	consecuencia	to drop	dejar caer [c
to consist	consistir	dull	aburrido, soso
to contain	contener		
to control	controlar	eastwards	al este
contrary	contrario	effect	efecto
correct	correcto, justo,	effort	empeño, esfuerzo
	exacto	either	tampoco
cottage	casita campestre	either ... or	o ... o
copper	cobre	to elect	elegir
council	consejo	electric	eléctrico
county	condado	else	otro, más
cover	cubierta	emperor	emperador
to cover	cubrir	ending	terminación
creature	criatura	to enjoy	gozar, disfrutar
cricket	juego de pelota in-	equal	igual
crop	cosecha [glés	equality	igualdad
crowd	muchedumbre, mul-	essential	esencial
to crowd	apretarse [titud	even	aun
crown	corona	event	evento, aconteci-
to cry	llorar, gritar, excla-		miento
cultural	cultural [mar	exactly	exactamente
cupboard	armario	to examine	examinar, registr
curious	curioso, extraño	except	salvo, excepto
curtain	cortina	to expect	esperar
cushion	cojín	to export	exportar
		to expose	exponer
damage	daño	eye	ojo
to damage	dañar, hacer daño		
damned	condenado	fact	hecho
damp	húmedo	famous	famoso
dead	muerto	far	lejos
deck	cubierta	fast	rápido, rápidame
to declare	declarar	fat	gordo

avourite	favorito
o feed*	nutrir, alimentar, dar de comer
o feel*	sentir, palpar
eeling	sentimiento
ierce	feroz
igure	cifra
o fill	llenar
lling-station	depósito de gasolina
inal	final
o finish	terminar, acabar
o fix	fijar
at	llano
at	piso
o follow	seguir
ol	tonto -a (subst.)
oreign	extranjero (adj.)
orge	fragua
o forget*	olvidar
ormula	fórmula
orward	adelante
ountain	fuente, surtidor
freeze*	helar, congelar
full	entero
furnish	amueblar
rniture	muebles
ture	futuro
llery	galería
rage	garaje
garden	cultivar el jardín
te	puerta exterior, cochera, verja
get on*	hacer progresos
nt	gigante
ad	contento, alegre
al	tanto
od	Dios
wn	toga
aduate	licenciado
avy	salsa
greet	saludar
eting	saludo
und floor	planta baja
grow*	crecer, cultivar
de	guía
n	cañón, fusil
fpenny	1/2 penique
l	comedor de colegio
handle	manejar
hang*	colgar, ahorcar
happen	ocurrir
dly	apenas
hate	odiar, detestar
d	cabeza
dquarters	cuartel general
lthy	saludable, sano
vy	pesado
oful	útil
hesitate	vacilar
to hide*	esconder
hint	consejo, aviso, su-
to hire	alquilar [gestión
historical	histórico
to hit*	golpear, pegar
hockey	hockey
to hold*	tener en la mano, tener, contener
honest	honrado
horrible	horrible
horror	horror
hors d'oeuvres	entremeses
hospital	hospital
housekeeper	ama de llaves
huge	enorme
to hurt*	hacer daño, doler
hypothesis	hipótesis
ice	hielo, helado
icicle	cerrión
identity	identidad
ill	enfermo
immediate	inmediato
important	importante
inch	pulgada
including	incluso, incluyendo
indeed	verdaderamente, de veras
independent	independiente
Indian	indio
indignant	indignado
indoors	en casa
information	informes
to insist	insistir
to intend	pensar, tener idea
intention	intención [de
interest	interés
interval	intervalo
intimate	íntimo
to introduce	presentar, introdu-
Ireland	Irlanda [dir
Irish	irlandés (adj.)
isle, island	isla
to isolate	aislar
jam	mermelada
job	trabajo, tarea
jug	jarro
just	sólo, solamente, precisamente
justice	justicia
key	llave
to kill	matar
knowledge	conocimiento(s)
lady	señora

lake	*lago*
lamb	*cordero*
language	*lenguaje, idioma*
large	*grande*
to last	*durar*
lately	*recientemente*
to laugh	*reír*
law	*ley*
lazy	*perezoso*
leader	*jefe, caudillo*
to lean*	*apoyarse, asomarse*
learned	*culto, sabio*
to leave out*	*omitir*
to lecture	*dar conferencias*
lecture	*conferencia*
left	*izquierdo*
to lend*	*prestar*
length	*longitud*
to let*	*dejar, permitir; arrendar, alquilar*
lettuce	*lechuga*
level	*nivel*
liberty	*libertad*
lo lie*	*yacer*
literally	*literalmente*
lobster	*langosta*
to lose*	*perder*
to love	*amar, encantar*
low	*bajo*
lucky	*afortunado*
maid	*criada*
manager	*director*
manageress	*directora*
manly	*viril, varonil*
marmalade	*mermelada de naranja*
marriage	*matrimonio, casamiento* [*miento*]
married	*casado*
match	*partido*
matter	*asunto*
mayonnaise	*mayonesa*
to mean*	*significar, querer decir* [*cir*]
member	*miembro*
to mention	*mencionar*
menu	*minuta, carta*
mercy	*misericordia*
to milk	*ordeñar*
mind	*mente*
to mind	*molestar, disgustar*
mistake	*falta, equivocación*
to make a mistake	
to make mistakes	} *equivocarse*
to mix	*mezclar*
moor	*páramo*
mountain	*montaña* [*ra*
mouth	*boca, desembocadu-*

movement	*movimiento*
mud	*barro*
musical	*musical*
native	*nativo, indígena*
naturally	*naturalmente*
nearly	*casi*
neighbour	*vecino* (subst.)
neighbouring	*vecino* (adj.)
nest	*nido*
neutral	*neutral*
noisy	*ruidoso*
northern	*del norte* (adj.)
note	*billete de banco*
to notice	*notar, observar, r•* *parar*
to obey	*obedecer*
object	*objeto, fin*
objection	*objeción*
observation	*observación*
to observe	*observar*
occasionally	*de vez en cuand•*
occur	*ocurrir*
ocean	*océano*
to offend	*ofender*
offer	*oferta*
to offer	*ofrecer*
to oil	*engrasar*
onion	*cebolla*
opinion	*opinión*
opportunity	*oportunidad, o•*
opposite	*en frente* [*si*
organisation	*organización*
origin	*origen*
ounce	*onza*
over	*encima, por encir• más de*
to owe	*deber, tener deu•*
own	*propio*
owner	*propietario*
to paint	*pintar*
parish	*parroquia*
park	*parque*
parson	*pastor*
patient	*paciente*
patrol	*patrulla*
pea	*guisante*
perfect	*perfecto*
to perfect	*perfeccionar*
permission	*permiso*
personal	*personal, partic•*
phenomenon	*fenómeno*
philosopher	*filósofo*
to pick	*coger, recoger*
pig	*cerdo*
pig-stye	*zahúrda*
pillow	*almohada*

latform	andén	to remind	recordar
layer	jugador	repair	reparo
leasant	agradable	to repair	reparar
leased	contento	reply	contestación
oet	poeta	to reply	contestar
olite	cortés	to rent	alquilar
oor	pobre	to return	volver, regresar
ope	Papa	rib	costilla
opularity	popularidad	rich	rico
opulation	población	to ride*	montar a caballo
ort	puerto	right	derecho, justo, correcto
orter's lodge	portería		
ossible	posible	to rise*	levantarse, salir -del
oultry	aves	roast	asado [sol
o pour	verter	rock	roca, peña
o prefer	preferir	room	cuarto, habitación;
reparation	preparación	root	raíz [sitio
resence	presencia	rose	rosa
reservation	preservación	rough	áspero
o preserve	preservar, conservar	rowing	remo
retentious	afectado, presumido	rug	estera, tapete
riest	cura		
rinciple	principio	to sacrifice	sacrificar
rison	cárcel	safe	seguro
o produce	realizar, poner en escena	safely	a salvo
		sail	vela
roduction	representación	to sail	navegar, zarpar
ogress	progreso	salad	ensalada
promise	prometer	salmon	salmón
oper	propio, conveniente	savage	salvaje
operty	propiedad	scenery	paisaje; decoraciones de teatro
ublic-house	taberna, bodega		
ulpit	púlpito	to score	marcar
uncture	pinchazo	Scotland	Escocia
uzzled	desconcertado, perplejo	scout	explorador
		secretary	secretario
uadrangle	patio	to separate	separar
uart	cerca 1 1/2 litros	separately	separadamente
uick	rápido	serious	serio
uiet	quieto, tranquilo	sermon	sermón
		service	servicio
gged	andrajoso	to settle	arreglar
raise	levantar	to set*	ponerse -del sol
t	rata	shadow	sombra
reach	alcanzar	to shake*	sacudir
ading-lamp	lámpara portátil	sheet	sábana
al	verdadero	shepherd	pastor
realize	darse cuenta	sherry	jerez
receive	recibir	ship	buque, barco
cital	recital	to shoot*	matar con un tiro, disparar
ference	referencia		
refuse	rehusar, negarse	on shore	a tierra, en tierra
gard	atención, considera-	sideways	de lado, de través
gistered	facturado [ción	sight	vista
hearsal	ensayo	sign	signo, seña, señal
ns	rienda	silver	plata
ation	relación, pariente [se	simply	simplemente, sencillamente
remember	recordarse, acordar-		

213

sincerely	sinceramente
to sing*	cantar
skill	destreza, habilidad
to smile	sonreír
society	sociedad
sofa	sofá
sole	lenguado
somewhere	en algún sitio
sound	sonido
to sound	sonar
space	espacio
Spaniard	español (subst.)
spare room	cuarto de huéspedes
special	especial
speech	discurso
to splash	salpicar
to spoil*	estropear
sport	deporte
to spread*	extender, esparcir
stage	escenario
staircase	escalera
stalk	tallo, tronco
to stamp	patalear
state	estado, condición
steak	biftek
to steal*	robar
steep	empinado
step	paso
to step	dar un paso, pisar
still	aún, todavía
stomach	estómago, vientre
stony	pedregoso
to stop	impedir, parar
stove	estufa
strange	extraño
stranger	forastero, descono-
to stretch	extenderse [cido
structure	estructura
subject	asunto, sujeto
suddenly	súbitamente, de repente
suffering	sufrimiento, pena,
to suggest	sugerir [dolor
suitable	conveniente, apro- piado, adecuado
to suppose	suponer
sure	seguro
to surprise	sorprender
sweet	postre, dulce
table-spoon	cuchara sopera
tail	cola, rabo
to take hold of	coger, agarrar
to teach*	enseñar
tea-cake	pasta de té
to tear*	despedazar, rasgar
tea-spoon	cucharilla
to tell*	decir, contar

tender	tierno
term	trimestre
test	prueba
to thank	agradecer, dar gra
to think*	pensar [cia
thought	pensamiento
threepenny	de tres peniques
to throw*	echar, tirar
to tie	atar, liar
title	título
toast	pan tostado
to toast	tostar
toe	dedo del pie
tradition	tradición
to travel	viajar
troop	tropa
trouble	disturbio, congoja, turbación, pena
true	verdadero, verídic
trunk	baúl
truth	verdad
to turn	volver(se), girar
tutor	director de estudic
typical	típico, característic
tyre	neumático
ugly	feo
uncomfortable	incómodo
undergraduate	estudiante
undulating	ondulante
unhappy	infeliz, desgraciac
uniform	uniforme
uninhabited	sin habitantes, inh bitado
unspoilt	inmaculado, libre d sin estropear
upon	en
uproar	tumulto
use	costumbre, uso
used	acostumbrado
useless	inútil
variety	variedad
vicar	vicario
vicarage	vicaría
villager	aldeano
voyage	viaje por mar
vulgar	vulgar, ordinario
Wales	país de Gales
wardrobe	ropero
warm	caliente
to watch	vigilar, observar,
weak	débil [mir
weight	peso
welcome	bienvenida
west	oeste
wheat	trigo

vheel	rueda
whip	látigo
vide	ancho
vild	salvaje, silvestre
villing	dispuesto
vish	deseo
o wish	desear
o wonder	preguntarse, maravillarse
o work	trabajar, funcionar
vorkman	obrero
o be worth	valer, valer la pena
rong	equivocado
ard	patio
et	todavía
orkshire	condado de Inglaterra

?. ESPAÑOL-INGLÉS.

ourrido	dull
cidente	accident
eptar	to accept
ontecimiento	event
orazado	battleship
ordarse	to remember
ostumbrado	used
tividad	activity
uerdo	accord, agreement
onerse de acuerdo	to agree
delante	forward
demás de	besides, as well as
dmitir	to admit
ectado	pretentious
ortunado	lucky
arrar	to take hold of*
radable	pleasant
radecer	to thank*
orcar	to hang
re	air
slar	to isolate
anzar	to reach
deano	villager
egre	glad, cheerful
ombra	carpet
ento	breath
mentar	to feed*
r allí	over there
nohada	pillow
uilar	to hire
a de llaves	housekeeper
able	kind
ar	to love
argo	bitter
ueblar	to furnish

ancho	wide
andén	platform
andrajoso	ragged
animal	animal
ante	in the presence of
anuncio	advertisement
aparecer	to appear
apenas	hardly
apoyado	leaning
apoyarse	to lean*
apretarse	to crowd
apuntar	to write down*
armario	cupboard
arquitectónico	architectural
arreglar	to settle
asado	roast
asistir a	to attend
asomarse	to lean*
aspecto	aspect
áspero	rough
asunto	subject, matter
atacar	to attack
atar	to tie
atónito	astonished
auditorio	audience
aún	even, still
autoridad	authority
aventura	adventure
aves	poultry
ayuda	aid, help
bajo	low
banco	bank
barba	beard
barro	mud
baúl	trunk
bautizar	to baptise
bienvenida	welcome
biftek	steak
billete de banco	note
bloquear	to block
a bordo	on board
bote	boat
Gran Bretaña	Great Britain
británico	British (adj.) / Briton (subs.)
buque	ship
a caballo	on horseback
cabeza	head
calendario	calendar
caliente	warm
cantar	to sing*
cañón, fusil	gun
carácter	character
cárcel	prison
cariñosamente	affectionately
carne de buey	beef

en casa	*indoors*	cubo	*bucket*
casado	*married*	cubrir	*to cover*
casita campestre	*cottage*	cuchara sopera	*table-spoon*
caso	*case*	cucharilla	*tea-spoon*
catedrático	*professor*	darse cuenta	*to realize*
causa	*cause*	cuerpo	*body*
a causa de	*because of*	cuidar	*to look after*
cavar	*to dig**	cultivar	*to grow*
cebolla	*onion*	cultivar el jardín	*to garden*
céltico	*Celtic*	cura	*priest*
cerdo	*pig*	curioso	*curious*
cerrar	*to close*		
ciego	*blind*	chimenea	*chimney*
cinturón	*belt*	chuleta	*chop*
cobre	*copper*		
claro	*clear*	dañar	*to damage*
clavel	*carnation*	daño	*damage*
coche	*carriage,* **car**	hacer daño	*to hurt**
cojín	*cushion*	deber	*to owe*
col	*cabbage*	débil	*weak*
cola	*tail*	decoraciones de	
cólera	*anger*	teatro	*scenery*
colgar	*to hang**	dejar	*to let**
dar de comer	*to feed**	dejar caer	*to drop*
cómoda	*chest of drawers*	delicioso	*delicious*
cómodo	*comfortable*	dentista	*dentist*
compañía	*company*	depender de	*to depend on*
compañero	*companion*	deporte	*sport*
común	*common*	depósito de ga-	
condado	*county*	solina	*filling-station*
conducir	*to drive**	desconcertado	*puzzled*
conferencia	*lecture*	desear	*to wish, to desire*
dar una confe-		desembocadura	*mouth*
rencia	*to lecture*	deseo	*desire, wish*
congelar	*to freeze**	desgraciado	*unhappy*
consecuencia	*consequence*	despedazar	*to tear**
consejo	*advice, council*	desventaja	*disadvantage*
consistir	*to consist*	detalle	*detail*
contar	*to tell**	dialecto	*dialect*
contener	*to hold, to contain*	dibujo	*drawing*
contento	*pleased, glad*	diferencia	*difference*
contestación	*reply*	difícil	*difficult*
contestar	*to reply*	dificultad	*difficulty*
contrario	*contrary*	Dios	*God*
controlar	*to control*	director	*manager*
cordero	*lamb*	directora	*manageress*
corona	*crown*	dirigir (una carta)	*to address*
correcto	*correct*	disciplina	*discipline*
cortés	*polite*	discurso	*speech*
cortina	*curtain*	diseñar	*to design*
cosecha	*crop*	disfrutar	*to enjoy*
costilla	*rib*	disparar	*to shoot**
creer	*to believe*	dispuesto	*willing*
criatura	*creature*	distraído	*absent-minded*
criada	*maid*	disturbio	*trouble*
cuanto más -más	*the more -the more*	diversión	*amusement*
cuartel general	*headquarters*	divertir	*to amuse*
cubierta	*cover, deck*	docena	*dozen*

doler	to hurt*, to ache
dolor	ache
dormirse	{ to go to sleep* / to fall asleep* }
dramático	dramatic
dudar	to doubt
durar	to last
efecto	effect
en efecto	in fact
por ejemplo	for example
elección	choice
eléctrico	electric
elegir	to elect
emperador	emperor
empinado	steep
enfadado	angry
enfermo	ill
enorme	huge
ensalada	salad
ensayo	rehearsal
enseñar	to teach, to show
entremeses	hors d'oeuvres
entretener	to amuse
equivocación	mistake
equivocado	wrong
equivocarse	to make mistakes*
escalera	staircase
escaparse	to run away*
escenario	stage
escocia	Scotland
escoger	to choose*
esconder	to hide*
escritorio	desk
esencial	essential
esfuerzo	effort
espacio	space
espalda	back
español	{ Spanish (adj.) / Spaniard (subs.) }
esparcir	to spread*
especial	special
esperar	{ to expect / to wait for / to hope }
estado	state
estallar	to burst*
estante	bookcase
este	eastwards
estómago	stomach
estorbar	to disturb
estrechar la mano	to shake hands*
estropear	to spoil*
estructura	structure
estudiante	student, undergraduate
estufa	stove
evitar	to avoid
exacto	exact
examinar	to examine
excepto	except
exclamar	to cry (out)
explorador	scout
exponer	to expose
exportar	to export
extender	to stretch, to spread*
extranjero	foreign
extraño	strange, curious
famoso	famous
favorito	favourite
felicidades	congratulations
feo	ugly
feroz	fierce
fijar	to fix
filósofo	philosopher
fin	object
final	final
al final	at last
forastero	stranger
fragua	forge
en frente	opposite
fresa	strawberry
fuente	fountain
funcionar	to work
futuro	future
galería	gallery
garaje	garage
gasolina	petrol
gigante	giant
gordo	fat
gorra	cap
gritar	to cry
guía	guide
guisante	pea
habilidad	skill
hacha	axe
hecho	fact
helado	ice
helar	to freeze*
herida	wound
herrero	blacksmith
hervir	to boil
hielo	ice
histórico	historical
honrado	honest
horrible	horrible
horror	horror
hospital	hospital
húmedo	damp
identidad	identity
idioma	language

igual	equal
igualdad	equality
impedir	to stop
importante	important
incluso	including
incómodo	uncomfortable
independiente	independent
indígena	native
indignado	indignant
indio	Indian
infeliz	unhappy
informes	information
inmediato	immediate
insistir en	to insist on
intención	intention
interés	interest
intervalo	interval
íntimo	intimate
inútil	useless
ira	anger
Irlanda	Ireland
Irlandés	{ Irish (adj.)
	{ Irishman (subs.)
isla	island
jarro	jug
jefe	leader, chief
jerez	sherry
judía	bean
jugador	player
justicia	justice
lago	lake
lámpara portátil	reading lamp
langosta	lobster
látigo	whip
latón	brass
lechuga	lettuce
lejos	far
lenguado	sole
levantar	to raise
ley	law
libertad	liberty
limpiar	to clean
lomo	back
longitud	length
luna	moon
llano	flat
llegar a ser	to become*
llenar	to fill
llevar	to carry
llorar	to cry
manejar	to handle
marroquí	Moroccan
más de	over
matar	to kill

matar de un tiro	to shoot*
matrimonio	marriage
mayonesa	mayonnaise
mencionar	to mention
menear	to wag
mente	mind
minuta	menu
mermelada	jam
mermelada de naranja	marmalade
mesita de noche	bedside table
mezclar	to mix
tener miedo	to be afraid
mirador	bow-window
molestar	to disturb, to mi
moneda	coin
montaña	mountain
montar a caballo	to ride*
morir	to die
movimiento	movement
muchedumbre	crowd
muebles	furniture
muerto	dead
musical	musical
nacer	to be born
natural	natural
navegar	to sail
necesitar	to be in need of, need
negarse	to refuse
neumático	tyre
nido	nest
nivel	level
nombrar	to appoint
nombre de pila	Christian name
obedecer	to obey
objeción	objection
objeto	object
obrero	workman
observación	observation
observar	to notice, to obse
ocasión	opportunity
océano	ocean
ocupado	busy
ocurrir	to happen, to oc
odiar	to hate
oeste	west
ofender	to offend
oferta	offer
ofrecer	to offer
o ... o	either ... or
ojo	eye
olvidar	to forget*
omitir	to leave out*
ondulante	undulating
onza	ounce

pinión	opinion
ambiar de opi-	
nión	to change one's mind
portunidad	opportunity
rdeñar	to milk
rganización	organisation
rigen	origin
so	bear
ro	other, else
aciente	patient
aisaje	scenery
apa	Pope
aramo	moor
recer	to look, to appear, to seem
ariente	relation
arque	park
rroco	vicar
artido	match
so	step
sta de té	tea-cake
stor	shepherd, parson
ata	paw
atalear	to stamp
atio	yard, quadrangle, court
atrulla	patrol
cho	chest
dregoso	stony
gar	to hit*
inadora	dressing-table
nsamiento	thought
nsar en	to think of*
rder	to lose*
rezoso	lazy
rfecto	perfect
rmiso	permission
permiso	on leave
sado	heavy
so	weight
nchazo	puncture
ntar	to paint
ar	to step
no	flat
ata	silver
olación	population
ore	poor
eta	poet
lo	chicken
nerse, del sol	to set*
oularidad	popularity
tería	porter's lodge
sible	possible
stre	sweet
cisamente	just
ferir	to prefer
guntarse	to wonder
paración	preparation

presentar	to introduce
al presente	at present
preservación	preservation
preservar	to preserve
presidente	chairman
tomar prestado	to borrow
prestar	to lend*
principio	principle
progreso	progress
prometer	to promise
propiedad	property
propietario	owner
propio	proper, own
a propósito	by the way
prueba	test, proof
puerta exterior	gate
pulgada	inch
puerto	port
púlpito	pulpit
quieto	quiet, still
quitarse	to take off*
raíz	root
rápido	fast, quick
rasgar	to tear*
rata	rat
recibir	to receive
recientemente	lately
recital	recital
recoger	to pick, to collect
recoger del suelo	to pick up
reconstruir	to rebuild*
recordar	to remind
recuerdo	wish
referencia	reference
regresar	to return
rehusar	to refuse
reír	to laugh
reírse de	to laugh at
remo	rowing
renunciar	to give up*
reparar	to repair
representar	to act
rico	rich
riendas	reins
riesgo	chance
robar	to steal*
roca	rock
ropero	wardrobe
rosa	rose
rueda	wheel
ruidoso	noisy
sabio	learned
sacrificar	to sacrifice
sacudir	to shake*
salir, del sol	to rise*

salmón	salmon	tampoco	either
salpicar	to splash	tanto como	as much as
salsa	gravy	tanto tiempo	
saludable	healthy	como	as long as
saludar	to greet	tapete	rug
saludo	greeting	tarea	job
salvaje	savage, wild	terminación	ending
a salvo	safely	terminar	to get through*, t
sangre	blood		finish
sangriento	bloody	tierno	tender
sano	healthy	a (en) tierra	on shore
secretario	secretary	tintorería	the cleaner's
seguir	to follow	típico	typical
según	according to	título	title
seguro	sure, safe	todavía	yet, still
sencillo	simple	tonto -a	fool
sentimiento	feeling	tostar	to toast
sentir	to feel*	pan tostado	toast
señas	address	tradición	tradition
señora	lady	tranquilo	quiet
separado	separate	de través	sideways
separar	to separate	trigo	wheat
serio	serious	trimestre	term
sermón	sermon	tropa	troop
servicio	service	tumulto	uproar
significar	to mean*		
signo	sign	uniforme	uniform
sincero	sincere	útil	useful, hepful
sitio	room		
en algún sitio	somewhere	vacilar	to hesitate
en cualquier sitio	anywhere	valer la pena	to be worth
sobre	envelope	variedad	variety
sociedad	society	varonil	manly
socio	member	vecino (subs.)	neighbour
sofá	sofa	vecino (adj.)	neighbouring
soldado	soldier	vela	sail
soltar	to let go of*	de veras	indeed
sollozar	to sob	verdad	truth
sombra	shadow	verdadero	real
sonar	to sound	verter	to pour
sonido	sound	de vez en cuando	from time to tir
sonreír	to smile		now and then,
sonrojar	to blush		casionally
soñar	to dream*	viajar	to travel
sorprender	to surprise	viaje (por mar)	voyage
súbitamente	suddenly	vigilar	to watch
suerte	chance	vista	sight
sufrimiento	suffering	vivo	alive
sugerir	to suggest	volver	to turn, to go b
superficie	area	vulgar	vulgar
suponer	to suppose		
suspirar	to sigh	yacer	to lie*
taberna	public house		
tallo	stalk	zahúrda	pig-stye

ÍNDICE